Evaluating
Behavior Therapy
Outcome

Ralph McMillan Turner, Ph.D., is an Associate Professor in the Department of Psychiatry at the Temple University School of Medicine. He received his degree from Temple University. His research interests are in the areas of assessment and treatment of anxiety and personality disorders, as well as quantitative research methods.

L. Michael Ascher, Ph.D., received his degree from the University of Pittsburgh. He presently holds the rank of Professor in the Department of Psychiatry at Temple University Health Sciences Center. In addition to supervision and private practice, he conducts research in the treatment of social phobia.

Evaluating
Behavior Therapy
Outcome

Ralph McMillan Turner, Ph.D.
L. Michael Ascher, Ph.D.

Editors

SP

SPRINGER PUBLISHING COMPANY
New York

Springer Publishing Company, Inc.
536 Broadway
New York, New York   10012

85   86   87   88   89   /   10   9   8   7   6   5   4   3   2   1

Library of Congress Cataloging in Publication Data

Main entry under title:
Evaluating behavior therapy outcome.
    Bibliography: p. Includes index.
     1. Behavior therapy—Evaluation.   I. Turner, Ralph McMillan.   II. Ascher,
L. Michael.
RC489.B4E95   1985   616.89'142   85–2798
ISBN 0–8261–4140–4

Printed in the United States of America

Contents

Foreword

This volume on outcome research in behavior therapy is exceptionally timely. In recent years, as the result of a drift in some quarters away from the experimental roots of behavior therapy (Skinner in 1953, Wolpe in 1958), more and more investigators have become careless of definition and have relaxed the scientific rigor that characterized early work in the field. This book is a significant step toward the restoration of this lost rigor. It offers a critique of methodology both in general and within the subdivisions of behavior therapy that are covered by individual chapters.

A methodological error in behavior therapy outcome research that has for years concerned me has been the practice of grouping cases as "the same" merely on the diagnostic label. To take an example, treatments of depression are compared by applying them to cases diagnosed as "depressed" without attention to the fact that the groups consist of heterogeneous assortments of situational, neurotic, and endogenous depressions. Such outcome research is as valueless as gynecological research would be that compared the effect on "vaginitis" of different therapeutic agents without first subdividing the cases into their causes, e.g., bacterial, fungal, or protozoal. I sincerely hope that this book will help to banish this kind of unscientific practice as well as correct the other methodological errors that it discusses.

Joseph Wolpe, M.D.
Professor of Psychiatry
Temple University Medical School and
Medical College of Pennsylvania

Contributors

L. MICHAEL ASCHER, Ph.D., Department of Psychiatry, Temple University School of Medicine, Philadelphia, Pennsylvania.

THOMAS L. BOYD, Ph.D., University of South Carolina at Aiken, Aiken, South Carolina.

JAMES P. CURRAN, Ph.D., Veterans Administration Medical Center, Brown University Medical School, Providence, Rhode Island.

M. DELUTY, Ph.D., Private Practice, New York, New York.

ROBERT A. DiTOMASSO, Ph.D., West Jersey Health System, Family Practice Residence, Tatem-Brown Family Practice Center, Voorhees, New Jersey.

BARBARA M. FLEMING, Ph.D., Department of Psychiatry, Case Western Reserve University, Cleveland, Ohio.

ALAN E. KAZDIN, Ph.D., Western Psychiatric Institute and Clinic, University of Pittsburgh School of Medicine, Pittsburgh, Pennsylvania.

PAUL R. LATIMER, M.D., Ph.D., Private Practice, Kelowna, British Columbia.

PAUL M. LEHRER, Ph.D., University of Medicine and Dentistry of New Jersey, Rutgers Medical School, Piscataway, New Jersey.

DONALD J. LEVIS, Ph.D., State University of New York at Binghamton, Binghamton, New York.

JOHNNY L. MATSON, Ph.D., Northern Illinois University, De-Kalb, Illinois.

KAREN M. SIMON, Ph.D., Center for Cognitive Therapy, University of Pennsylvania, Philadelphia, Pennsylvania.

ANDREW A. SWEET, Psy.D., Behavior Therapy Institute of Colorado, Denver, Colorado.

RALPH McMILLAN TURNER, Ph.D., Department of Psychiatry, Temple University School of Medicine, Philadelphia, Pennsylvania.

ROBERT L. WOOLFOLK, Ph.D., Rutgers, The State University of New Jersey, New Brunswick, New Jersey.

1

Behavior Therapy Outcome Research: Some Methodological Issues

RALPH McMILLAN TURNER AND L. MICHAEL ASCHER

In the last decade, the applications of behavior therapy interventions have increased markedly, and the range of disorders for which behavioral procedures have been found effective has expanded. In addition, a proliferation of specific techniques included under the aegis of behavior therapy has occurred. One result of this explosion of treatments and applications is that it has become difficult for the practicing clinician to determine which behavioral intervention strategy works for what specifiable problem. The purpose of this book is to examine from a methodological perspective the efficacy of some of the most popular behavioral techniques. In addition, we wish to set a standard, or at least to support the existing standard, of sound methodological analysis and to delineate future research directions in behavior therapy outcome research.

There are many salient reasons why such a review is important. Foremost is the current stress from governmental agencies and health insurers for documentation of the effectiveness of psychotherapy. As this increased push for accountability becomes implemented, it will become crucial to develop carefully detailed and methodologically sound reviews of interventions. Historically, research in behavior therapy has emphasized the evaluation of treatment strategies. Consequently, behavior therapy researchers will have a unique opportunity to lead the field in documenting effectiveness. Thus, the aim of the current project is to systematically specify a core set of procedures and to identify those mental health problems which respond optimally to those procedures. Furthermore, the interactions of these specific behavioral techniques with other interventions (e.g., drugs) and the side-effects or other deleterious consequences of the techniques will be specified.

There are common methodological themes which run through the following chapters. Thus, difficulties one encounters in conducting research on social skills training are quite similar to the problems involved with research on systematic desensitization or, for that matter, on psychotherapy in general.

The Experimental Paradigm

Any substantive analysis, of course, must first focus upon experimental design issues. Randomization of subjects to experimental groups is the sin qua non of clinical trials. The process of randomization helps to prevent patient characteristics (e.g., socioeconomic status, IQ, presence of secondary disorders) from confounding the therapeutic effects. It is assumed that all extraneous variables will be equally distributed across experimental groups by assigning subjects to treatments at random. Assuming that the random assignment procedure is effective in initially equating groups of subjects on the relevant parameters, then any differences arising among treatment groups at the termination of therapy can unequivocally be attributed to the effects of treatments. Since the principle goal of psychotherapy outcome research is to make refined statements about treatment efficacy, random assignment can be thought of as the cornerstone of the process.

It is appropriate that discussions of the randomization procedure lead to a discussion of experimental controls. The randomization procedure is important because it helps to eliminate (controls) certain plausible alternative hypotheses as explanations for the results of an experiment. Since randomization can occur only in the context of multiple experimental groups, research design must be beyond the single-group (uncontrolled) type. Use of multiple groups is, then, the corollary to randomization in good design. If one of the groups is a no-treatment control group and subjects are assigned at random, then all of the threats to internal validity listed by Campbell and Stanley (1963) are controlled. These two essential ingredients allow for control of (1) history, (2) maturation, (3) testing, (4) instrumentation, (5) regression, (6) selection, (7) mortality, and (8) the interaction of selection, maturation, and other effects (Campbell & Stanley, 1963). Thus, as we review the experimental literature on the efficacy of behavior therapy techniques, attention will quite naturally focus on the interconnected issues of randomization, multiple comparison groups, and no-treatment control groups. By emphasizing the multiple group contrast design, we are stressing the point that one-group, pretest–posttest, and posttest-only designs are unacceptable. The strategy of using subjects as their own controls is subject to every source of threat to internal and external validity which Campbell and Stanley (1963) list except the selection and mortality factors. Thus, an essential ingredient of good therapy outcome research is multiple comparison groups.

Our insistence upon multiple comparison groups does not necessitate the use of the traditional experimental design notion of a no-treatment control group or placebo group, a modification with which most therapy researchers agree (Karasu, 1982; Kazdin & Wilson, 1978; O'Leary & Borkovec, 1978). Both ethical and pragmatic difficulties are involved in the use of attention-placebo and no-treatment controls. Ethically, it is difficult to justify either withholding treatment or providing inferior treatment to individuals requesting therapy. The untoward side-effects and loss of confidence in therapy may not be reversible. Pragmatically, patients who are told they must wait for treatment often will simply seek it elsewhere. When high levels of attrition occur in this way, the resulting subject samples are biased and there is virtually no way the experimenter can resolve the problem (Imber, 1978; Karasu, 1982).

As the paradigmatic view of experimental control has evolved, alternative control strategies have been developed. Research in natural clinic environments sometimes precludes randomization, but nevertheless the treatment clinic represents an important setting for testing the impact of therapeutic techniques. Under such circumstances, the use of intact groups, such as patients on two different wards or children in two different classes, is the best alternative. This is not a unique problem in psychological research, however. Educational psychologists have long worked with intact groups of subjects as a necessary feature of their medium, and Campbell and Stanley (1963) have suggested some quasi-experimental design strategies for such applied settings. These quasi-experimental designs control many sources of internal and external threats to validity and yield meaningful conclusions. Thus, even though randomization of subjects to treatment groups is the hallmark of good research design, alternative strategies do exist for establishing control in applied research.

Quasi-experimental designs, for one, include (1) time series, (2) equivalent samples, (3) nonequivalent control group, (4) counterbalanced designs or crossover, (5) the separate sample pretest–posttest design, (6) multiple time series, (7) recurrent institutional cycle designs, and (8) ex post facto correlational designs. Each of these designs takes advantage of factors in the in situ situation and brings some degree of control into the procedure. Because these designs are open to threats to internal or external validity, the research process becomes a step-by-step task of eliminating the extant alternative explanations of the findings.

Other alternative solutions to the traditional model are (1) component-control comparisons, (2) alternative-treatment control groups, and (3) the development of community norms. In the component-control strategy, the total treatment procedure is compared to its subcomponents. It has been discussed as the dismantling strategy (Kazdin & Wilson, 1978) and has been utilized by Lang, Lazovic, and Reynolds (1965).

The alternative treatment process contrasts a behavior therapy technique with a specified alternative therapy procedure. This process actually gets at the heart of many controversial issues in the therapy outcome literature, but it is plagued by problems similar to those of other omnibus comparisons (Karasu, 1982; Kazdin & Wilson, 1978; Smith & Glass, 1977).

A more recent innovation is the use of community controls. In actuality, this procedure is not new, but is simply the establishment of a normative sample. Treatment groups are then compared with the normative sample to determine the impact of the therapy. Thus, instead of researchers gathering their own control data, they would utilize the normative sample. A problem with this approach is that possible discrepancies in variables such as age and IQ can exist between the experimental and control group; however, it has the advantage of reflecting when therapy has had a positive impact on patients by bringing about improvement in the symptoms that brought them to therapy.

On the whole, these alternative treatment designs do control for a substantial number of threats to validity. Specifically the alternative treatment strategy can be set up to contrast the best available treatment with the experimental treatment. In this way, a direct indication of the treatment of choice is obtained.

Thus far we have emphasized multiple subject and group research. However, behavior therapy outcome researchers have pursued issues of control even in the case study. Single-case experimental designs have been developed (Hersen & Barlow, 1976; Kazdin, 1982) and utilized to assess treatment strategies. Single-case designs originated with operantly oriented therapists whose goals were to demonstrate the efficacy of a specific intervention for controlling problem behavior. Control in this type of design is achieved by showing that only when the intervention is actively in place is there a diminution of problem behavior; when the treatment is removed, the problem returns. In recent years, elaborations on the basic single-case design have been made that allow us to consider certain single-case experiments to be as meaningful as controlled group studies (Hersen & Barlow, 1976; Kazdin, 1980). Consequently, the reviews of treatment strategies will give merit to single-case as well as group designs.

Assessment and Diagnosis

One of the criticisms most often leveled against behavior therapy is the lack of emphasis upon treating standard diagnostic disorders. Much behavioral research has focused upon analogue, college student populations and not patients with real *DSM III* diagnoses. While this is true to some extent, there are many examples of work with autistic and mentally retarded children, individuals with sexual disorders and deviations, agoraphobics, obsessive-compulsives, and schizophrenics.

One aspect that has been lacking in the outcome studies is the incorporation of a standardized procedure for making diagnoses. The same criticism can be made of much psychotherapy outcome research in general, but it is particularly striking in the behavior therapy literature. This is due, in part, to early behavior therapists' rejection of diagnostic labeling and psychiatric diagnosis. However, more recently, we see many more studies focusing upon such diagnostic entities as agoraphobia or obsessive-compulsive disorder. If behavioral therapists are to continue developing and researching treatment strategies for diagnostic classes, then we will need to incorporate standardized diagnostic procedures into our outcome research strategies. For instance, the National Institute of Mental Health has developed the computerized *Diagnostic Interview Schedule* which standardizes *DSM III* diagnosis (Robins, Helzer, Croughan, Williams, & Spitzer, 1981). The hope is that by utilizing a standardized procedure to diagnose clients, research findings can be amalgamated across studies with greater generalizability. The reduction in ambiguity concerning type and severity of diagnostic entities under treatment will be of tremendous value. If behavior therapists wish to have an impact on the field in general, then we will have to incorporate systems that will allow us to communicate our findings to other professionals.

An associated assessment issue which surfaces in the methodological reviews focuses upon behavior analysis. Early behavior therapists emphasized a focus on the adaptiveness and adequacy of behavior. However, there are difficulties in defining adequate behavior. For instance, what specifically constitutes socially skilled behavior? For the most part, researchers have developed idiosyncratic definitions and have conducted studies utilizing their own definitions. Future behavioral research will surely be involved with the development of assessment strategies which will clearly define target behaviors in order to resolve these problems.

The Outcome Criterion Problem

Perhaps one of the longest-standing methodological problems in psychotherapy research is the task of determining when clients are improved. This is also true for research on behavioral techniques. Naturally, this problem is closely tied to difficulties the researcher encounters in behavioral assessment. For instance, just what constitutes interpersonal skillfulness and deficit? When is a psychiatric diagnosis no longer warranted? How much fear is too much? What are the implications of dyschrony between fear and avoidance for assessing the impact of an intervention? The reader will find these issues arising again and again in the chapters that follow.

Early in the history of behavior therapy, it seemed that the very essence of the focus upon behavior solved the outcome-criterion problem. The researcher simply observed and counted the frequency of the target behavior. There was no need to debate different measures or modes of measurement. This was particularly true for many childhood disorders, behavioral problems associated with autism or mental retardation, and behavioral manifestations of schizophrenia. Anxiety disorders proved to be more difficult to assess in this manner, since one cannot objectively measure anxiety. Thus, early researchers asked clients to rate their subjective units of discomfort or they assessed avoidance as distance from a feared object or psychophysiological response to that feared object. Unfortunately, none of these measures of fear correlated strongly with the others. Thus was borne the tripartite model of fear assessment and doubts as to the absolute objectivity of behavioral assessment. Then researchers began to discover that even behavioral observation is fraught with technical difficulties and biases that, at times, can lead to problems with reliability and validity (Cone, 1979).

As we peruse the behavioral literature in almost any area, we quickly discover that there has been a significant reliance upon uncontrolled self-reports of improvement by patients. This has occurred as the result of the implicit assumption of behavior therapy that procedures and not dependent measures were to be tested. Seldom did investigators assess the reliability and validity of these self-report instruments. Thus, the utility of many studies is limited.

At the other extreme, some researchers did utilize direct observation. However, sometimes the observations occurred in contrived, artificially designed settings. While the data obtained from such an assessment are often very reliable, their practical utility, social validity, and generalizability to everyday life have been found to be lacking (Bellack, Hersen, & Turner, 1978; Curran, 1978).

In the future, behavior therapists will increasingly focus upon the social validation of dependent assessments (Kazdin, 1980). The removal of a psychiatric diagnosis and improvement in the quality of life are becoming key indicators in outcome research (Steinmetz, Lewinsohn, & Antonuccio, 1983). In addition, as behavior therapy research integrates with the mainstream of clinical psychiatric and psychological research, more studies will need to be conducted which emphasize general experimental principles of clinical trials research such as independent evaluations by professionals. Also, a broader scope of assessment procedures will be emphasized. Behaviors, cognitions, feelings, sense of well-being, and the reports of significant others regarding aspects of the patient's functioning will be assessed. In a real sense, the research will be health-oriented, not simply symptom-oriented.

Integrity of Subjects

One very controversial issue involved with evaluating behavior therapy interventions is whether experimental subjects are actual patients presenting at clinics for treatment or are college student volunteers who may show only mild forms of the disorder of interest. This refers to the controversy regarding research conducted with actual clinical variables versus analogue clinical variables. At issue is the relevance and generalizability of findings of outcome experiments for clinical practice. Since the focus of the present book is on determining the efficacy of behavioral interventions for clinical practice, the issue of generalizability is of central importance.

Analogue studies are ideally suited for abstracting the clinical environment in order to obtain tight control over both the experimental and extraneous variables. The function of analogue studies is that of unequivocally assessing the impact of the therapeutic process. Lang and Lazovik's (1963) and Lang, Lazovik, and Reynolds' (1965) classic studies on systematic desensitization treatment of snake phobia are a superb example of analogue research. Under tightly controlled conditions, these researchers were able to demonstrate that desensitization lowered subjects' fearfulness of snakes and that the result was due to the active therapeutic ingredients in the behavioral technique. Later research by Lang, Melamed, and Hart (1970) demonstrated that those subjects who actually show physiological responses to the relaxation component are the ones who show overall reductions in fearfulness. Such findings are highly significant for increased understanding of the theoretical mechanisms by which systematic desensitization works, as well as for suggesting methods for maximizing the clinical efficacy of the procedures. It is in this regard that analogue studies have their strength. Attempting to unravel therapeutic mechanisms in the clinic setting with its myriad of uncontrolled factors would be laborious at best. Thus, with regard to conducting therapy process research, the analogue model is superior.

However, when it comes to establishing the effectiveness of interventions, experiments conducted in natural clinic settings are usually superior to analogue studies. First and foremost, there is no way to be sure that subclinical analogue subjects are in any way similar to clinical patients. Research on agoraphobia clearly demonstrates this phenomenon (Mathews, 1978). Agoraphobics exhibit a constellation of symptoms organized into an interlocking syndrome, whereas analogue clients typically show a monosymptomatic profile which is more amenable to a single therapeutic intervention. The clinic outcome data, to date, indicate that agoraphobics require a multicomponent, long-term intensive therapy in contrast to analogue studies, which show that simple exposure works adequately to reduce fears (Mathews, 1978).

Experiments conducted with clinically significant problems also bring into play a host of potentially limiting factors inherent to the true therapeutic context. There is less control over subject resistance, follow-through, and motivation for change. Real-world problems, such as family support, vocational difficulties, and financial constraints, are brought to bear on the final judgment of effectiveness. In sum, *in vivo* studies reflect real-life clinical practice, which is the essence of determining clinical efficacy. In order to make informed judgments as to which technique to use with a specific patient, the clinician needs to know which procedures have been shown to be effective under similar conditions. Thus, the *in vivo* research model makes its contribution to the outcome problem.

Consequently, the analogue versus *in vivo* controversy can be solved by realizing that each model has its strengths and weaknesses. Process questions are best answered through analogue experiments. Outcome effectiveness of techniques for specific disorders are best answered by *in vivo* studies assessing the specific treatment for the specific disorder. Consequently, because of the aims of the present book, the reviews of behavioral strategies will focus upon *in vivo* research.

Integrity of Treatments

The issue of treatment integrity emphasizes that what a research report describes as the components and sequence of therapy should indeed be what occurs in each and every session. It has recently been pointed out that often deviations in the plan occur spontaneously (Kazdin, 1980). Clinicians are independent individuals and vary the game plan according to the immediate exigencies of the therapeutic situation. While this may be the best and most ethical strategy, it causes severe problems in interpreting outcome findings and making definitive judgments about the relative effectiveness of therapeutic interventions. For instance, the reason a success rate of 60% is obtained for social skills training instead of 80% might be that talk therapy occurred in 5 of 10 sessions. The patient or patients may have come to the clinic in a crisis state and the clinician decided to allow the patient to emote and work through the problem instead of following the game plan. Such well-meaning deviations greatly reduce the accuracy and utility of the subsequent findings. Thus, studies which monitor the integrity of treatment administered will be emphasized in the reviews. In point of fact, very few behavioral outcome studies have controlled for this factor. Thus, a general direction for the future of behavioral outcome research might be reevaluations of past research in terms of the integrity of the treatments.

In addition to "doing what we say we do," the integrity of treatments issue touches upon the experience of the treating clinician, the length of therapy, the interaction of the specific intervention within a comprehensive treatment plan, and potential side-effects. In many behavioral outcome studies, the treating clinicians have been graduate students. It is not that graduate students cannot be good clinicians; in fact, they often are more enthusiastic and spend more time focusing upon individual patients than do more experienced but possibly jaded clinicians. Since initial clinical contacts are an exciting learning experience which is highly valued by most clinical students, this is not surprising. But certain factors involved with handling patients' resistance and the knowledge of the sporadic developmental course in therapy can be obtained only through experience. Thus, if we wish to determine strategies for general clinical use, we should conduct the experiments in a manner which reflects the mainstream of clinical practice. In other words, there is an advantage to utilizing experienced clinicians in outcome research. Actually, there is important information to be obtained in utilizing both novice and established clinicians to determine the importance of this factor (see Turner & Ascher, 1982).

The length of therapy is another important aspect of treatment integrity. Many behavioral studies have been of relatively short duration and lacked long-term follow-through. This does not reflect realistic therapy, which is generally long-term, including behavior therapy. An ancillary problem is that treatment is often scheduled for a prespecified period of time as opposed to continuing until the patient is clinically better. Of course, to conduct experiments in which patients are treated for differential periods of time would confound the type of treatment with duration. This would result in a loss of control of historical, maturational, and motivational factors. Consequently, rigor and preestablished control are to be emphasized over these naturalistic issues. However, after relative superiority of a treatment is established, issues of the length of therapy, or dosage required to achieve, say, an 80% success rate, should be conducted. The methodological and statistical techniques of probit analysis (Finney, 1971) provide the structure for answering such questions. As important as these questions are, surprisingly no such dosage studies of behavioral interventions have occurred.

Finally, in the actual clinical situation very few patients are treated exclusively with a single therapeutic procedure. Rather, a combination of these interventions is used as part of a comprehensive treatment program involving medication, supportive counseling, vocational counseling, social work interventions, and the ubiquitous homework practice. Little behavioral outcome research reflects this reality. Certainly, in the early stages of assessing the effectiveness of a technique, experiments should limit themselves to focusing upon the intervention alone. However, follow-up research should be conducted to assess the treatment in combination with other commonly used treatment modalities. The researcher also needs to assess the occurrence of any untoward side-effects of the intervention or of its combination with the comprehensive treatment components. Knowing the conditions which preclude using an intervention are as crucial as knowing when to utilize it. The reviews that follow will emphasize these issues.

Statistical and Clinical Efficacy

As has been noted by Kazdin (1980), the level of statistical significance of an outcome finding tells us nothing about the magnitude of the actual effect. What behavioral research typically wants to demonstrate is that an intervention makes a symptomatic individual nonsymptomatic. Thus, there will be an emphasis throughout the book on determining the clinical efficacy of the behavioral interventions. However, to date, studies focusing upon clinical significance are few. This issue, then, represents another significant area of investigation for future research.

Behavioral Interventions

The range of behavioral interventions is varied. We have chosen to focus upon a core set of procedures which reflect the behavioral treatments of choice for common mental health problems. In planning this book we had considered the option of presenting each of the contributors with a relatively rigid outline which each was to use in preparing the chapters. However, our decision was to forgo the positive benefits which such a procedure would have in order to avoid its potentially greater negative aspects in this context. Although there are common issues and considerations among the different procedures, there are numerous characteristic differences which are important but might be lost if the same format were required for each review.

Chapter 2 reviews systematic desensitization, the progenitor of the field. The range of application of systematic desensitization is exceedingly wide and consequently more space is required to review this procedure than some others. Closely allied to systematic desensitization is flooding. Flooding has also been utilized extensively, so there is copious material to be reviewed. Levis and Boyd present their extinction model of flooding in order to elucidate future research directions. Next Lehrer and Woolfolk review the relaxation therapy literature. They scientifically focus upon progressive relaxation, autogenic training, and meditation. Following the chapter on relaxation therapy, Curran discusses the origins of the interpersonal skill training model and reviews the evidence for the efficacy of this intervention.

The next section of the book deals with the treatment outcome results of cognitive behavioral techniques. Because there has been a sudden and dramatic increase in research on cognitive techniques, as well as much controversy as to their efficacy, we have devoted several chapters to this topic. First, Simon and Fleming review the studies assessing the Beck type of cognitive therapy. This chapter is particularly focused on the treatment of depression. The following chapter by Latimer and Sweet criticizes the cognitive-behavioral data and concludes that the effective ingredients of the cognitive-behavioral approach are singularly the behavioral components. Finally Ascher and DiTomasso overview the developing evidence for paradoxical interventions in behavior therapy. Although the literature on paradox is small, it is promising.

The final two chapters of the book deal with the operant strategies of the token economy and punishment. Kazdin emphasizes the role single-case experimental designs play in studying the impact of token economy procedure and historically ties this characteristic element of token economy research to its operant origin. Matson then presents an exhaustive review of the utility of punishment procedures in treating maladaptive behaviors. Both Kazdin and Matson discuss the legal and ethical issues and implications involved with the use of the token economy or punishment procedures.

After studying these chapters, our hope is that the reader will have a grasp of the clinical effectiveness of these core behavioral interventions, a greater appreciation of the mechanics and difficulties of conducing outcome research, and a clear direction to follow for pursuing research on any of these procedures.

References

Bellack, A. S., Hersen, M., & Turner, S. M. Role play tests for assessing social skills: Are they valid? *Behavior Therapy,* 1978, *9,* 448–461.

Campbell, D. T., & Stanley, J. C. *Experimental and quasi-experimental designs for research.* Chicago: Rand McNally and Company, 1963.

Cone, J. D. Confounded comparisons in triple response mode assessment research. *Behavioral Assessment,* 1979, *1,* 85–95.

Curran, J. P. Comments on Bellack, Hersen & Turner's paper on the validity of role play tests. *Behavior Therapy,* 1978, *9,* 462–468.

Finney, D. J. *Probit analysis* (3rd ed.). Cambridge: Cambridge University Press, 1971.

Hersen, M., & Barlow, D. H. *Single case experimental designs: Strategies for studying behavior change.* New York: Pergamon Press, 1976.

Imber, S. D. Some research issues in psychotherapy. In J. D. Frank, R. Hoehn-Sanc, S. D. Imber, B. L. Liberman, & A. R. Stone (Eds.), *Effective ingredients of successful psychotherapy.* New York: Brunner/Mazel, 1978, pp. 130–154.

Karasu, T. B. (Ed.). *Psychotherapy research: Methodological and efficacy issues.* Washington: American Psychiatric Association, 1982.

Kazdin, A. E. *Research design in clinical psychology.* New York: Harper & Row, 1980.

Kazdin, A. E. *Single-case research designs methods for clinical and applied settings.* New York: Oxford University Press, 1982.

Kazdin, A. E., & Wilson, G. T. *Evaluation of behavior therapy: Issues, evidence, and research strategies.* Cambridge, Mass.: Ballinger Publishing Company, 1978.

Lang, P. J., & Lazovik, A. D. Experimental desensitization of a phobia. *Journal of Abnormal and Social Psychology,* 1963, *66,* 519–525.

Lang, P. J., Lazovik, A. D., & Reynolds, D. J. Desensitization, suggestibility, and pseudotherapy. *Journal of Abnormal Psychology,* 1965, *70,* 395–402.

Lang, P. J. Melamed, B. G., & Hart, J. A psychophysiological analysis of fear modification using an automated desensitization procedure. *Journal of Abnormal Psychology,* 1970, *76,* 220–234.

Mathews, A. Fear-reduction research and clinical phobias. *Psychological Bulletin,* 1978, *85,* 390–404.

O'Leary, K. D., & Borkovec, T. D. Conceptual, methodological, and ethical problems of placebo groups in psychotherapy research. *American Psychologist,* 1978, *9,* 821, 830.

Robins, Lee, N., Helzer, J. E., Croughan, J., Williams, J. R. W., & Spitzer, R. L. *NIMH Diagnostic Interview Schedule: Version III.* NIMH Division of Biometry and Epidemiology, Contract MH 278-79-00 17DB and Research Grant MH 33583. Department of Health & Human Services, NIMH, Rockville, MD, 1981.

Smith, M. L., & Glass, G. V. Meta-analysis of psychotherapy outcome studies. *American Psychologist*, 1977, *32*, 752–760.

Steinmetz, J. L., Lewinsohn, P. M., & Antonuccio, D. O. Prediction of individual outcome in a group intervention for depression. *Journal of Consulting and Clinical Psychology*, 1983, *51*, 331–337.

Turner, R. M., & Ascher, L. M. Therapist factor in the treatment of insomnia. *Behavior Research & Therapy*, 1982, *20*, 33–40.

2

Systematic Desensitization

RALPH McMILLAN TURNER, ROBERT A. DiTOMASSO,
AND M. DELUTY

Introduction

Systematic desensitization is a therapeutic intervention designed to
eradicate fear behavior and avoidance syndromes associated with
psychological disturbances. The procedure is composed of two distinct
components. The first component consists of teaching the patient a
response counter to anxiety. Progressive relaxation, or some other
general relaxation procedure, is typically utilized for this purpose,
although any counteranxiety response the patient makes, such as
assertion, will suffice. For instance, an assertive response inhibits
the experience of anxiety and consequently would adequately serve
as a counteranxiety agent. The second component of systematic desensitization involves graduated exposure to the fear-eliciting stimulus. Exposure may be accomplished either imaginally or *in vivo*.

The empirical literature on systematic desensitization is too
extensive to review in its entirety in a textbook format. Thus, in this
chapter, we will focus on the efficacy of systematic desensitization
with regard to *specific disorders*.

Historical Development

J. Wolpe (1958) originated systematic desensitization as a method of
reducing anxiety reactions. The procedure relies on the principles of
classical conditioning which were developed by I. V. Pavlov (1927).
The basic assumption underlying desensitization is that an anxiety

15

response to a fear-evoking stimulus can be eliminated or weakened by generating a counteranxiety response. Any response which is incompatible with anxiety may be utilized to inhibit the anxiety response.

Prior to Wolpe's work, several researchers had set the stage for the study of experimentally induced neurosis (Gantt, 1944; Masserman, 1943; Pavlov, 1927, 1941). The discovery inherent in all of the work was that laboratory animals would develop fear associations between a fearsome event and contextual cues in which these aversive conditions were presented. In the typical paradigm, animals in a particular experimental chamber would repeatedly receive electric shock while engaging in a desired behavior. Consequently, the animals would develop "anxiety-like" behavior patterns while in the chamber, such as the inability to eat, even when very hungry.

John B. Watson (1925), using the Pavlovian conditioning paradigm, demonstrated that the fears and phobias children show early in life are not inherited, but learned through conditioning. The most famous of Watson's experiments demonstrated the conditioning of a fear response to a white rat in an infant boy named Albert. During a sequence of eight laboratory trials, Watson was able to generate a fear response by striking a steel bar with a carpenter's hammer as Albert reached to touch a white rat. Additional testing showed a spread or transfer of the conditioned emotional response to a rabbit, dog, fur coat, cotton, wool, and even Watson's own graying hair. Watson argued strongly that the experimentally conditioned emotional response paradigm explained the development of all anxiety disorders.

Wolpe's major contributions to the field of experimental neurosis were expanding the empirical base supporting the notion that anxiety reactions can be conditioned to contextual cues in animals; developing a procedure for deconditioning the anxiety response; and, more importantly, extending these findings to human beings. In his first experiment, Wolpe replicated the earlier experimental neurosis findings which demonstrated that applying mild electric shocks to an animal's cage could reliably inhibit its eating and lead to the development of other anxiety symptoms. Wolpe next devised a treatment to eliminate the conditioned fear response. Based upon Sherrington's (1906) notion of reciprocal inhibition, Wolpe deduced that treatment must consist of somehow inhibiting the animal's anxiety response and then gradually moving the animal physically closer and closer to the cage and to the experimental area associated with the shock. Wolpe, who performed his experiments with cats, selected food as the method of inhibiting anxiety, because it is easy to administer and produces a potent calmness in cats. His speculations proved correct. The neurotic symptoms in every experimental animal were alleviated through the combination of gradual exposure to the feared object plus the inhibition of anxiety through feeding.

Next, Wolpe turned his attention to the treatment of human neurosis. Following the earlier lead of Watson and Rayner (1920), Wolpe developed his procedure of systematic desensitization. The therapeutic technique worked quickly and thoroughly. This set the stage for the revolution in the treatment of neurotic anxiety-based disorders that followed.

At the present time, there are literally hundreds of experiments and case reports assessing the efficacy of desensitization. It is, without a doubt, the most researched psychotherapeutic technique in existence. In the remainder of this chapter, then, we will attempt to delineate the disorders for which systematic desensitization is the treatment of choice. From a theoretical perspective, there is great controversy as to the actual therapeutic mechanism responsible for behavior change with desensitization. We will address this issue more thoroughly in a later section. Suffice it to say that these controversies over the mechanism of change have served to broaden the range of application of the procedure, as well as to permit creative usages of it which even Wolpe could not have foreseen.

The Procedure of Systematic Desensitization

Systematic desensitization is composed of three principal components: (1) teaching the patient a relaxation response, (2) developing a hierarchy of anxiety-eliciting stimuli, and (3) exposing the relaxed patient to the eliciting stimuli in imagination or *in vivo*.

The traditional method for generating a relaxation response is to train the patient in Jacobson's (1938) progressive muscle relaxation. Progressive relaxation is based on the notion that stress or anxiety is caused by tension in the muscular system. This actual physical tenseness leads to felt anxiety. Jacobson (1938) developed a method of muscle-tension release to reduce this experienced anxiety. First, the patient contracts his hand into a fist and holds it tightly for 20 seconds. Second, he gradually unclenches his hand. And third, while sitting calmly for two minutes, he focuses attention upon the experienced difference between tension and relaxation. This process is repeated three to four times. After this initial step, the individual continues this process throughout every major muscle grouping in the body. A total of 10 relaxation training sessions is typically required to enable the patient to achieve a reliable relaxation response.

Other means are available for developing the relaxation response. Wolpe (1958) has suggested anxiolytic agents and carbon dioxide inhalation. Additionally, other forms of relaxation, such as meditation or hypnosis, may be utilized. Furthermore, some experts have suggested that no relaxation response is necessary at all (Rimm & Masters, 1974). In this case, the therapist need only concern himself with constructing the hierarchy of phobic-eliciting stimuli and then exposing the patient to these stimuli.

The second component of systematic desensitization is the creation of the hierarchy of phobic-eliciting stimuli. This hierarchy consists of all those stimuli, situations, events, thoughts, and persons which are associated with the fear response. After the therapist obtains all of the relevant elements and sets their parameters, he must then arrange the hierarchy items in an order which reflects increasing levels of fear arousal. In the therapy itself, this allows for a gradual exposure of the patient to the phobic stimuli. For example, an elevator-phobic may become progressively more anxious as he approaches an elevator. In this case, the hierarchy would most probably consist of scenes in which the patient finds himself closer and closer to the elevator and ultimately rides on the elevator. This is an example of a physical distance hierarchy.

Hierarchy development is perhaps the most difficult aspect of the procedure. Often the patient is unaware of eliciting stimuli and unable to articulate clearly the sequence of events leading to the emotional response. A therapist needs much training and experience to master this component of the technique.

After the patient has learned a reliable relaxation response and the hierarchy is developed, the next stage of therapy involves gradually exposing the patient to the phobic-eliciting stimuli, while maintaining the state of physiological relaxation. This is done by having the patient come into contact with the stimuli either in imagination or in reality. The exposures become increasingly more difficult, beginning with the least anxiety-provoking situations or aspects of the hierarchy and concluding with the most fearful stimuli. Consequently, therapy proceeds step by small step. This allows the patient to gain confidence with early successes. The result of repeatedly exposing the patient to the anxiety-eliciting stimuli while keeping him relaxed is the eventual disappearance of the anxiety reaction altogether.

For more detailed descriptions of the systematic desensitization procedure, refer to Wolpe (1958) and to Rimm and Masters (1974).

Anxiety Disorders

Childhood Phobias

The first documented case of successful classical conditioning for the treatment of childhood fears was as early as Jones (1924). In it, she paired a fear-evoking stimulus (rabbit) with its antithesis, a pleasure-eliciting stimulation (eating). Through graduated exposure, Jones arranged treatment so that the intensity of the fear was always less than the intensity of the pleasure.

In another case study, Garvey and Hegreaves (1966) used *in vivo* desensitization in the treatment of a school-phobic 10-year-old boy. Gradational *in vivo* exposure was conducted over a 20-day period by the therapist, then by the child's father, and finally by the principal.

In a treatment outcome study conducted by Hampe, Noble, Miller, and Barrett (1973), phobic children were exposed to either reciprocal inhibition therapy, psychotherapy, or no therapy. Interestingly enough, treatment and nontreatment techniques proved to be equally effective. Follow-ups at one and two years led to the conclusion that childhood phobias tend to remit by themselves, but that desensitization does facilitate a more rapid recovery.

In light of the uncontrolled nature of the single case studies reported and the equivocal findings of Hampe et al. (1973), desensitization cannot be considered the unequivocal treatment of choice for childhood phobias.

Phobias

In one of the earliest studies of a phobic population, Lazarus (1961) tested a variation of systematic desensitization in a group setting and compared this to group insight therapy. Thirty-five phobics, including acrophobics, claustrophobics, sexual phobics, and mixed phobics, were selected from a group of volunteer patients on the basis of whether their specific phobia produced the required dysfunctions: (1) severe limitation of social mobility; (2) interference with interpersonal relationships; and (3) restriction of the patient's constructive abilities. The nature and severity of each individual's phobia had already been confirmed through pretreatment behavioral assessment, and patients who had received psychiatric treatment were excluded. The phobics were matched together by sex and age (within a four-year range), as well as by the nature and severity of the problem, and then randomly assigned to groups, where they were treated with peers who shared the same phobic reaction. (Several months into the study, the author apparently decided to add an additional treatment team utilizing group insight therapy plus relaxation.)

Posttreatment recovery was evaluated by an objective behavioral assessment test for the specific type of phobia in question, with the exclusion of the sex and mixed phobics. Patient self-reports were also used. Outcome of therapy was categorized as either complete recovery (i.e., absolute neutrality to the original conditioned stimulus constellation) or failure. The data supported the effectiveness of desensitization in comparison to the other two treatments—group insight and group insight plus relaxation.

Although the original data were reported in frequencies, a more accurate manner of describing the results is by percentage of patients recovered. Seventy-five percent of the desensitized patients recovered, while 0% of the group insight and 25% of the group insight plus relaxation patients recovered. Of the initially recovered subjects, 23% relapsed with desensitization, 50% with group interpretation plus relaxation. Although all the results do indeed appear to support desensitization, there are some flaws with this study, including the lack of a placebo control group and the fact that the investigator treated all subjects.

Gelder, Marks, and Wolff (1967) matched a group of phobics (agoraphobics, social phobics, and specific phobics) by age, vocabulary level, and severity of symptoms, and assigned them to one of three groups: systematic desensitization, group psychotherapy, or/ and individual psychotherapy. Outcome measures, gathered before and after treatment and during follow-up, included ratings on a variety of variables (e.g., phobia, anxiety) by the patients, therapists, and an independent observer/rater. The patients also completed several questionnaires. When evaluating successful treatment of the main phobia, patient, therapist, and assessor responses showed significant differences between the desensitization and the psychotherapy groups in favor of desensitization. Moreover, at a six-month follow-up patients continued to rank desensitization as better than the other two treatments. Finally, ratings after an average of seven months follow-up by an independent psychiatric social worker, who was kept intentionally uninformed about the treatment condition, also revealed that most symptom improvement occurred in the desensitized patients.

The results of this study must be considered in light of the following methodological problems. First, because the psychotherapy groups and desensitization groups were conducted by numerous physicians and psychiatrists, respectively, treatment effects are confounded with therapist effects. Moreover, one doctor treated both individual and group psychotherapy subjects. Second, the length of each treatment session and the duration of the overall treatment were not standardized. Desensitization patients met for one hour once a week for an average of 12 months; and group psychotherapy patients, 1.5 hours a week for an average of 18 months. Third, the outcome ratings were subjective in nature, leaving their validity in question. Fourth, the absence of a placebo group leads one to query whether the results may be attributable solely to attention by a therapist. Fifth, the failure to gather credibility ratings masks whether the treatments were differentially perceived by patients. Finally, from a statistical standpoint, Univariate Analysis of Variance was used to evaluate outcome on numerous measures. In order to avoid probability pyramiding, multivariate statistics would have been more appropriate here.

Seven treatment failures from these psychotherapy conditions were later studied by Gelder and Marks (1968). Subjects included five agoraphobics, one thunder phobic, and one social phobic. Assessment ratings of six groups of symptoms relating to the primary phobias were made by the patient, therapist, and two independent evaluators. The authors concluded that, on the average, the patients' phobias improved approximately three times as much as they did in the previous two years, which included 18 months of psychotherapy and a six-month waiting period.

The conclusions of this study warrant careful consideration. Number one, a crossover design was used which, although efficient for a small group of subjects, does not allow one to separate the interactive effects of each treatment. Number two, definitive comparisons cannot be made because of the absence of a placebo and an untreated control group. Number three, two of the therapists were the authors, who were not appropriately incognizant to the purposes of the study, and finally, two of the patients were on medication (chlordiazepoxide) at the time of the investigation, intermixing drug effects with treatment effects.

Marks, Gelder, and Edwards (1968) utilized a crossover design and randomly allocated agoraphobics, social phobics, and similar phobics to either systematic desensitization or hypnosis for 12 weeks of treatment. After the 12 weeks, patient, therapist, and an independent psychiatric assessor rated six outcome variables (e.g., main phobia, other phobias) on a five-point scale. If two of the three raters did not agree that the patient had improved by one or more points on the rating scale, treatment was discontinued for 6 weeks, and if during that time no change had occurred, the alternate treatment was put into effect. The following findings emerged regarding the main phobia: (1) in the original groups, no significant differences between the treatments were evident on the ratings; (2) following crossover, only patient ratings indicated that desensitization was more effective than hypnosis; (3) combining the original plus crossover data, desensitized patients reported significantly more improvement on ratings than the other patients; (4) combining the original and crossover related t tests (pre–post change), significant improvement was evident in desensitized patients.

As in the previous two studies, a methodological overview of this study indicates that we find the same methodological difficulties.

In a study by Benjamin, Marks, and Huson (1972), eight patients with incapacitating phobic disorders (agoraphobic, social, thunder, frogs, and sex) were distributed alternately to two groups in a balanced crossover design. All psychotropic medications were discontinued during the course of therapy, except for one patient, who was instructed never to take his Valium within 36 hours of treatment. All patients received an initial interview, hierarchy construction, one session of relaxation, and an initial assessment. Then one group received six sessions of systematic desensitization, while the other received six sessions of graduated imaginal exposure (without relaxation). A second assessment was then obtained, after which groups crossed over to alternative treatment for six sessions, followed by a final assessment. Outcome measures included galvanic skin response, heart rate, and subjective clinical ratings made by the patient, therapist, and an independent medical assessor. The results indicated that both treatments produced significant improvements in phobic anxiety, avoidance, and subjective anxiety. No changes were observed in the physiological measures. Moreover, no differences between treatments were noted in the clinical and physiological measures. It is interesting that in view of the methodological limitations of this study, pre–post differences were restricted to the subjective measures.

In a later study by Gillan and Rachman (1974), 32 multiphobic psychiatric outpatients were matched by age and IQ, and by duration and severity of phobia, then randomly assigned to one of four conditions: systematic desensitization; individual psychotherapy; relaxation and pseudotherapy; and desensitization in the absence of relaxation (hierarchy only). Patients were allowed to continue only their sleep medication during treatment, and no drugs were permitted for the 24-hour period preceding a treatment session. Pre- and posttreatment and three follow-up assessments were obtained. Outcome measures included subjective ratings by the patient, therapist, and a blind independent assessor; the Eysenck Personality Inventory; a behavioral avoidance test; a subjective estimate (fear thermometer); and a physiological measure. On a total phobic score, the evaluations of those patients who received desensitization and desensitization without relaxation were significantly superior to those of the pseudotherapy and psychotherapy patients. Therapists' ratings of the total and main phobias also indicated that desensitized subjects experienced greater benefit. Furthermore, when it came time for posttreatment and follow-up, patients who received desensitization experienced significantly less anxiety than those given pseudotherapy and psychotherapy. On the avoidance test, desensitized subjects stayed longer in the situation that was most feared than those who received psychotherapy.

Finally, on the fear thermometer, desensitization and hierarchy-only patients experienced more fear reduction than the pseudotherapy group. The authors concluded that systematic desensitization was most effective at posttreatment and follow-up, but not significantly better than the hierarchy-only group. A noteworthy aspect of this study is the use of a placebo condition; however, in the absence of credibility ratings, one is forced to question whether the placebo condition was perceived as a credible treatment. This point is especially important in light of the fact that in the pseudotherapy condition the phobic situation was never discussed. Therapists were instructed to veer the conversation away from that subject whenever it was mentioned by a patient who was presumably there to be treated for a phobia. Moreover, treatment conditions confounded with therapist personality and investigator expectancy as six therapists delivered the psychotherapy condition, whereas the author delivered all remaining treatments. To confound the results even further, numerous outcome measures were evaluated by univariate statistics, which increases the probability of Type I error.

In two investigations, desensitization and flooding were compared. In the first study, Marks, Boulougouris, and Marset (1971) randomly assigned 16 phobic subjects (severe phobics) to two treatment order groups. Half the patients received six sessions of systematic desensitization, followed by six sessions of flooding, and vice versa. Both treatments included therapist-accompanied *in vivo* exposure. Pre- and post-subjective ratings were made by the patient, therapist, and an independent medical assessor on several variables (e.g., main phobia, other phobias), and physiological measures were taken. The year-long follow-up included ratings by the patient and therapist at three-month intervals and an interview with a psychiatric social worker. The results indicated the following: (1) on the therapist evaluations of the main phobia, total phobias, heart rate, and skin conductance, flooding was significantly superior to desensitization; (2) the heart rate increase observed prior to treatment during the main phobic fantasy and phobic talk disappeared after treatment by flooding, but not by desensitization; (3) on therapist's ratings of the main phobia, patients who received flooding followed by desensitization did better than those given the reverse order; (4) several indicators of clinical severity and physiological arousal correlated positively with outcome after flooding. Many of the limitations discussed previously are evident also in this study, including crossover design flaws, statistical problems, and absence of a placebo group.

In the second study by this group, Gelder et al. (1973) divided 36 patients into agoraphobic and nonagoraphobic groups and then randomly assigned them to one of three treatments (nonspecific control, desensitization, and flooding) and to one of three therapists with different orientations (eclectic, analytic, and behavioral). One outstanding feature bears note: to standardize treatments, all three therapists had received four months of training. Multiple outcome measures were obtained by subjective ratings, behavioral testing, psychological testing, and physiological reactivity. Assessments were conducted by the patient, therapists, a psychiatric appraiser, a psychologist, and a social worker, the last three blind to both treatment and therapist, and were gathered pretreatment, posttreatment, and at a six-month follow-up. The findings reached four conclusions: (1) desensitization and flooding proved more effective than the control treatment; (2) on psychiatric ratings of the main phobia and patient ratings of self-improvement, flooding was significantly better than the control group and equal to desensitization; (3) on ratings of social adjustment, all three treatments were equally effective; (4)

behavioral testing indicated that patients who were flooded and desensitized could do more and experienced less anxiety than the control subject, but not by significant proportions.

Actually, the only significant finding here was that flooding patients moved significantly higher up the hierarchy than controls. On ratings of how much fear and somatic complaints patients expected to experience in situations on the behavioral hierarchy, each treatment group differed from controls. On the Fear Survey Schedule, desensitization resulted in a significant reduction in agoraphobic and social phobic symptoms as compared to controls. There are several points in this study that merit special consideration. First, on a positive note, the amount of contact with the therapist and the discussions of symptoms and life situation, goal setting, and positive encouragement were standardized. However, multivariate analysis should have been employed. Finally, no credibility ratings were obtained across the treatments.

Of the seven clinical outcome studies reviewed here, all support the efficacy of systematic desensitization for phobias. However, one study advocates the superiority of flooding over desensitization. We listed a number of limitations on both the internal and external validity of these studies. Future research in this area will have to utilize *DSM III* criteria and more clearly define the patient's specific disorder.

Agoraphobia

Desensitization has been shown to be relatively ineffective in the treatment of agoraphobia. Specifically, four studies (Gelder & Marks, 1966; Lipsedge et al., 1973; Yorkston, Sergeant, & Rachman, 1968; Zitrin, Klein, & Woerner, 1978) found that the procedure does not have impact on agoraphobic symptoms. (Only one study, by Gelder et al., 1973, found desensitization to effect improvement over an attention control condition.) While there are some experimental confounds in these studies, such as Zitrin et al.'s subjects receiving desensitization mixed with supportive therapy, they are methodologically sound investigations. Consequently, it is apparent that systematic desensitization is not the treatment of choice for agoraphobia. Recent reviews of the agoraphobic literature by Mathews, Gelder, and Johnstone (1981) and Jansson and Öst (1982) arrived at the same conclusion.

Social-Evaluative Anxiety

The application of systematic desensitization to the problem of social-evaluative anxiety was carefully analyzed in a series of studies by Paul (1966, 1967, 1968; Paul & Shannon, 1966). Paul's now classic 1966 experiment is one of the most frequently cited studies in behavior therapy literature, and it represents the first well-controlled comparison of systematic desensitization with traditional psychotherapy.

For a variety of reasons, Paul's (1966) investigation is an exemplary methodological study. First, it is important to note that, for the subjects, interpersonal performance anxiety was a clinical problem. For example, at the time of the investigation, one of the main course requirements for graduation at the University of Illinois was public speaking. Second, of a total of 380 volunteers, only the most severely affected subjects were selected for participation. Subjects were carefully screened to exclude those individuals with any of the following characteristics: high falsification scores; a history of previous treatment; little motivation for therapy; psychotic features; and a primary problem other than social-evaluative anxiety. Moreover, the problem duration for the sample ranged from 2 to 20 years and was reported to be most intense in public speaking circumstances. Thus, there was little doubt that the subjects' anxiety was of clinical proportions. Third, multimodal dependent measures, which assessed the cognitive, physiological, and behavioral components of anxiety, were used. Fourth, five experienced and specially trained psychotherapists administered therapy with the following methodological controls strictly adhered to throughout the experiment: (1) random selection ensured that therapist characteristics were not confounded with treatment condition; (2) the use of more than one therapist and the fact of their experience met external validity requirements; (3) uniform desensitization and placebo treatment manuals and tape-recorded monitoring of sessions standardized the presentation; (4) while the order of treatment sessions was counterbalanced among therapists, each treatment was delivered with equal frequency under three different settings. Fifth, Paul compared desensitization to three control conditions: attention placebo; a wait-list control group; and a no-contact control. These conditions allowed the evaluation of nonspecific attention effects; the subjects' participation in the experiment; and the possible outcome of completing therapeutic assessment instruments. Sixth, short-term six-week follow-up measures were gathered as a means of determining whether the effects of therapy were durable.

In view of the well-controlled nature of this investigation, the clinical efficacy of systematic desensitization was firmly established. Systematic desensitization was significantly superior to the no-treatment control condition on cognitive, physiological, and behavioral indices of anxiety. Also, desensitization was superior to traditional psychotherapy and the placebo therapy.

Paul (1967) later published a two-year follow-up study showing that systematic desensitization produced the greatest benefits in comparison to insight therapy, attention placebo, and untreated controls. These findings were consistent with the original findings.

In another study, Paul and Shannon (1966) assessed the efficacy of group desensitization for interpersonal-evaluative anxiety relative to a no-treatment control condition. The 10 subjects chosen had failed to improve in the wait-list control group of Paul's (1966) earlier study and were matched on a pretherapy measure of performance anxiety with 10 subjects in each of Paul's (1966) active treatment conditions. In addition, a control group was formed in order to assess the effects of desensitization upon academic performance. The results indicated that group desensitization produced significant improvement in social-evaluative and general anxiety. Grade point average comparisons dramatized significant differences between desensitization and untreated subjects, with desensitization by far the preferred treatment. Paul's (1968) two-year follow-up of the group-desensitized subjects further supported the durability of improvement on public speaking anxiety, as well as other areas of anxiety such as test and global anxiety. Again, the subjects exhibited no relapses or symptom substitution, and last, in relation to the controls, more than twice as many of the desensitized subjects were succeeding academically. One of the major limitations of this investigation was that the investigators served as the therapists.

Test Anxiety

Systematic desensitization has been frequently employed in the treatment of test anxiety. In an extensive review of the subject, DiTomasso (1980) summarized and methodologically critiqued all of the then available experimental outcome research, dividing the studies into six areas for evaluation: (1) the type of desensitization hierarchy; (2) individual versus group desensitization; (3) additional variations of the desensitization paradigm; (4) the components of the desensitization package; (5) traditional versus self-control desensitization; (6) and desensitization versus other behavioral and cognitive treatments. The following conclusions were drawn: first, variations of both the desensitization hierarchy (individualized versus standard) and the manner of imaginal scene presentation (maximal versus progressive) yielded comparable positive outcomes; second, individually administered and group-administered desensitization produced improvements in both self-reported test anxiety and general anxiety; third, variations of the desensitization paradigm, including marathon group desensitization, massed group desensitization, accelerated massed desensitization, and automated desensitization, were effective in reducing self-reported test anxiety and were analogous to the results obtained with the standard Wolpean treatment format; fourth, relaxation and desensitization generated similar effects; fifth, the incorporation of an active coping skill component in the desensitization program mitigated both test anxiety and, like the standard passive counterconditioning paradigm, general non-targeted anxiety; sixth, combining desensitization with study skills produced anxiety reduction and improved academic performance; and seventh, cognitive behavior modification might be more effective than desensitization.

DiTomasso (1980) took his investigation of the test anxiety literature one step further with an analysis of 51 methodological criteria. An interesting pattern of the strengths and shortcomings of the literature emerged. On the one hand, investigators in general attended to issues of theoretical validity; followed certain commonly acceptable statistical practices; clearly specified the subjects' characteristics, as well as the dependent and independent variables; and standardized their procedures. On the other hand, these same scientists fell into the trap of methodological negligence, which DiTomasso divided into four major categories: (1) subject biases (e.g., motivational biases for participation, mortality effects); (2) therapist-related issues (e.g., failure to monitor treatment delivery); (3) statistical issues (e.g., failure to use multivariate analyses when indicated); and (4) control group issues (e.g., lack of attention–placebo comparisons). Therefore, DiTomasso could draw but one conclusion: the effectiveness of desensitization for test anxiety has not been definitively demonstrated.

Dental Phobia

Dental phobia, the fear and avoidance of dentists, dental procedures, and other stimuli related to dental situations, is quite a common problem. In fact, an estimated 5 million individuals avoid dental care as a result of fear and anxiety. For instance, in a national survey, Friedson and Feldman (1958) discovered that more than half of their sample failed to visit the dentist on a regular basis, and of those individuals, 9% reported fear as the main inhibition. Thus, the considerable efforts given to the modification of dental anxiety are well-founded (Ayer, 1981), especially in view of the risks associated with poor oral health behavior.

With the above facts in mind, it is clear why systematic desensitization has been applied here. An early case report by Gale and Ayer (1969) demonstrated the successful application of desensitization with a patient who had avoided dentists for many years. However, it was not until the work of Shaw and Thoresen (1974) that a controlled evaluation was conducted. In this study, Shaw and Thoresen treated individuals who exhibited clinical levels of dental phobia. Subjects were recruited through local newspaper advertisements and selected on the basis of four criteria: (1) need for dental work; (2) ability to pay for dental care; (3) avoidance of the dentist for at least one year; and (4) refusal during behavioral assessment of an anesthetic injection and the drilling of a small cavity. Thirty-six subjects were randomly assigned to four treatment groups: modeling (relaxation, video-presented social models, and imagined self-modeling); desensitization; placebo; and a wait-list control. To guarantee therapist objectivity, each therapist treated only half of the subjects in each condition. Pretreatment and posttreatment self-report assessments included fear and attitude measures especially developed for the study. In addition, the Fear Survey Schedule II and IPAT Anxiety Scale Questionnaire were administered to evaluate generalization of treatment effects. Finally, at three months, posttreatment subjects were asked whether they had visited a dentist and whether they had had work done. On the basis of their responses, subjects were then categorized as complete successes, partial successes, or failures. Also, to ensure similarity of the treatment protocols, every therapist mutually monitored the other's sessions. Unfortunately, treatment credibility ratings were not obtained.

On the arousal and attitude measures, desensitization and modeling were each significantly superior to the placebo and assessment control conditions. On the more rigorous behavioral measure, however, the modeling treatment yielded more complete success, but not significantly more, than desensitization. Only one of the placebo subjects and none of the wait-list controls achieved complete success. Statistical comparisons between groups showed that while modeling was far more effective than either control, desensitization was decidedly better than the assessment control only. Therefore, in light of the strong effects of the modeling procedure, desensitization, though of value, cannot be considered the treatment of choice for dental phobia.

Obsessive-Compulsive Disorders

Unfortunately, as with many other clinical disorders, there have been no controlled experimental investigations into the efficacy of desensitization for the obsessive-compulsive phenomenon. At this time, only 21 cases treated by 12 therapists have been reported (Beech & Vaughan, 1978), with imaginal and *in vivo* desensitization the procedures used in 50% of these cases. Beech and Vaughan catalogued 11 successes, 5 moderate successes, and 5 complete failures, and after combining the latter two designations into one comprehensive failure category, determined that there is a 52% success rate for systematic desensitization in the treatment of obsessive-compulsive disorders. However, because of the absence of any controlled experimental trials; these conclusions are limited. We cannot conclude that desensitization is effective for obsessive-compulsive disorder.

Depression

Wolpe (1979) has argued that neurotic anxiety is the basis of reactive depression. He has classified such depression into four types, one of which is a reactive depression due to conditioned emotional responses. For such a depressive disorder, he maintains that systematic desensitization is often the appropriate treatment. Case reports do provide some support for this position (e.g., cf. Hollon 1981; Wanderer, 1972; Wolpe, 1979), but in the absence of controlled studies, the efficacy of desensitization in this area remains as yet undemonstrated.

Psychophysiological Disorders

Asthma

Systematic desensitization has also been used in the treatment of asthmatics in whom there is evidence of a psychosomatic component. A psychosomatic illness can be conceptualized as a real physical condition in which an individual's anxiety responses to psychological events become manifested in a periodic overreactivity of some biologically vulnerable organ (Alexander, 1981; Wolpe, 1980). Presumably, the elimination of the anxiety responses will in turn eliminate the hyperreactivity in the target organ.

The first controlled clinical investigation of desensitization with asthmatics was conducted by Moore (1965), who compared systematic desensitization, relaxation training, and relaxation plus suggestions of symptom relief in a balanced incomplete block design. The subjects included six children and six adults, severe asthmatics not currently on steroid medication with a prognosis of reversible obstruction of the airways. There was one child and one adult per block, and each received a combination of two of the treatments, all delivered by the investigator. The dependent measures were the number of asthma attacks (subjective) and the maximum peak flow of inspired air (objective). Despite the encouraging findings that only desensitization produced significantly more improvement in maximum peak flow, Alexander (1981) has criticized the study for obtaining its pulmonary measures on only a weekly basis. Thus, both the periodic nature of asthma and the study's relatively infrequent measurements limit a strong efficacy conclusion.

In a later study, Yorkston, McHugh, Brady, Serber, and Sergeant (1974) randomly assigned 14 adult asthmatics, whose asthma was stabilized on drugs, to two treatments: systematic desensitization ($n = 6$) and relaxation ($n = 8$). Subjects received six half-hourly therapy sessions over a period of two weeks, administered by three psychiatrists experienced with behavior therapy techniques. Relaxation subjects were exposed to standard relaxation exercises in which they were asked to imagine scenes unrelated to asthma and then to practice relaxation in the circumstances depicted by the scenes. The remaining group was systematically desensitized to four themes and visualizations: symptoms of asthma and tensions (e.g., breathlessness, wheezing); the patient's personal description of an attack; distressing thought during an attack; situations in attacks that had personally occurred; and finally, a combination of all four themes. These same subjects were next encouraged to practice *in vivo* desensitization by approaching previously avoided situations.

For both groups, forced expiratory volumes in one-second measures were obtained before and after each session. Patients also rated their own outcome. Finally, one of the original psychiatrists rated each patient, and then his notes were judged by an independent evaluator. At follow-up two years later, the evaluator was kept blind to treatment, therapist, and medication changes.

The authors divided their findings into short-term and long-term effects. In the short term, only verbally desensitized subjects showed significant progress on forced expiratory volume. However, with regard to independent evaluators and subject ratings, although both groups had improved, there were no *significant* differences between groups. In the long term, desensitized subjects showed greater gains than the relaxation group and a greater reduction in the use of all drugs (e.g., steroids).

In the more comprehensive Denver study, Miklich et al. (1977) set out to discover whether systematic desensitization would offer any clinical benefit over and above the standard medical management of asthma. Subjects were juvenile inpatients at a treatment and rehabilitation facility for chronic asthmatic children and met the following criteria: (1) a well-established diagnosis of moderate to severe perennial asthma and (2) at least some evidence that emotional arousal may have precipitated symptoms. Of the total sample of 26 children, 19 received desensitization, and 7 served as controls. Control subjects were determined by the unavailability of a therapist when the child was ready to receive treatment. An elaborate array of outcome measures was gathered, including one-second forced expiratory volume twice a day every day, types of medications and inhaled treatments, number of days hospitalized, and symptom frequency. The frequency of symptoms (i.e., wheezing, chest tightness) was collected by research assistants, who checked on subjects every 30 minutes during the 4 hours preceding bedtime. Furthermore, both the nurses who administered medications and treatments and the desensitization therapists were kept unaware of the subject's status in the study.

Desensitized subjects were exposed to at least five hierarchies from four areas: (1) sensation during an attack; (2) situations in which subjects experienced arousal in response to having or thinking about asthma; (3) reports by the patients or their parents about emotional precipitants; and (4) nonemotional precipitants. In addition, all treated subjects received Jacobsonian relaxation.

Moreover, for some subjects, EMG biofeedback provided further help, while for others, EMG potentials gathered at the therapists' discretion served solely to aid the therapist. To control for therapist effects, five experienced clinical psychologists treated patients. Unfortunately, though the portioning of patients was not uniform, one therapist treated as many as seven subjects while another treated only two subjects. To standardize therapy, only one procedural manual was used, and sessions were monitored periodically. The number of sessions across patients, however, was not standardized.

The results of this study are as follows: during all phases of the experiment (treatment, posttreatment, and follow-up) desensitized subjects had significantly greater change in forced expiratory volume scores than control subjects. This was attributed to a decline on the part of controls. (Interestingly, only on symptom frequency were control subjects more improved than desensitized subjects.) From this, the authors determined that (1) mean improvement in desensitized subjects was clinically insignificant and (2) desensitization may help patients tolerate a reduction in maintenance medication and thereby serve only an ancillary role. Interestingly, individual patient analysis revealed that five subjects showed greater than average progress. This can be interpreted to mean that for some subjects, reducing anxiety and panic about asthma attacks may be clinically helpful.

Muscle Contraction Headache

Daniels (1973) described the case of a 23-year-old female graduate student and teacher. She had for six years suffered from an acute onset of hives (prior to seeking treatment) as well as from severe headaches of two years' duration. The headaches ceased two months prior to treatment, which not incidentally coincided with the closing of school for summer vacation. The headaches resumed one month after school opened in the fall and were associated with poor supervisory evaluations of her. This patient was treated with both covert modeling and systematic desensitization, and the headaches stopped after two months. The patient was symptom-free at a 22-month follow-up. Since uncontrolled case studies preclude conclusions about cause–effect relationships between treatment and outcome, further controlled single-case studies and also experimental outcome studies are sorely needed in this area. Until this happens, the efficacy of desensitization for muscle contraction headache remains undemonstrated.

Migraine Headaches

Systematic desensitization has usually been included as part of a more comprehensive treatment package for migraine headache sufferers. In an investigation with chronic migraine sufferers, Mitchell and Mitchell (1971) conducted two controlled experiments in which a comprehensive behavior therapy package was compared to the component procedures. In Study I, the therapeutic effectiveness of applied relaxation and a combined program (systematic desensitization, applied relaxation, and assertive training) were evaluated with patients who had suffered from migraines for an average of eight years. There were 17 subjects (including university staff and students) with a mean age of approximately 23 years; a medical diagnosis certifying their condition; and a total number of pretreatment frequency of attacks from 3 to 56 (mean = 11.1) per eight weeks. Prior to the study all of the subjects had been taking medication for acute attacks, while three-fourths of the participants also took sleeping agents or tranquilizers. The drugs were either reduced or eliminated for the treatment subjects; for the controls, no changes were made. Subjects were randomly assigned to groups and received 15 sessions (50–60 minutes in length). Pre- and posttreatment measures were obtained on a variety of variables, including frequency and duration of migraines.

Mitchell and Mitchell found that the comprehensive-package patients demonstrated significant reductions in frequency and duration of headaches over a 32-week period. No changes were evident in either the applied relaxation or the control group. These results indicate that combining desensitization with assertiveness may be an effective protocol for reducing the frequency and duration of migraine headaches.

Study II, which utilized a similar experiment format to that of Study I, compared systematic desensitization alone with the combined program. The combined desensitization group had significantly fewer headaches than either the systematic desensitization or no-treatment controls. No significant differences were observed between the systematic desensitization group and controls.

In a later study, Mitchell and White (1977) used a sequential dismantling strategy with 12 individuals diagnosed with migraine, who suffered an average of 13.6 episodes per month. Mean amount of time since the onset of the problem was seven years. Subjects were randomly assigned to four conditions: (1) self-recording; (2) self-monitoring; (3) self-monitoring plus skill acquisition (audio training sessions for cue-controlled relaxation, mental relaxation, self-desensitization); and (4) self-monitoring plus controlled relaxation and mental relaxation. The results showed the self-monitoring plus skill acquisition group to be superior to the other interventions. Thus, overall, systematic desensitization in combination with assertiveness training and cue-controlled relaxation training is an effective treatment for migraine headaches.

Alcoholism

Hedberg and Campbell (1974) investigated the efficacy of systematic desensitization with alcoholics. Participating in this study were 49 outpatient chronic alcoholics who were referred to a mental health center. Each patient could choose either abstinence or controlled drinking as the treatment goal and then was randomly assigned to one of four groups: systematic desensitization, behavioral family counseling, covert sensitization, or aversion therapy. Results were reported in a percentage of subjects by treatment groups who had attained their treatment goal. At a six-month follow-up, both systematic desensitization and behavioral family counseling produced comparable results with regard to the percentage of subjects who attained their goal (67% and 74%, respectively) and those who were much improved (20% and 13%, respectively). The study presents us with its share of pluses and minuses. As a noteworthy feature, the patients received only one treatment, and the order and frequency of sessions were standardized across groups. Unfortunately, the study also suffers from some serious flaws. First, the authors provide insufficient information as to the therapists' background, saying only that they were paraprofessionals. No mention is made as to whether and how the paraprofessionals were trained in the procedures, nor is there an indication that the treatments were monitored. Second, the absence of an attention-placebo group undermined the conclusion that desensitization is potent with alcoholics. One must then suspect that therapist contact was solely answerable for the results. Third, the failure to obtain credibility ratings precludes any conclusion that the treatments were perceived as equally potent across groups. The fact that 66% of the aversion therapy patients left the group clearly indicates that this treatment was differentially perceived and reacted to by patients. Fourth, the criteria for defining a patient as "much improved" are not operationally defined. Finally, the use of a six-month follow-up period with an alcoholic population is insufficient time to evaluate the therapy. It is evident that desensitization is not an effective treatment for alcoholism.

Sexual Disorders

Sexual Deviations

Imaginal or *in vivo* desensitization, when it is either the sole treatment or combined with other behavioral techniques, has been reported to be effective in many case studies of sexual deviations. These include homosexuality (Di Scipio, 1968; Gold & Neufeld, 1965; Gray, 1970; Huff, 1970; Kraft, 1967a, 1967b, 1969; Latimer, 1977; Levin, Hirsch, Shugar, & Kapche, 1968; Lo Piccolo, 1971); exhibitionism (Bond & Hutchinson, 1960; Dengrove, 1967; Wickramasekera, 1968; Wolpe, 1958, 1976; cf. Quirk, 1974, 1982); fetishism (Cooper, 1973; Marquis, 1970); and homosexual pedophilia (Kohlenberg, 1974). In controlled studies of homosexuality, Bancroft (1974) has found desensitization and electrical aversion equally effective. However, there are no controlled experiments demonstrating that systematic desensitization has reliable, profound, and durable effects upon patients presenting with sexual deviations.

Sexual Dysfunctions

In case reports, systematic desensitization has been successful in the treatment of male and female sexual dysfunctions (Hogan, 1978; Wolpe, 1958, 1973, 1982). In controlled studies, desensitization has surpassed control groups, both as the only therapy used (Asirdas & Beech, 1975; Auerbach & Kilman, 1977; Huste, 1975; Kockott, Dittman, & Nusselt, 1975; O'Gorman, 1978; Sotile & Kilmann, 1978) and merged with other behavioral techniques (Munjack et al., 1976; Obler, 1973).

Likewise in the treatment of orgasmic dysfunction related to sexual anxiety, desensitization has generally produced positive results (e.g., Everaerd & Dekker, 1982). However, a number of studies have shown also that decreases in heterosexual anxiety do not always result in very significant improvement in orgasmic functioning (Husted, 1975; Nemetz, Cristol, & Reith, 1978; Wincze & Caird (1976). For example, in the Wincze study, both video-mediated desensitization and systematic desensitization were effective in diminishing sexual anxiety, but for both groups only 25% of the nonorgasmic women became orgasmic.

In two other studies (Everaerd and Dekker, 1982; Mathews et al., 1976), desensitization was not significantly different from a treatment program based on research by Masters and Johnson (1970), while directed masturbation was reported to be better than desensitization for increasing orgasmic functioning. We cannot definitively confirm the effectiveness of desensitization with regard to orgasmic dysfunctions, because all of the related studies have the following methodological difficulties: no groups to control for expectancy effect; the use of inappropriate statistical procedures; and the absence of patient ratings to ensure equal credibility of the treatments.

Other Disorders

Gilles de la Tourette's Syndrome

Thomas, Abrams, and Johnson (1971) used self-monitoring and reciprocal inhibition therapy to successfully eliminate multiple tics in an 18-year-old hospitalized patient, who was currently being treated with haloperidol. The experimenters used a modified multiple baseline design, whereby first a vocal tic and then a newly developed minor vocal sound and neck tic were baselined and modified. Interestingly, the experimenters were able to obtain independent observations in real-life situations and *in vivo* exposure. Thus, they concluded that self-monitoring, reciprocal inhibition therapy, and haloperidol all contributed to improvement in the symptoms, but more specifically, that because relaxation and reciprocal inhibition were introduced prior to self-monitoring, these techniques may have been the primary behavior modifiers. Due to the manner in which the treatments were presented and the fact that when haloperidol was removed the patient worsened, it is difficult to draw any firm conclusion from this case. The use of other controlled single-case experimental designs and controlled-between-subjects studies would prove helpful.

Seizure

It is common knowledge that in some individuals, emotional tension can precipitate seizures. The learning model of seizures suggests that pathological neural responses could be conditioned to visual and auditory stimuli (Efron, 1957). In a case study, Parrino (1971) employed systematic desensitization and self-desensitization in a 36-year-old male who suffered an average of 58 seizures per day. The seizures were triggered by anxiety-provoking situations of a social nature. At a five-month follow-up, the patient was seizure-free. Forster (1966) anecdotally described the case of a patient whose seizures were elicited by the music of Debussy and Sibelius and only when performed by several instruments or instruments with voice. Treatment consisted of the *in vivo* presentation of a graduated hierarchy of increasing orchestration, and after only 50 hours the patient could listen without seizures. Subsequently, male and female voices were added to the orchestration. The patient's sensitivity to the music was totally eliminated. Additional work with desensitization for seizure disorders is needed.

Combination with Drug Treatments

In four investigations (Friedman, 1966; Hafner & Marks, 1976; Mawson, 1970; Yorkston, Sergeant, & Rachman, 1968) the effects of combining desensitization with barbiturates or tranquilizers were evaluated. Yorkston et al. (1968) treated 12 severely agoraphobic men and women with a mean problem duration of approximately five and one-half years whose occupational and social activities were radically altered. In a balanced crossover design, patients received two of the following treatments: methohexitone and desensitization; verbal relaxation, saline, and desensitization; verbal relaxation and desensitization; and methohexitone alone. Two psychiatrists treated six patients each one hour daily for five days. Pre- and posttreatment measures were obtained on several questionnaires, symptom checklists, phobia ratings, fear thermometer (distress score), and a behavioral test. None of the groups was observed to improve significantly.

Later, Mawson (1970), in a controlled crossover trial with 12 moderately severe phobics, compared the effects of methohexitone-assisted desensitization and conventional desensitization. The duration of the phobias ranged from 1 to 15 years. The patients' personal, professional, and leisure activities were interfered with quite severely, and five of them reported suffering high levels of general anxiety. Patients received a total of 12 one-hour weekly sessions with a crossover after the sixth session. The severity of the phobia and degree of general anxiety were assessed prior to treatment, at crossover, and posttreatment. Ratings were provided by the patients, therapists, and an independent blind clinician. The findings revealed that phobias improved more during the drug plus desensitization condition and that this combination may increase the number of phobic patients responsive to treatment.

In an uncontrolled multiple-case study, Friedman and Silverstone (1967) treated 20 male and female phobics with a mean symptom duration of about five years with methohexitone-assisted desensitization. Presenting symptoms included travel phobia, claustrophobia, agoraphobia, and other circumscribed phobias. Patients were treated weekly by the senior author while the other author assessed improvement at the end of treatment. Patients received between 5 and 22 sessions lasting 15 to 20 minutes. At posttreatment, all patients were categorized as much improved, while five were symptom-free. At follow-up, an average of 10.5 months posttreatment, 83% of the patients were rated as much improved or recovered.

In an independent review of the above-listed suggestions, Hollon and Beck (1978) have concluded, "These studies suggest that drug-assisted desensitization may, under certain conditions, prove more effective or at least more rapid, than conventional relaxation training plus desensitization" (p. 469). We should add here that none of these studies incorporated a placebo-control condition and therefore the findings could be attributed merely to therapist attention. Moreover, in some of these studies the limitations of the crossover design are evident.

In two other studies, desensitization was combined with drugs and compared with drug treatments alone. We will briefly review these studies. Lipsedge et al. (1973) evaluated the effects of drug-desensitization combinations in a 3×2 factorial design with 71 severely agoraphobia patients. The six conditions were as follows: (1) methohexitone-assisted systematic desensitization plus iproniazid (25–50 mg $t.d.s.$), (2) methohexitone-assisted systematic desensitization plus placebo pill, (3) standard systematic desensitization (including relaxation training) plus iproniazid, (4) standard systematic desensitization plus placebo pill, (5) iproniazid, and (6) placebo pill. Patients were randomly assigned to one of the conditions. Treatment consisted of 30-minute sessions for eight weeks. Outcome was determined through the use of patient and clinician ratings of degree of anxiety and avoidance. The findings showed that the drug treatment and the drug plus desensitization treatment were effective in reducing avoidance.

Zitrin et al. (1976) conducted a comprehensive controlled investigation of the effects of combining behavioral and drug therapies in treating outpatient phobics. The subjects were divided into three groups: agoraphobics, phobic neurotics (circumscribed), and mixed phobics (e.g., claustrophobics with panic attacks who have no travel restrictions). Random assignment to one of three conditions was made: behavior therapy plus imipramine; behavior therapy plus placebo; and supportive psychotherapy plus imipramine. The first two conditions were double-blind while the last condition was single-blind. Each patient was administered 25 mg of imipramine or placebo initially and the dosage was increased by 25 mg every other day to a maximum of 150 mg daily. Behavior therapy patients received systematic desensitization imaginally and *in vivo* as well as assertive training. Patients who received supportive psychotherapy focused upon obtaining insight into the causes of their behavior through interpretation, confrontation, and reality testing. All patients received weekly 45-minute sessions over the course of a 26-week period. At pretreatment and at other points during treatment, patients were evaluated by the therapist and by an independent assessor both of whom were blind to the medication condition. In addition, patient self-evaluations and those of a spouse or significant other were obtained. Follow-up data were collected at three and six months, as well as yearly follow-ups for five years subsequent to treatment.

Zitrin et al. (1976) have reported their findings on 57 subjects who had completed at least one-half of their treatment. The mean problem duration for this group was 8.8 years (range of 2 to 37 years) and three-fourths of these individuals had previously received about an average of two years of traditional psychotherapy (range of 3 weeks to 8 years). These authors hypothesized that for agoraphobics and mixed phobics, both of whom suffer spontaneous panic attacks, imipramine would inhibit panic while behavior therapy would eliminate anticipatory anxiety. In addition, for those phobics who experienced no panic, behavior therapy plus imipramine would be equal to behavior therapy plus placebo. Finally, behavior therapy was hypothesized to be more effective than supportive psychotherapy. The preliminary findings at the end of the 13th session indicated that (1) agoraphobics and mixed phobics showed more improvement than phobic neurotics on imipramine, whereas the agoraphobics and mixed phobics were most unimproved with the placebo; (2) for agoraphobics and mixed phobics combined, those receiving behavior therapy plus imipramine did significantly better than those who received behavior therapy plus placebo; (3) imipramine-treated patients did significantly better than those treated with behavior therapy plus placebo; (4) for mixed and agoraphobic patients no differences emerged between behavior therapy plus imipramine and supportive therapy plus imipramine; (5) for phobic neurosis there was no difference between behavior therapy plus imipramine and behavior therapy plus placebo; and (6) for phobic neurosis patients, no difference between imipramine and placebo patients was observed.

The findings of this investigation, however, must be viewed with certain methodological considerations in mind. We are in agreement with Hollon and Beck (1978), who have criticized the manner in which comparisons were made in this investigation. First, they argued that the investigators appear to equate behavior therapy with behavior therapy plus placebo. This assumption is faulty, thereby necessitating the addition of a behavior therapy-only group. Second, Hollon and Beck (1978) point out the unjustifiability of collapsing over behavior therapy plus imipramine and supportive therapy plus imipramine in order to evaluate the effects of imipramine versus the placebo drug. Possible interactions between the drug and one or the other psychological treatments may account for the results. These criticisms would call into question conclusions 1, 3, and 6 described above. Finally, we would caution the reader from a statistical standpoint. Numerous *t* tests were calculated instead of the preferred multivariate analysis.

Despite these cautions, our review indicates that systematic desensitization does mix well with pharmacological interventions. How well desensitization combines with other psychological techniques (such as insight psychotherapy) is yet to be determined.

Mechanisms of Action

Over the years, a number of theories have been proposed to explain the efficacy of systematic desensitization. These include reciprocal inhibition, exposure accounts, and processing accounts of various sorts.

Reciprocal Inhibition

It has been Wolpe's (e.g., 1958, 1973, 1976, 1981) position over the years that *reciprocal inhibition* underlies systematic desensitization: if one behavior increases in strength, then other behaviors, in compensation, must decrease in strength. For example, relaxation and anxiety are responses that reciprocally inhibit one another. As a result, if an anxiety-arousing stimulus that is weak in strength is presented when the patient is relaxed, counterconditioning will occur. The particular stimulus will no longer elicit anxiety, but will instead elicit the relaxation response. Other responses, besides relaxation, may also inhibit anxiety (see Wolpe, 1973).

Pavlovian counterconditioning is a robust phenomenon that occurs in a number of animal conditioning preparations (e.g., Pavlov, 1927; Pearce & Dickinson, 1975). A number of learning theorists have suggested, moreover, that reciprocal inhibition underlies counterconditioning (e.g., Estes, 1969). In addition, in the past decade, a number of quantitative models of operant and Pavlovian conditioning have been proposed. Despite the diversity of models that have been proposed, they all assume reciprocal inhibition. This is not to say that all that is involved in operant or Pavlovian conditioning is reciprocal inhibition. But it appears that reciprocal inhibition is an important aspect of learning. Of all the models that have been proposed, there are two that have been the most influential. In the case of operant conditioning, it is the one proposed by Herrnstein (1979). In the case of Pavlovian conditioning, it is the model proposed by Rescorla and Wagner (1972) and Wagner and Rescorla (1972).

Exposure

Other accounts of systematic desensitization challenge the theory of reciprocal inhibition. It has been suggested that it is simply the *exposure* to the feared stimulus by the patient that results in the decrease in anxiety (e.g., Marks, 1981). The exposure results in the extinction of habituation of the anxiety response (Delprato, 1973; Kazdin & Wilcoxon, 1976; Lader & Matthew, 1968; Waters, McDonald, & Koreska, 1972; Watts, 1979).

Processing

In the past decade, processing explanations of various kinds have been proposed. The cognitive explanations suggest that desensitization restructures the patients' cognitions (e.g., Beck, 1976) or changes his self-efficacy (Bandura, 1977) so that he is nò longer anxious in the presence of the feared stimulus. Rachman (1980) has suggested that desensitization allows emotional processing to occur so that the anxiety-arousing stimuli are satisfactorily absorbed and integrated by the patient (Lang, 1977).

Self-Control

An understanding of desensitization in terms of a coping or self-control mechanism has been offered by Goldfried (1971). Finally, it should be noted that a psychoanalytic explanation (Silverman, Frank, & Dachinger, 1974) in terms of the patient's "unconscious merging fantasies" with the therapist has been presented, but there is evidence against it (Condon & Allen, 1980; Emmelkamp & Straatman, 1976).

Side Effects

The issue of side effects in behavior therapy has indeed been a controversial one. From the psychoanalytic perspective, systematic desensitization, like other behavioral interventions, is a treatment aimed at the alleviation of a symptom (e.g., fear) without regard for the underlying psychic cause of the syndrome. Presumably, the failure to treat the underlying psychodynamic cause results in "symptom substitution," i.e., the reappearance of the original symptom or the appearance of a new substitute program.

Kazdin (1978) has astutely criticized the concept of symptom substitution. He points out that psychodynamic theorists invoke the concept despite their failure to specify (1) how to determine when the phenomenon occurs, (2) the types of symptoms that should occur, (3) the conditions under which the symptoms arise, and (4) the interval of time one must wait for symptoms to appear. Nonetheless, efforts aimed at evaluating the viability of symptom substitution have yielded extremely discouraging results. Review of case studies and controlled investigations argue against symptom substitution (Kazdin, 1978; Rimm & Masters, 1974).

Thus, there appear to be no adverse side effects in employing systematic desensitization. In fact, there is some evidence to suggest that the benefits of desensitization may generalize to other untreated (nontargeted) but related problems (e.g., test anxiety and public speaking anxiety) (Zemore, 1975).

Contraindications

Clinical experience and research have revealed several contraindications for systematic desensitization (Rimm & Masters, 1974). We have conveniently divided contraindications into three areas: the patient's presenting complaint(s), the patient's ability to imagine, and the patient's ability to relax.

The number and types of problems with which a patient presents have been shown to affect the course of outcome with desensitization. In an early study, Lang and Lazovik (1963) reported an inverse relationship with desensitization. The implication of this finding is that patients with relatively fewer phobias may be expected to obtain greater benefits from desensitization than those who suffer from many phobias.

There is also evidence available which suggests that desensitization may be relatively more cost effective for some types of complaints than others. These data are reviewed in the separate sections on clinical problems. In sum, it is safe to conclude that desensitization is not indicated for patients with free-floating anxiety (Foa, Steketee, & Ascher, 1980) and that it is of only limited value in the treatment of obsessive-compulsives (Foa & Tillmanns, 1980) and agoraphobics (Foa et al., 1980).

Finally, Rimm and Masters (1974) emphasize the importance of the patient possessing the prerequisite skills for confronting the feared target. Thus, desensitization alone is contraindicated in treating patients who lack the necessary skills to cope with the target situation. For example, no amount of desensitization is expected to cure a social phobic whose learning history reveals a decisive social skills deficit.

The inability of a client to clearly and vividly imagine hierarchy scenes with appropriate emotion is another contraindication for systematic desensitization. Clients who have difficulty imagining scenes clearly are unlikely to benefit from a procedure based upon the use of imagery. Moreover, a positive relationship exists between the rated degree of clarity of a fearful image and the amount of physiologically measured anxiety (Grossberg & Wilson, 1968; Rimm & Bottrell, 1969). *In vivo* desensitization provides a useful alternative for patients who have difficulty imagining scenes.

A final contraindication for desensitization is the inability of a patient to respond to relaxation (Rimm & Masters, 1974). Medication is sometimes used to facilitate relaxation or an alternative to relaxation that is also incompatible with anxiety must be found.

Conclusions

The purpose of this chapter was to review the evidence for the effectiveness of systematic desensitization and to delineate the specific disorders for which it is the treatment of choice.

Because the literature on desensitization is truly voluminous, we, at first, thought to easily demarcate those psychological problems for which it is an effective treatment from those for which it is not, especially in view of several important critical review papers which supported the efficacy of systematic desensitization (Kazdin & Wilcoxin, 1976; McGlynn, Mealiea, & Landau, 1981; Paul, 1969). However, much to our surprise, only a small proportion of the studies yielded unambiguous results.

The principal problem with the desensitization literature is that it consists of uncontrolled case studies. While case studies serve the important function of generating ideas and useful research directions, they cannot serve as definitive evidence of merit. The exception to this rule is the single-case experimental design since there is controlled manipulation of the treatment condition, which ensures that causal relationships are clearly evident (Hersen & Barlow, 1976). Unfortunately, the desensitization case studies reviewed here are not of this type. Thus, one clear direction for future research on systematic desensitization is replication of much of the case study literature in the single-case experimental design format.

When experimental trials have been conducted, they generally suffer from methodological problems inherent in much of psychotherapy research: (1) the lack of experimental controls, such as wait-list controls and placebo groups; (2) the use of assessment measures which have no established validity and reliability properties; (3) the reliance upon self-report measures in lieu of behavioral avoidance and psychophysiological evaluations (the rare exemplary exception is the study by Paul, 1966); and (4) the absence of sound diagnostic procedures.

Outcome research on systematic desensitization has also assumed that patients and therapists were interchangeable, thus adhering to dangers of the uniformity myth described by Kiesler (1971) and Turner and Ascher (1982). As Paul (1966) so cogently argued, the task for research is to determine what patient working with which therapist responds to systematic desensitization.

Finally, a number of procedural problems have invalidated the desensitization studies. Seldom have researchers verified the psychological credibility of the alternative treatments to which desensitization has been compared (Kazdin & Wilcoxin, 1976), unfortunately raising the question of whether the technique was actually more effective than a realistic placebo manipulation. In addition, the desensitization literature is replete with the use of liberal statistical procedures, which only inflate the probability of obtaining significant findings. In most studies where multiple outcome measures were utilized, multivariate statistical analyses should have been used. This error is not seriously misleading, but unlike a more conservative perspective, it can permit an interpretation of major experimental effects where actually there are none (Turner, 1978).

Now we come to the task of determining exactly for which psychiatric disorders desensitization would be the preferred treatment. Childhood phobias require far more specific research. There have been nonexperimental case studies and only one experiment by Miller et al. (1972) which showed no difference between systematic desensitization and a no-treatment control condition. Subjects in both conditions improved; however, desensitization patients responded more quickly.

On the other hand, there is strong evidence that desensitization can abate adult phobic disorders. As you will recall from the section on phobias, there are methodological problems with many of these studies. Nevertheless, we should listen to Smith and Glass (1977) and Rosenthal (1978), who wisely argue that when many studies point to the same conclusion, we have detected a reliable trend. The strengths and limitations of the aggregate studies compensate for one another and cancel out external validity violations. In fact, under such varied conditions, the external validity of the findings is in fact greatly strengthened. Thus the weight of the evidence supports systematic desensitization as an effective treatment for adult phobias. The agoraphobic response to desensitization presents another picture. The studies accumulated to date indicate that the procedure is not generally successful for this disorder.

Speech anxiety appears to respond very well to systematic desensitization. The work of Gordon Paul (1966), with its methodological rigor and soundness, is a model for all therapy outcome research.

With regard to test anxiety, the studies generally indicate that desensitization is an effective treatment; but, as we pointed out, there are severe drawbacks to this group of studies.

Dental phobia is shown by one experiment to improve with treatment by desensitization. More specific research will have to be conducted in this area to allow anything other than a cautious conclusion.

With regard to obsessive-compulsive disorder, there have been no controlled experimental studies assessing the impact of systematic desensitization. Numerous uncontrolled case studies abound which suggest a positive treatment effect, but in the absence of controlled experimental trials, we can make no definite judgments.

The situation with depression is much the same as with obsessive-compulsive disorder. In the absence of controlled experimental trials, the efficacy of desensitization treatment for depression remains undemonstrated.

Asthma responds well to desensitization in an ancillary fashion. Several case studies and controlled experimental investigations suggest that psychogenic components of the asthmatic disorder, for patients treated with desensitization, can be utilized in an ancillary fashion to help reduce the amount of medication required to control the patient's symptoms. Further research will need to focus on delineating specific patient types who best respond to treatment.

There are three other disorders which have received attention through case studies but have not been experimentally examined: muscle contraction headaches; Gilles de la Tourette's syndrome; and seizure disorders.

Desensitization plays an important ancillary role in the successful treatment of sexual disorders. Although there are deficiencies in the studies of sexual deviations and sexual dysfunctions, the procedure does produce reductions in heterosexual anxiety, if not improvements in performance.

You can now see why no omnibus statement concerning the efficacy of systematic desensitization is possible. In some cases, the evidence is pro and con, while in others it is undetermined. This situation ensues from the overreporting of uncontrolled case studies.

Because individual cases present the greatest opportunity for obtaining treatment outcome data, in the future clinician investigators will need to make more use of single-case experimental designs.

References

Alexander, A. B. Asthma. In S. N. Haynes & L. Gannon. *Psychosomatic disorders*. New York: Praeger Publishers, 1981.

Asirdas, S., & Beech, H. R. The behavioral treatment of sexual inadequacy. *Journal of Psychosomatic Research*, 1975, *19*, 345–353.

Auerbach, R., & Kilman, P. R. The effects of group systematic desensitization on secondary erectile failure. *Behavior Therapy*, 1977, *8*, 330–339.

Ayer, W. A. Dental providers and oral health behavior. *Journal of Behavioral Medicine*, 1981, *4*(3), 272–282.

Bancroft, J. *Deviant sexual behaviours: Modification and assessment*. Oxford: Clarendon, 1974.

Bandura, A. Self-efficacy: Toward a unifying theory of behavioral change. *Psychological Review*, 1977, *84*, 191–215.

Beck, A. T. *Cognitive therapy and the emotional disorders*. New York: International Universities Press, 1976.

Beech, H. R., & Vaughan, M. *Behavioral treatment of obsessional states*. New York: Wiley, 1978.

Benjamin, S., Marks, I. M., & Huson, J. Active muscular relaxation in desensitization of phobic patients. *Psychological Medicine*, 1972, *2*, 381–390.

Bond, I. K., & Hutchison, H. C. Application of reciprocal inhibition therapy to exhibitionism. *Canadian Medical Association Journal*, 1960, *83*, 23–25.

Condon, T. J., & Allen, G. J. The role of psychoanalytic merging fantasies in systematic desensitization: A rigorous methodological examination. *Journal of Abnormal Psychology*, 1980, *89*, 437–443.

Cooper, A. J. A case of fetishism and impotence treated by behavior therapy. *British Journal of Psychiatry*, 1973, *109*, 649–652.

Daniels, L. Treatment of uticaria and severe headache by behavior therapy. *Psychosomatics*, 1973, *14*, 347–351.

Delprato, D. J. Exposure to the aversive stimulus in an animal analogue to systematic desensitization. *Behaviour Research and Therapy*, 1973, *11*, 187–192.

Dengrove, E. Behavior therapy of the sexual disorders. *The Journal of Sex Research*, 1967, *3*, 49–61.

Di Scipio, W. Modified progressive desensitization and homosexuality. *British Journal of Medical Psychology*, 1968, *41*, 267–272.

DiTomasso, R. A. A meta-analyses of therapy outcome research with test anxious college students. Unpublished doctoral dissertation, University of Pennsylvania, 1980.

Efron, R. Conditioned inhibition of uncinate fits. *Brain,* 1957, *80,* 251, 262.

Emmelkamp, P. M., & Straatman, H. A psychoanalytic reinterpretation of the effectiveness of systematic desensitization. Fact or fiction? *Behaviour Research and Therapy,* 1976, *14,* 245–249.

Estes, W. K. Outline of a theory of punishment. In B. A. Campbell & R. M. Church (Eds.), *Punishment and aversive behavior.* New York: Appleton-Century-Crofts, 1969.

Everaerd, W., & Dekker, J. Treatment of secondary orgasmic dysfunction: A comparison of systematic desensitization and sex therapy. *Behaviour Research and Therapy,* 1982, *20,* 269–274.

Foa, E. B., Grayson, J. B., Steketee, G. S., Doppelt, H. G., Turner, R. M., & Latimer, P. R. Success and failure in the behavioral treatment of obsessive-compulsives. *Journal of Consulting and Clinical Psychology,* 1983, *51,* 287–297.

Foa, E., Steketee, G., & Ascher, L. M. Systematic desensitization. In A. Goldstein & E. Foa (Eds.), *Handbook of behavioral intervention.* New York: Wiley, 1980.

Foa, E., & Tillmanns, A. The treatment of obsessive-compulsive neurosis. In A. Goldstein & E. Foa (Eds.), *Handbook of behavioral intervention.* New York: Wiley, 1980.

Forster, F. M. Conditioning in sensory evoked seizures. *Conditioned Reflex* 1966, *1,* 4.

Friedman, D. A new technique for the systematic desensitization of phobic symptoms. *Behavior Research and Therapy,* 1966, *4,* 139–140.

Friedman, D. E. I., & Silverstone, J. T. Treatment of phobic patients by systematic desensitization. *Lancet,* 1967, *1,* 470–472.

Friedson, E., & Feldman, J. Public looks at dental care. *Journal of the American Dental Association,* 1958, *57,* 325–331.

Gale, E., & Ayer, N. M. Treatment of dental phobias. *Journal of the American Dental Association,* 1969, *73,* 1304–1307.

Gantt, W. H. Experimental basis for neurotic behavior. *Psychosomatic Medicine Mongraph, 3,* Nos. 3 and 4, 1944.

Garvey, W. P., & Hegreaves, J. R. Desensitization techniques in the treatment of school phobia. *American Journal of Orthopsychiatry,* 1966, *36,* 147–152.

Gelder, M. G., Bancroft, J. H. J., Gath, D. H., Johnson, D. W., Mathews, A. M., & Shaw, P. M. Specific and nonspecific factors in behavior therapy. *British Journal of Psychiatry,* 1973, *123,* 445.

Gelder, M. G., & Marks, I. M. Severe agoraphobia: A controlled prospective trial of behavior therapy. *British Journal of Psychiatry,* 1966, *112,* 309–319.

Gelder, M. G., Marks, I. M., & Wolff, H. Desensitization and psychotherapy in phobic states: A controlled enquiry. *British Journal of Psychiatry,* 1967, *113,* 53.

Gelder, M. G., & Marks, I. M. A crossover study of desensitization in phobias. *British Journal of Psychiatry,* 1968, *114,* 323–328.

Gillan, P., & Rachman, S. An experimental investigation of behavior therapy in phobic patients. *British Journal of Psychiatry,* 1974, *124,* 392.

Gold, S., & Neufeld, I. L. A learning approach to the treatment of homosexuality. *Behaviour Research and Therapy,* 1965, *2,* 201–204.

Goldfried, M. R. Systematic desensitization as training in self-control. *Journal of Consulting and Clinical Psychology,* 1971, *37,* 228–234.

Gray, J. J. Case conference: Behavior therapy in a patient with homosexual fantasies and heterosexual anxieties. *Journal of Behavior Therapy and Experimental Psychiatry,* 1970, *1,* 225, 232.

Grossberg, J. M., & Wilson, H. K. Physiological changes accompanying the visualization of fearful and neutral situations. *Journal of Personality and Social Psychology,* 1968, *10,* 124–133.

Hafner, J., & Marks, I. Exposure in vivo of agoraphobics: Contributions of diazepam group exposure and anxiety evocation. *Psychological Medicine,* 1976, *6,* 71–88.

Hampe, E., Noble, H., Miller, L. C., & Barrett, C. L. Phobic children one and two years posttreatment. *Journal of Abnormal Psychology,* 1973, *82,* 446–453.

Hedberg, A. G., & Campbell, L. A. A comparison of four behavioral treatments of alcoholism. *Journal of Behavior Therapy and Experimental Psychiatry,* 1974, *5,* 251–256.

Herrnstein, R. J. Derivatives of matching. *Psychological Review,* 1979, *86,* 486–495.

Hersen, M., & Barlow, D. H. *Single case experimental designs.* New York: Pergamon, 1976.

Hogan, D. R. The effectiveness of sex therapy: A review of the literature. In J. LoPiccolo & L. LoPiccolo (Eds.), *Handbook of sex therapy.* New York: Plenum, 1978.

Hollon, S. D. Comparisons and combinations with alternative approaches. In L. P. Rehm (Ed.), *Behavior therapy for depression.* New York: Academic Press, 1981.

Hollon, S. D., & Beck, A. T. Psychotherapy and drug therapy: Comparison and combinations. In S. L. Garfield & A. E. Bergin (Eds.), *Handbook of psychotherapy and behavior change: An empirical analysis.* New York: Wiley, 1978.

Huff, F. The desensitization of a homosexual. *Behavior Research and Therapy,* 1970, *8,* 99–102.

Husted, J. R. Desensitization procedures in dealing with female sexual dysfunction. *The Counseling Psychologist,* 1975, *5,* 30–37.

Jacobson, E. *Progressive relaxation.* Chicago: University of Chicago Press, 1938.

Jansson, L., & Öst, L. G. Behavioral treatments for agoraphobia: An evaluative review. *Clinical Psychology Review,* 1982, *2,* 311–336.

Jones, M. C. A laboratory study of fear: The case of Peter. *Pediatrics Seminar,* 1924, *31,* 308–315.

Kazdin, A. E. *History of behavior modification: Experimental foundations of contemporary research.* Baltimore: University Park Press, 1978.

Kazdin, A. E., & Wilcoxon, L. A. Systematic desensitization and nonspecific treatment effects: A methodological evaluation. *Psychological Bulletin,* 1976, *83,* 729–758.

Kiesler, D. J. Experimental designs in psychotherapy research. In A. E. Bergen & S. L. Garfield (Eds.), *Handbook of psychotherapy and behavior change.* New York: Wiley, 1971.

Kockott, G., Dittman, F., & Nusselt, L. Systematic desensitization of erectile impotence: A controlled study. *Archives of Sexual Behavior,* 1975, *4,* 493–500.

Kohlenberg, R. J. Treatment of a homosexual pedophiliac using in vivo desensitization: A case study. *Journal of Abnormal Psychology,* 1974, *83,* 182–195.

Kraft, T. A case of homosexuality treated by systematic desensitization. *American Journal of Psychotherapy,* 1967, *21,* 815–821. (a)

Kraft, T. Behavior therapy and the treatment of sexual perversions. *Psychotherapy and Psychosomatics,* 1967, *15,* 351–357. (b)

Kraft, T. Desensitization and the treatment of sexual disorders. *The Journal of Sex Research,* 1969, *5,* 130–134.

Lader, M. H., & Mathews, A. M. A physiological model of phobic anxiety and desensitization. *Behavior Research and Therapy,* 1968, *6,* 411–424.

Lang, P. J. Imagery in therapy: An information processing analysis of fear. *Behavior Therapy,* 1977, *8,* 862–886.

Lang, P. J., & Lazovik, A. D. Experimental desensitization of a phobia. *Journal of Abnormal and Social Psychology,* 1963, *66,* 519–525.

Latimer, P. A case of homosexuality treated by in vivo desensitization and assertive training. *Canadian Psychiatric Association Journal,* 1977, *22,* 185–189.

Lazarus, A. A. Group therapy of phobic disorders by systematic desensitization. *Journal of Abnormal and Social Psychology,* 1961, *63,* 504–510.

Levin, S., Hirsch, I., Shugar, G., & Kapche, R. Treatment of homosexuality and heterosexual anxieties with avoidance conditioning and systematic desensitization: Data and case report. *Psychotherapy: Theory, Research, and Practice,* 1968, *5,* 160–168.

Lipsedge, M., Hajioff, J., Huggins, P., Napier, L., Pearce, J., Pike, D. J., & Rich, M. The management of severe agoraphobia: A comparison of iproniazid and systematic desensitization. *Psycho-Pharmacologia,* 1973, *32,* 67–80.

LoPiccolo, J. Case study: Systematic desensitization of homosexuality. *Behavior Therapy,* 1971, *2,* 394–399.

Marks, I. *Cure and care of neuroses: Theory and practice of behavioral psychotherapy.* New York: Wiley, 1981.

Marks, I., Boulougouris, J., & Marset, P. Flooding versus desensitization in the treatment of phobic patients: A crossover study. *British Journal of Psychiatry,* 1971, *119,* 353–375.

Marks, I., Gelder, M. G., & Edwards, G. Hypnosis and desensitization for phobias. A controlled prospective trial. *British Journal of Psychiatry,* 1968, *114,* 1263–1274.

Marquis, J. N. Orgasmic reconditioning: Changing sexual object through controlling masturbation fantasies. *Journal of Behavior Therapy and Experimental Psychiatry,* 1970, *1,* 263–271.

Masserman, T. H., *Behavior and neurosis.* Chicago: University of Chicago Press, 1943.

Masters, W. H., & Johnson, V. E. *Human sexual inadequacy.* Boston: Little, Brown, 1970.

Mathews, A., Bancroft, J., Whitehead, A., Hackman, A., Julier, D., Bancroft, J., Goth, D., & Shaw, P. The behavioural treatment of sexual inadequacy: A comparative study. *Behaviour Research and Therapy,* 1976, *14,* 427–436.

Mathews, A. M., Gelder, M. G., & Johnston, D. W. *Agoraphobia Nature and Treatment.* New York: Guilford Press, 1981.

Mawson, A. B. Methohexitone-assisted desensitization in treatment of phobias. *Lancet,* 1970, *1,* 1084–1086.

McGlynn, F. D., Mealiea, W. L., & Landau, D. L. The current status of systematic desensitization. *Clinical Psychology Review,* 1981, *1,* 149–179.

Miklich, D. R., Renne, C. M., Creer, T. L., Alexander, A. B., Chai, H., Davis, M. H., Hoffman, A., & Danker-Brown, P. The clinical utility of behavior therapy as an adjunctive treatment for asthma. *Journal of Allergy and Clinical Immunology,* 1977, *60,* 285–294.

Miller, L. D., Barrett, C. L., Hampe, E., & Noble, H. Comparison of reciprocal inhibition, psychotherapy, and waiting list control for phobic children. *Journal of Abnormal Psychology,* 1972, *79,* 269–279.

Mitchell, K. R., & Mitchell, D. M. Migraine: An exploratory treatment application of programmed behavior therapy techniques. *Journal of Psychosomatic Research,* 1971, *15,* 137–157.

Mitchell, K. R., & White, R. G. Behavioral self-management: An application to the problem of migraine headaches. *Behavior Therapy,* 1977, *98,* 213–221.

Moore, N. Behavior therapy in bronchial asthma: A controlled study. *Journal of Psychosomatic Research,* 1965, *9,* 257–276.

Munjack, D., Cristol, A., Goldstein, A., Phillips, D., Goldberg, A., Whipple, K., Staples, F., & Konno, P. Behavioural treatment of orgasmic dysfunction: A controlled study. *British Journal of Psychiatry,* 1976, *129,* 497–502.

Nemetz, G. H., Craig, K. D., & Reith, G. Treatment of female sexual dysfunction through symbolic modeling. *Journal of Consulting and Clinical Psychology,* 1978, *46,* 62–73.

Obler, M. Systematic desensitization in sexual disorders. *Journal of Behavior Therapy and Experimental Psychiatry,* 1973, *4,* 93–101.

O'Gorman, E. C. The treatment of frigidity: A comparative study of group and individual desensitization. *The British Journal of Psychiatry*, 1978, *132*, 580–584.

Parrino, J. J. Reduction of seizures by desensitization. *Journal of Behavior Therapy and Experimental Psychiatry*, 1971, *2*, 215–218.

Paul, G. L. *Insight vs. desensitization in psychotherapy. An experiment in anxiety reduction.* Stanford, CA: Stanford University Press, 1966.

Paul, G. Insight vs. desensitization in psychotherapy two years after termination. *Journal of Consulting Psychology*, 1967, *31*, 333–348.

Paul, G. A two year follow-up of systematic desensitization in therapy groups. *Journal of Abnormal Psychology*, 1968, *73*, 119–130.

Paul, G. L. Outcome of systematic desensitization. In C. M. Franks (Ed.), *Behavior therapy: Appraisal and status.* New York: McGraw-Hill, 1969.

Paul, G. L., & Shannon, D. T. Treatment of anxiety through systematic desensitization in therapy groups. *Journal of Abnormal Psychology*, 1966,*71*, 124–135.

Pavlov, I. P. *Conditioned reflexes.* London: Oxford University Press, 1927.

Pavlov, I. P. *Conditioned reflexes and psychiatry.* W. H. Gantt (trans.). New York: International, 1941.

Pearce, J. M., & Dickinson, A. Pavlovian counterconditioning: Changing the suppressive properties of shock by association with food. *Journal of Experimental Psychology: Animal Behavior Processes*, 1975,*1*, 170–177.

Quirk, D. A. A follow-up on the Bond-Hutchison case of systematic desensitization with an exhibitionist. *Behavior Therapy*, 1974, *5*, 428–431.

Quirk, D. A. A second decade follow-up of the Bond-Hutchison case of systematic desensitization with an exhibitionist. *Behavior Therapist*, 1982, *5*, 46–47.

Rachman, S. Emotional processing. *Behaviour Research and Therapy*, 1980, *18*, 51–60.

Rescorla, R. A., & Wagner, A. R. A theory of Pavlovian conditioning: Variations in the effectiveness of reinforcement and nonreinforcement. In A. H. Black & W. F. Prokasy (Eds.), *Classical conditioning, II. Current research and theory.* New York: Appleton-Century-Crofts, 1972.

Rimm, D. C., & Bottrell, J. Four measures of visual imagination. *Behavior, Research and Therapy*, 1969, *7*, 63–69.

Rimm, D. C., & Masters, J. C. *Behavior therapy: Techniques and empirical findings.* New York: Academic Press, 1974.

Rosenthal, R. Combining results of independent studies. *Psychological Bulletin*, 1978, *85*, 185–193.

Shaw, D., & Thoresen, C. Effects of modeling and desensitization in reducing dental phobia. *Journal of Counseling Psychology*, 1974, *21*, 415–420.

Sherrington, C. S. *Integrative action of the nervous system.* New Haven, CT: Yale University Press, 1906.

Silverman, L. H., Frank, S., & Dachinger, P. Psychoanalytic reinterpretation of the effectiveness of systematic desensitization: Experimental data bearing on the role of merging fantasies. *Journal of Abnormal Psychology*, 1974, *83*, 313–318.

Smith, M. L., & Glass, G. V. Meta-analysis of psychotherapy outcome studies. *American Psychologist*, 1977, *32*, 752–760.

Sotile, W. M., & Kilmann, P. R. The effects of group systematic desensitization of orgasmic dysfunction. *Archives of Sexual Behavior*, 1978, *7*, 477–491.

Thomas, E. J., Abrams, K. S., & Johnson, J. B. Self-monitoring and reciprocal inhibition in the modification of multiple tics of Gilles de la Tourette's Syndrome. *Journal of Behavior Therapy and Experimental Psychiatry*, 1971, *2*, 159–171.

Turner, R. M. Multivariate assessment of therapy outcome research. *Journal of Behavior Therapy and Experimental Psychiatry*, 1978, *9*, 309–314.

Turner, R. M., & Ascher, L. M. Therapist factor in the treatment of insomnia. *Behavior, Research and Therapy*, 1982, *20*, 33–40.

Wagner, A. R., & Rescorla, R. A. Inhibition in Pavlovian conditioning: Applications of a theory. In R. A. Bookes & M. S. Halliday (Eds.), *Inhibition and learning*. New York: Academic Press, 1972.

Wanderer, Z. W. Existential depression treated by desensitization of phobias: Strategy and transcript. *Journal of Behavior Therapy and Experimental Psychiatry*, 1972, *3*, 111–116.

Waters, W. F., McDonald, D. G., & Koresko, R. L. Psychophysiological responses during analogue systematic desensitization and non-relaxation control procedures. *Behaviour Research and Therapy*, 1972, *10*, 381–394.

Watson, J. B. *Behaviourism*. New York: W. W. Norton, 1925.

Watson, J. B., & Rayner, R. Conditioned emotional reactions. *Journal of Experimental Psychology*, 1920, *3*, 1–14.

Watts, F. N. Habituation model of systematic desensitization. *Psychological Bulletin*, 1979, *86*, 627–637.

Wickramasekera, I. The application of learning theory to the treatment of a case of sexual exhibitionism. *Psychotherapy: Theory, Research and Practice*, 1968, *5*, 108–112.

Wincze, J. P., & Caird, W. K. The effect of systematic desensitization and video desensitization on the treatment of essential sexual dysfunction in women. *Behavior Therapy*, 1976, *7*, 335–342.

Wolpe, J. *Psychotherapy by reciprocal inhibition*. Stanford: Stanford University Press, 1958.

Wolpe, J. *The practice of behavior therapy* (2nd ed.). New York: Pergamon Press, 1973.

Wolpe, J. *Theme and variations: A behavior therapy casebook*. New York: Pergamon, 1976.

Wolpe, J. The experimental model and treatment of neurotic depression. *Behaviour Research and Therapy*, 1979, *17*, 555–565.

Wolpe, J. Reciprocal inhibition and therapeutic change. *Journal of Behavior Therapy and Experimental Psychiatry*, 1981, *12*, 185–188.

Wolpe, J. *The practice of behavior therapy* (3rd ed.). New York: Pergamon Press, 1982.

Yorkston, N. J., McHugh, R. B., Brady, R., Serber, M., & Sergeant, H. G. S. Verbal desensitization in bronchial asthma. *Journal of Psychosomatic Research*, 1974, *18*, 371.

Yorkston, N., Sergeant, H., & Rachman, S. Methohexitone relaxation for desensitizing agoraphobic patients. *Lancet*, 1968, *2*, 651–653.

Zemore, R. Systematic desensitization as a method of teaching a general anxiety reducing skill. *Journal of Consulting and Clinical Psychology*, 1975, *43*, 157–161.

Zitrin, C. M., Klein, D. F., Lindemann, C., Tobak, P., Roch, M., Kaplan, J. H., & Ganz, V. H. Comparisons of short-term treatment regimens in phobic patients. In R. L. Spitzer & D. F. Klein (Eds.), *Evaluation of psychological therapies*. Baltimore: Johns Hopkins University Press, 1976.

Zitrin, C. M., Klein, D. F., & Woerner, M. G. Behavior therapy, supportive psychotherapy, imiprimine and phobias. *Archives of General Psychiatry*, 1978, *35*, 307.

3

The CS Exposure Approach of Implosive (Flooding) Therapy

DONALD J. LEVIS AND THOMAS L. BOYD

From the arsenal of available psychotherapeutic techniques, perhaps no other approach to psychopathology offers a more comprehensive, unique, and direct strategy to treatment than that provided by Implosive (flooding) Therapy (IT). This behavioral approach, which is based upon the Pavlovian principle of direct experimental extinction, is designed to treat severe neurotic psychopathology. Successful application of the implosive procedure has been reported for a wide variety of cases including phobic responding, obsessive-compulsive behavior, hysterical reactions, pervasive anxiety attacks, affective, dissociative, and conversion reactions, psychosomatic disorders, and psychotic reactions including schizophrenia.

The Implosive Therapy technique represents a logical extension of a comprehensive theory of psychopathology designed to explain symptom development, maintenance, and removal. The approach is unique in that it resolves a number of critical issues related to symptom maintenance, incorporates recent contributions in the area of memory encoding and reactivation, and provides a comprehensive analysis of the role various stimulus patterns play in maintaining a particular behavioral symptom.

The purpose of this chapter is to provide an outline of the theoretical model supporting the IT technique as well as to provide a critical but constructive review of the existing literature dealing with the effectiveness of the implosive and related extinction techniques. As will become apparent in this chapter, a credible evaluation of the treatment literature cannot be made in the absence of a thorough understanding of the theoretical rationale underlying the technique. Previous reviews of the implosive literature (Ayres, 1972; Frankel, 1972; Marshall, Gauthier, & Gordon, 1979; McNamara, 1972; Morganstern, 1973; Smith, Dickson, & Sheppard, 1973) frequently have failed to consider whether important points of the procedure were incorporated into a given research design. Unfortunately, this lack of understanding of the conceptual model has led to a number of theoretical misconceptions and erroneous conclusions as well as to frequent misapplications of the IT procedure. Not only will an attempt be made to correct such misinformation, but the critical issues in need of study will be outlined. Furthermore, a suggested methodological strategy designed to resolve some of the critical issues facing the implosive and other behavioral approaches will be presented.

Historical Developments

Prior to providing an outline of the relevant features of the IT model, a brief history of the rationale behind the development of the technique should prove useful. The IT theory and technique was conceptualized by Thomas G. Stampfl in 1957. Stampfl was greatly influenced by the infrahuman avoidance learning literature and especially by the theoretical writing of O. H. Mowrer, Clark Hull, Neal Miller, and John Dollard. But perhaps more than any other factor, it was his own extensive clinical experience with severely disturbed children that led him to conclude that experimental extinction was the primary causal agent for producing corrective behavioral change.

According to Stampfl (1966) the therapeutic system was initiated by two general observations. The first observation evolved from his conducting play therapy with children. Therapeutic success seemed to depend on the degree to which emotional responding accompanied the child's play patterns during the session. The second major factor influencing Stampfl was Maslow and Mittleman's (1951) insistence that the neurotic's symptoms, defense mechanisms, and general maladaptive behavior resulted from anticipation or expectation of some catastrophe, which was usually unspecific or unidentifiable by the neurotic. A variety of catastrophic expectations appeared to occur. These included the anticipation of abandonment, injury, and annihilation, condemnation and disapproval, humiliation, enslavement, loss of love, loss of control, and utter deprivation.

For Stampfl, the critical importance of the Maslow–Mittleman interpretation was that it deemphasized the viewpoint, common to many dynamic and personality treatment systems, that impulses to act in sexual or aggressive ways are the main stimuli to which the anxiety reaction is conditioned. Rather, Maslow and Mittleman strongly suggested a dimension of stimulus complexity as a critical variable in any learning analysis of a given problem. This interpretation dovetailed with Stampfl's clinical experience and led to a theoretical conceptualization of psychopathology based on an extension of Mowrer's (1947) two-factor theory of avoidance learning. Symptoms were conceptualized as avoidance behavior designed to escape a variety of aversive conditioned stimuli. Once psychopathology was viewed as an outgrowth of aversive conditioning sequences, it seemed straightforward to Stampfl to draw upon Pavlov's (1927) original principle of experimental extinction. That is to say, the repeated presentation of the conditioned stimulus in the absence of the unconditioned stimulus will lead to the weakening and removal of the learned response. This principle has been established as one of the most reliable and virtually unquestioned formulations of the experimental laboratory. The technique he developed to implement this principle represents an attempt to re-present, re-reinstate, or symbolically reproduce those emotionally evoking cues motivating symptomatology.

The technique, itself, first evolved in the late 1950s as an *in vivo* approach exposing patients to cues correlated with symptom onset. By encouraging subjects to block symptomatic behavior, CS exposure occurred and with repetition resulted in the extinction of the symptomatic behavior. But Stampfl quickly realized that with more severe pathology, full CS exposure to some of the avoided CS patterns could not be reproduced by *in vivo* exposure. He then developed an imagery approach which permitted full exposure to anticipated events as well as hypothesized past conditioning events believed to be encoded in memory and still functioning as an active CS pattern.

The presentation of these hypothesized internal cues appeared at times to reactivate an internal associative chain of avoided stimuli, the exposure of which produced an intensely strong affective discharge. It was precisely this observed release of intense emotional reactions accompanied by a host of reportable internal thoughts and memories that led Stampfl to label his technique Implosive Therapy. The term *implosion* is borrowed from physics. It reflects an attempt through analogy to depict the internal process of associative chaining and uncovering of "hidden" stimuli which leads to a discharge of internally stored emotional energy. In the same vein, others have used the term *flooding* to describe the process of confronting the patient with a host of emotionally loaded avoided cues in order to maximize and facilitate the extinction process.

As Levis and Hare (1977) noted, the terms *flooding* and *implo-*

sion appeared to be used indiscriminantly depending on the author's preference. However, the term *flooding* is rarely used in studies that introduce cues other than those correlated with symptom onset. The techniques clearly are not different in the sense that the same principle of therapeutic change, direct experimental extinction, is applied and both use *in vivo* as well as an imagery approach. Since the question of what cues need to be extinguished is clearly an empirical question, the terms will be used interchangeably for the purpose of this chapter. It is unfortunate that some behavior therapists shy away from the term *implosion* because of the use of hypothesized cues which apparently for them elicit "ghost of Freudian" theory. As will be seen in this chapter, IT theory is an S-R approach couched in modern learning terminology, with a feedback technique that is specifiable in operational terms and experimentally testable.

The Origin and Development of Psychopathology

The development as well as the effective use of a given therapeutic technique rests, in part, on how one conceptualizes psychopathology. In the following sections, the rationale underlying the IT technique will be provided by describing a conceptual framework for understanding symptom development, maintenance, and removal. As noted earlier, Mowrer's (1947, 1960) two-factor theory of avoidance learning provides the structure upon which the theory is developed. However, it also should be recognized that the theory is influenced by Miller's (1951) and Brown's (1961) theory of conflict, Solomon and Wynne's (1954) conservation of anxiety hypothesis, Amsel's (1958) theory of frustration, and the conceptualizations of Dollard and Miller (1950). Since the theory has been described in detail elsewhere (Levis, 1979a, 1980a, 1981; Levis & Hare, 1977; Stampfl, 1970; Stampfl & Levis, 1967, 1969, 1973, 1976), an attempt will be made to state only the main points of the model.

Psychopathology is viewed as learned behavior resulting from the organism's exposure to past, specific aversive conditioning experiences. Inherent in its development is the learning of two response classes. The first involves the conditioning of an aversive emotional state via the principles of classical conditioning. The second involves learned behavior designed to reduce or remove the negative effects of the first response class via the principles of instrumental or avoidance learning. The above-stated proposition follows a two-factor theoretical framework (Mowrer, 1947, 1960), which conceptualizes psychopathology as an emotional as opposed to a cognitive disorder. Conditioning of an aversive emotional reaction involves the pairing of a nonharmful stimulus with a primary drive state, an unconditioned stimulus (UCS) producing pain, fear, frustration, or severe states of deprivation. Through repeated pairings of the nonharmful stimulus with the UCS, conditioning occurs with the nonharmful stimulus, now referred to as conditioned stimulus (CS), becoming capable of eliciting aversive motivational or secondary drive states labeled fear (anxiety) or frustration (Amsel & Maltzman, 1950; Brown, Kalish, & Farber, 1951). All conditioning events associated with psychopathology are assumed to be encoded in long-term memory with the resulting representations being capable of reactivation or retrieval. As will be seen later, memory storage of past conditioning events is a critical factor for providing an explanation of symptom maintenance and in analyzing the total CS complex motivating symptom behavior.

A key component of the IT model is the importance it places on viewing aversive conditioning as occurring to a complex set of stimuli comprising both external and internal CS patterns. The above statement needs to be stressed since some behavior therapists take a rather naive viewpoint in analyzing what CSs are motivating maladaptive behavior. The false assumption frequently is made that the conditioned CS patterns involve only those cues correlated with the onset of emotional responding. For example, in a case involving a car or airplane phobia, the *in vivo* stimulus (car or airplane) is viewed as the only critical stimulus in need of extinction. Yet in the vast majority of such cases a careful history reveals no direct conditioning events to these stimuli and suggests that anticipated cues elicited by exposure to the phobic stimulus (e.g., bodily injury, death, or loss of control) are also part of the CS complex.

The model also assumes that central state constructs such as images, thoughts, and memories can function as conditioned cues and in many cases represent the major art of the stimulus complex maintaining human psychopathology. In theory, images, thoughts, and memories can become part of the conditioned complex in at least three ways. First, repeated fear-conditioning trials may elicit images and thoughts directly. For example, punishment may be preceded by sexual fantasies, images or thoughts of parental acceptance, or anticipatory images or memories of repeated punishment trials. When these internal events are directly followed by punishment, such internal cues will become part of the CS complex. Second, the external stimuli associated with a conditioning trial (e.g., punishment administered by a father) may reactivate imaginal representation of past punishment trials stored in memory, which not only adds to the fear level of the conditioning sequences but if followed by pain become strengthened through reconditioning. Third, anticipated images of the punishment to be received may involve cues associated with an emotional feeling which is in excess of the pain produced in the actual conditioning trial. For example, an anticipatory image may develop in a child that the angry father may kill or seriously injure the child. Although the actual UCS may not involve serious bodily injury, these anticipatory cues, because they have been followed by aversiveness, can become part of the CS complex.

It should be emphasized that internal cognitive processes labeled thoughts, images, and memories which produced an aversive reaction function as CSs, not UCSs. Images, thoughts, and memories are not inherently aversive primary reinforcers, and if they possess aversive properties, the effect has been imposed by a conditioning sequence. Considerable confusion exists on this point in the behavior therapy literature in which writers like Morganstern (1973) and Foa, Blau, Prout, and Latimer (1977) have expressed concern over the implosive therapist's attempts to present to their clients aversive images which they labeled as "horrifying" and "cruel." This viewpoint represents a gross misunderstanding of the conditioning approach and the implosive procedure (Levis, 1974). What is a "horrifying" scene to one person is not to another and the difference in reactivity can be found in differences in conditioning histories. If a subject does respond to such material, the assumption is made that conditioning of these cues has occurred. The greater the response, the greater the degree of past conditioning effects. Words, thoughts, memories, or images which elicit fearful responses are not, in and of themselves, capable of eliciting unconditioned responses (i.e., producing physical pain). They acquire their affective aversive reactions by being paired with another CS or CS sequence which was at some point in time paired with a UCS.

It should be noted, however, that CSs, if not extinguished, can produce, upon exposure, strong conditioned reactions which, in turn, can function as powerful secondary reinforcers for the learning of new behavior to remove such stimulation. A great deal of human aversive emotional learning becomes conditioned through association or pairing with other aversive CSs. The learning principles involved in this transfer include the process of secondary condition-

ing, higher-order conditioning, primary stimulus generalization, re-
sponse-mediated generalization, semantic and symbolic mediated
conditioning, and memory reactivation or reintegration of past aversive agents. Such principles are needed to explain, for example, why
children fear ghosts and skeletons when they have not been directly
hurt by them, or why many adults fear riding in an airplane or being
exposed to a spider, rat, or snake when such an experience has never
been followed by bodily injury or physical pain (Miller & Kraeling,
1950).

Symptom Development

As noted earlier, learned behaviors labeled psychological symptoms
are functionally designed to avoid or escape conditioned aversive
stimulation that signals the potential occurrence of a catastrophic
event. In theory such behavior is reinforced by the resulting reduction in aversive stimulation. Psychopathology is assumed to occur
when a very low or zero correlation exists between the occurrence of
the avoidance response (symptom) and the potential presence of
physical danger (UCS) to the organism. Such behaviors are labeled
maladaptive because their occurrence is not biologically protective,
is usually not under the individual's control, and frequently inter-
feres with the functioning of desired, socially adaptive responses.
Overt avoidance behaviors involving the skeletal nervous system can
be seen in flight responses, aggressive acts, and compulsive rituals.
These behaviors are subject to direct measurement. Covert avoidance
behavior mainly involves the classic cognitive defense mechanisms
such as repression (not thinking or remembering), rationalization,
intellectualization, projection, suppression, and denial. Unfortunately, direct or indirect measurement of covert activity represents a
difficult methodological hurdle for the behaviorist. But the least
understood and studied avoidance behavior is that which involves
the autonomic nervous system. Most therapists look at the repeated
occurrence of an autonomic reaction as a failure in avoidance such as
occurs with cases of pervasive anxiety. But clinical experience suggests that in such cases the anxiety reaction itself helps the individual turn his or her attention away from confronting the cue
patterns responsible for eliciting the reaction (for a detailed analysis
of pervasive anxiety see Hare & Levis, 1981). The use of autonomic
reactions as avoidance behavior also occurs in cases where anger is

continually felt and expressed. When one is angry, cues associated with rejection, failure, individual responsibility, and guilt can be masked and avoided (see Levis, 1980b). The emotional reaction of the depressive response can also function in this matter by preventing an individual from avoidance feelings of anger, guilt, or rejection (see Boyd & Levis, 1980).

The topography of overt and covert human avoidance behavior can also be classified as active or passive avoidance responding which follows the corresponding established experimental laws for these behaviors. Active overt avoidance responding can be seen in the flight response of a phobic, in the rituals of an obsessive, and in the conversion reaction of an hysteric. Active covert responding is seen in activation of cognitive defenses like rationalization, intellectualization, and projection. Passive overt avoidance responding can be seen in individuals who fail to engage in behaviors which elicit fear and in depressive responding. Covert passive avoidance responding is seen in the execution of cognitive defense mechanisms such as denial and repression.

The development of a given set of symptoms is not seen as a random process. It is maintained that symptoms make sense in a functional way if the source of conditioned aversive stimulation and reinforcement effects are taken into consideration. The most obvious examples of symptom utility can be found in cases of hysterical conversion reactions where a combat soldier, for example, develops a paralyzed leg or a combat aviator develops blindness or a disturbance in depth perception or night vision. Another example is seen in an obsessive who counts his heartbeats in order to avoid fearful sexual thoughts or in cases of depression or agoraphobia where an individual attempts to avoid cues associated with rejection, sexuality, or fears of failure in work or interpersonal relationships. Symptoms are not an effect or outgrowth of anxiety but rather a stratagem to circumvent, suppress, or avoid painful CS cues (see Levis, 1980a). They can be understood more easily following a thorough analysis of the array of conditioned stimuli driving the individual's symptomatology.

Finally, etiology of human symptom formation can be motivated by more than a single drive state and in most cases can be best described in the context of a multiprocess approach—an avoidance conflict paradigm involving two or more primary drive states. The interested reader is referred to the Levis and Hare (1977) article, in which four conflict models believed responsible for generating psychopathology have been outlined.

Symptom Maintenance and Symptom Extinction

In the quest to develop effective techniques to reduce or eliminate fear and resulting symptomatic behavior, the authors believe, it is essential to have an understanding of the principles responsible for maintaining such behavior. Perhaps no other issue has plagued a behavorial viewpoint of psychopathology more than symptom maintenance. Central to the issue is the observation that human avoidance behavior (symptoms) in patients appear to last for years in the absence of the UCS, yet the weight of laboratory data suggest that conditioned human and infrahuman avoidance behavior tends to extinguish fairly rapidly with UCS removal. Theorists concerned with addressing this issue recognize the above paradox (Eysenck, 1979; Rachman, 1976; Seligman, 1975). For example, Eysenck (1979) concluded that the classic law of extinction fails to explain why with many neuroses, the unreinforced CS appears not to extinguish but rather results in an enhancement of symptom maintenance. Theoretical attempts at explaining extreme avoidance maintenance have largely abandoned a traditional S-R viewpoint in favor of such concepts as partial irreversibility (Solomon & Wynne, 1954), automatization (Kimble & Perlmuter, 1970), CS incubation (Eysenck, 1979), uncontrollability (Seligman, 1975), and cognitive expectancy (Seligman & Johnston, 1973).

Extreme resistance to extinction of an avoidance response, indeed, is problematic for two-factor theory as presented by Mowrer (1947). Clinical evidence also suggests that when a patient attempts to block symptomatic behavior, the failure to avoid usually results in an unbearable increase in anxiety which frequently progresses to a panic-like intensity. Rather than producing a decrease in anxiety as theory would suggest, it appears that the individual is punished for trying to prevent symptom onset by the resulting increase in anxiety (Stampfl & Levis, 1976).

Symptom Maintenance

Perhaps one of Stampfl's greatest contributions is his theoretical rationale for explaining this seeming paradox at both the infrahuman and clinical levels without abandoning the two-factor theoretical framework. To achieve this objective Stampfl built upon Solomon and Wynne's (1954) now classic conservation of anxiety hypothesis. Stampfl (see Levis, 1966) reasoned that one could maximize resistance to extinction in the laboratory by dividing the CS–UCS interval into distinctive components and ordering them sequentially. He hypothesized that after the attainment of short latency responses to the first stimulus component of the sequence, S_1, subsequent extinction effects to this component would result in less generalization of extinction effects to the second component in the sequence, S_2, if the S_2 segment is highly dissimilar to the S_1 segment. The greater the shift in generalization of extinction effect from the early part of the CS–UCS interval to the later portions, the greater the amount of anxiety that will be moved to the components closer to the UCS onset. With extinction of fear to the S_1 stimulus, the avoidance response latencies will become longer, resulting in the exposure of S_2. The stimulus change from a low-fear state to a high-fear state results in a secondary conditioning effect, recharging the S_1 segment. This process will continue to repeat itself until S_2 is sufficiently exposed to produce a full extinction effect. By adding additional distinctive cues (S_3, S_4) to the CS chain, the probability of increasing resistance to extinction will be maximized by generating a greater percentage of short latency avoidance responses via the principles of anxiety conservation and secondary intermittent reinforcement. Considerable research has been conducted in support of the above theory and the interested reader is referred to the following articles: Boyd and Levis (1976), Dubin and Levis (1973), Kostanek and Sawrey (1965), Levis (1966, 1970), Levis and Boyd (1973, 1979), Levis and Dubin (1973), Levis and Stampfl (1972), Levis, Bouska, Eron, and McIlhan (1970), and Shipley (1974).

Thus, human conditioning resulting in psychopathology is not viewed as a function of a simple conditioning episode to one CS element but rather comprises many CS components that are ordered in a serial or sequential manner in terms of accessibility. By adding the concepts of memory encoding of conditioning sequences, memory summation, and memory reactivation, a powerful explanatory model can be put in place that not only explains symptom maintenance but parallels existing clinical observations. In other words, symptoms are maintained by a network of previously conditioned cue patterns which are interconnected with each other in a sequential associative linkage in terms of accessibility to the level of verbal report. This chain of associative linkage is ordered in terms of accessibility from least to most aversive, with the most aversive patterns representing stored memories of past conditioning sequences involving UCS presentation. According to this viewpoint, the role of external stimuli that are correlated directly with symptom onset is seen mainly as a mediator or reactivator (retrieval cue) involving a network of stored memories of past conditioning events which are affectively encoded and represented in the form of images, thoughts, or impulses.

The implosive procedure can be viewed as a memory reactivation technique; numerous clinical examples reflecting the position adopted above already have been reported (see Levis, 1980a; Stampfl, 1970; Stampfl & Levis, 1969, 1973). What is interesting is that the content of the avoided memories is frequently correlated with a particular symptom. Following exposure to the phobic object, phobic individuals often report memories of past conditioning events where the fear of bodily injury or death was heightened. Handwashers frequently report the recall of past sexual memories (e.g., semen on the hand) which elicits thoughts of being exposed and punished and which they attribute to the start of their handwashing compulsion. Hysterics frequently report memories following therapy in which they experience strong sexual feeling for the opposite sex parent, and so on.

The model goes on to state that, excluding effects from generalization of extinction, all unexposed components of the conditioning complex associated with maladaptive behavior will maintain or conserve their aversive loading until such exposure occurs. Furthermore, extinction of the cues correlated with symptom onset can result in the reactivation of the next set of cues in the chain. Their exposure can lead to an increase in emotional responding and, if paired with the earlier part of the chain, can produce a secondary conditioning effect which reestablishes responding of the symptomatic behavior to the previously extinguished cues. Clinically this is seen when patients try to stop their symptoms by not engaging in them when fear is elicited. Such attempts frequently result in an unbearable increase in anxiety, forcing the patient to return to the symptomatic behavior in order to reduce this new increase in anxiety.

Although the reactivated stimulus increases the level of aversiveness and although it can recondition the early part of the chain, any exposure to this stimulus results in a weakening effect (extinction) of the secondary drive source attached to this stimulus. With sufficient exposure a new part of the stimulus chain will be exposed. Although symptom behavior is primarily reinforced by the resulting reduction in aversive stimulation, such behavior also can be reinforced if it produces a positive secondary gain effect. Many patients are positively reinforced for symptom behavior. Such behavior may elicit in significant others behavior which demonstrates support, love, or caring feelings. In other cases the patient's work load may be reduced or direct financial gain may be received because of the disability. In still other cases symptom behavior may be reinforced because it hurts an individual toward whom the patient feels anger. Such reinforcement can help perpetuate the maintenance of mal-adaptive behavior.

By extending the conservation of anxiety hypothesis to account for human symptom maintenance, the tenets of two-factor theory are preserved, and the need to appeal to nontraditional learning con-structs like CS incubation, expectancy, and partial irreversibility is unwarranted. It seems fitting at this point to briefly comment on another attack made against conditioning theory by the concept of "preparedness" introduced by Seligman (1971) and incorporated by Eysenck (1979). Basically, the preparedness hypothesis suggests that the most frequently experienced phobic fears are attached to situations that threatened the survival of our ancestors and that there is a genetic predisposition for acquiring these fears. From this analysis, prepared stimuli such as fear of the dark, snakes, and heights are more readily acquired and more resistant to extinction than unprepared stimuli like tones, shoes, and color. In Seligman's (1971, p. 312) words: "And only rarely, if ever, do we have pyjama phobias, grass phobias, electric-outlet phobias, hammer phobias, even though these things are likely to be associated with trauma in our world." What Seligman and Eysenck fail to consider is that phobias of electric outlets and hammers are rare because such stimuli are frequently exposed throughout life in nonaversive settings. Not only do any past conditioning effects to these stimuli have a chance to undergo extinction and latent inhibition effects, but considerable discrimination training is given in how to use these objects properly to avoid danger. On the other hand, the sensory consequence of common phobias that are characterized as prepared are more readily avoided, reducing CS exposure and exposure to other aversive asso-ciative cues stored in memory that comprise the total CS complex. For a more detailed critique of this and other related issues see Levis (1979b).

Symptom Extinction

Returning to the issue of unlearning symptom behavior, it will be recalled that implosive (flooding) therapy is a technique designed to maximize the principle of direct experimental extinction. This basic principle of psychology states that the presentation of the CS in the absence of the UCS will lead to extinction of the conditioned response. As noted earlier psychopathology involves two response classes: emotional responding and avoidance behavior. From a two-factor position one needs to extinguish only the conditioned emotional response. According to Mowrer's theory (1947, 1960), the repeated presentation of the total CS complex will result in extinction of the conditioned emotional response. Once the drive value of the CS has been eliminated, CS presentation will cease to motivate the avoidance behavior. Ample experimental research has corroborated this interpretation (Baum, 1970; Black, 1958; Denny, Koons, & Mason, 1959; Hunt, Jernberg, & Brady, 1952; Knapp, 1965; Weinberger, 1965). Strong evidence at the infrahuman level exists which suggests that forced exposure to the total CS markedly extinguishes both fear and avoidance behavior (Shipley, Mock, & Levis, 1971). It is maintained that this extinction principle of the laboratory can be applied readily to the treatment of maladaptive behavior by using the technique of implosive or flooding therapy.

To maximize the extinction effect, repeated exposure should be given not only to CS patterns directly correlated with symptom onset but also to all the cues reactivated by the exposure procedure and those hypothesized to be responsible for symptom development. It is not essential that all external or encoded conditioning patterns be presented or that their presentation be completely accurate. Extinction effects resulting from the presentation of one cue pattern can generalize as a function of stimulus similarity to other unexposed patterns. The principle of generalization of extinction appears to be a powerful principle which helps facilitate the extinction process. Further, extinction of the conditioned emotional response appears to be directly related to the total amount of CS exposure. Although this principle of total amount of CS exposure is still debated at the infrahuman level, experimental support for the principle has been obtained (e.g., Shearman, 1970; Shipley, 1974; Shipley et al., 1971).

The model also suggests that the stronger the emotional responses elicited by the presentation of a CS pattern, the greater the degree of emotional extinction obtained. It would also follow that the more clearly the subject perceives the aversive-eliciting stimuli when followed by nonreinforcement, the more rapid will be the extinction of the emotional response. The above corollary is supported by the experimental work of Lowenfeld, Rubenfeld, and Guthrie (1956) and by Wall and Guthrie (1959).

It is important to remember that greater emotional responding and extinction will occur with the presentation of cues directly correlated with the development of symptomatic behavior. This is the main reason why the implosive therapist introduces cues reactivated in memory by the implosive procedure and cues that are hypothesized to be correlated with symptom development. An attempt is made to get the subject to reexperience the original conditioning events through the use of an imagery technique. To obtain the best results it is important to re-present an image of the subject being exposed to the hypothesized UCS. A mental or imaginal representation of the UCS functions as a CS and is capable, by repeated exposure, of being extinguished. This is why implosive therapists frequently introduce scenes in which the subject imagines himself or herself being exposed to punishment or bodily injury cues. It should be remembered that it is critical that the emotional response be elicited if extinction of this response is to occur. Failure to achieve this objective should result in failure of the technique to remove symptom behavior.

Therapeutic Extension of the Model

As noted in the previous section, symptoms can be removed by extinguishing the conditioned stimulus complexes which provide the motivation for symptom occurrence and maintenance. To achieve this goal in therapy, the therapist must represent, reinstate, or symbolically reproduce in the absence of physical pain (UCS) the cue pattern to which the symptomatology has been conditioned. In those cases where symptom-correlated cue patterns involve discrete external stimuli, *in vivo* exposure to these cues has been found very effective and may be the only form of cue presentation necessary, especially in cases where psychopathology is not severe. *In vivo* CS exposure should function as an activator of other internally coded cues which, if elicited, will themselves undergo an extinction effect, mitigating the need for presentation by the therapist. Furthermore, extinction effects to one set of cues can generalize to other non-presented sets of cues. The extent of the generalization of extinction effect is a function of the degree of stimulus similarity between the sets of cues.

However, in many cases, especially those involving severe psychopathology, presentation of the external cues correlated with symptom onset will not be sufficient to produce symptom removal. In such cases or in cases where *in vivo* exposure is difficult, an imagery method of cue presentation is used. Such a method is especially needed for the presentation of those internal cues believed to include neural representation of specific past events involving pain and punishment. Through verbal instruction to imagine, scenes are presented to the patient which include the various stimuli (visual, auditory, tactile) hypothesized to be linked to the original conditioning events. The position is taken that all cues reproduced in imagery which elicit negative affect do so because of previous learning and thus are extinguishable. Images function as CSs since they are not inherently aversive.

The therapist's task is to present to the client as many of the cue patterns as possible that comprise the total avoided CS complex. Complete accuracy in reconstructing the original conditioning events is not essential since some effect, through the principle of generalization of extinction, would be expected when an approximation is presented. In the interest of efficiency and to reduce resistance, symptom-correlated cues are presented first, followed by cues reported by the patient, and then by hypothesized cues. Belief or acceptance of the themes introduced in a cognitive sense is not required.

The therapist attempts to maximize emotional arousal (anxiety, anger, guilt, etc.) by describing the avoided cues as vividly and realistically as possible. By repeating the scene over and over again, the emotional response elicited should become less and less until complete extinction occurs. Repetition of the main components of the avoided CS complex introduced is followed by progressive expansion to other sets of cues hypothesized to be related to the patient's symptom. Any attempt on the patient's part to avoid the imagined aversive stimuli is matched by the therapist's attempt to circumvent or discourage such behavior. The essence of the procedure is to repeatedly expose the aversive stimuli underlying the patient's difficulties until an extinction effect is obtained and symptomatic behavior is markedly reduced or eliminated. To increase CS exposure and maximize the extinction effect, the patient is assigned "homework" scenes. These assignments also help to bring the process under personal control.

Prior to administering the technique, a session of "neutral" imagery training is given to help establish a baseline for the ability of the client to imagine various stimuli. Since it is critical for the therapist to have a clear understanding of what cues are being avoided, a good historical work-up and behavioral assessment of the patient's problem is needed prior to starting therapy. The therapist should also remember that since the original aversive conditioning events are assumed to result from contiguity of stimuli with physical injury or pain, it would follow that cues immediately associated with these events will carry a greater weight in evoking the anxiety response.

It should be kept in mind that the implosive procedure is an operational procedure involving feedback from the patient. The validity of the content of a given scene is determined by the patient's autonomic response to the scene. The greater the emotional respond- ing elicited, the stronger the support for introducing the cues pre- sented. By soliciting verbal feedback following a given scene as to what feelings and thoughts were experienced, new material for addi- tional scenes can be obtained. It is common following scene presenta- tions to have patients report new memories and feelings associated with their symptom development. For a detailed description of the IT procedure and technique the reader is referred to Levis, 1980a (also see Stampfl, 1970; Stampfl & Levis, 1967, 1969, 1973, 1976).

Evidence for Efficacy

In a comprehensive review of the implosive (flooding) therapy litera- ture, Levis and Hare (1977) identified over 60 articles involving case reports, analogue research, and patient outcome research. Since that time, the total research output has more than doubled (approximate- ly 135 reports). A decided shift in emphasis from analogue to clinical outcome research has occurred. This literature confirms the effec- tiveness of CS exposure therapy on the treatment of feared anxiety, as well as on collateral emotions. Some badly needed parametric work has been conducted, but overall the research continues to dis- play methodological weaknesses, both in experimental design and in execution of the treatment procedure.

Because of space limitations, a greater emphasis in this review will be placed upon outcome effectiveness for selected disorders in patient populations. Since the Levis and Hare (1977) review, a dramatic increase in patient-outcome studies has appeared. For the most part, these experimental efforts have concentrated upon obses- sive-compulsive patient populations, diverse phobic patients, and agoraphobics. Two studies will also be reviewed which deal with alcoholics and insomniacs. The major shift in emphasis of the more recent outcome research has involved an attempt to evaluate the effects of exposure treatment in the context of a group setting, the effects of patient characteristics on exposure treatment, and the interactive effects of exposure and psychopharmacological treatment. Finally, a brief review will be made of key experiments which have attempted to evaluate a number of procedural details associated with extinction-based treatments. These procedural details include: (1) stimulus content or cue category, (2) mode of stimulus presentation, and (3) duration of stimulus material presented and strength of the fear response.

Outcome Effectiveness: Patient Population Research

In the Levis and Hare (1977) review, 16 studies examining the effectiveness of implosive-flooding procedures with psychiatric patients were evaluated (Boudewyns, 1975; Boudewyns & Levis, 1975; Boudewyns & Wilson, 1972; Boulougouris & Marks, 1969; Boulougouris, Marks, & Marset, 1971; Crowe, Marks, Agras, & Leitenberg, 1972; Emmelkamp, 1974; Emmelkamp & Wessels, 1975; Hodgson & Rachman, 1970; Hogan, 1966; Hussain, 1971; Levis & Carrera, 1967; Newton & Stein, 1974; Rachman, Marks, & Hodgson, 1973; Watson, Gaind, & Marks, 1972; Watson & Marks, 1971; Watson, Mullet, & Pillay, 1973). Except for one study (Newton & Stein, 1974) using an alcoholic population, the exposure-based extinction approach was found to be reliably superior to a controlled condition. Improvement was reported on a variety of dependent measures and with a variety of clinical problems. As a whole, this early patient research suffered from the absence of behaviorally based outcome measures, an absence of a systematic separation of treatment effect through use of matched group designs, a lack of control of stimulus exposure times across groups, and a confounding of follow-up data with subsequent treatments. Nonetheless, the consistent finding of changes in outcome across studies is impressive.

   While the implosive-flooding procedure is not theoretically limited in its potential application to circumscribed diagnostic populations, the major research efforts have concentrated upon obsessive-compulsive, diverse phobic, and agoraphobic patient populations.

Obsessive-Compulsive Populations

A total of eight patient-outcome studies utilizing obsessive-compulsive populations were reviewed. The major research question addressed by these experiments concerned the relative effectiveness of *in vivo* modes of stimulus exposure to alternate imaginal and/or physical stimulus presentations in reducing obsessive-compulsive images and behavioral rituals. In reviewing these studies, it is apparent that while exposure-based treatment strategies are effective with obsessive-compulsive patients, the most effective method of stimulus exposure remains uncertain.

Foa, Steketee, Turner, and Fischer (1980) examined the combined effects of imaginal and *in vivo* exposure to "feared catastrophies," as compared with *in vivo* exposure alone in 15 obsessive-compulsives with checking rituals. As rated by an independent assessor on six scales of depression, anxiety, and obsessive/ritualistic behavior, exposure resulted in significant relative gains for both treatment conditions. These groups did not differ at posttreatment, but did at follow-up: the *in vivo*-alone exposure group partially relapsed on four of the six measures.

Rabavilas, Boulougouris, and Stefanis (1976) exposed 12 obsessive-compulsive patients to treatment conditions varying in mode of exposure (*in vivo* versus fantasy) and duration of exposure in a Latin-square design. The treatment condition in which long fantasy preceded long *in vivo* exposure resulted in the greatest amount of improvements in subjective and physiological recording. Finally, Emmelkamp, van der Helms, van Zanten, and Plochq (1980) failed to find any differences between *in vivo* plus self-instructional exposure (imagery) in obsessive-compulsive rituals at posttest and at follow-ups of one and six months' duration. Both groups did improve on a variety of subjective ratings by therapist, patient, and independent assessor.

A separate yet related procedural issue has been that of self-imposed versus therapist-controlled *in vivo* exposure. Bandura (1977) has argued that the most effective procedure for fear reduction would be an initial utilization of therapist-controlled induction aids to obtain initial performance of the feared response. After performance is obtained, Bandura (1977) recommended that the therapist be removed in a type of self-directed masking phase of treatment in order to enhance treatment gains through self-efficacy. Accordingly, Emmelkamp and Kraanen (1977) exposed 14 obsessive-compulsive patients to either therapist-controlled or self-controlled *in vivo* exposure in the home setting. While both treatment conditions revealed significant gains, no differential group effects were obtained at posttest or at 1-month or 3.5-month follow-ups as measured by patient, therapist, and observer evaluations.

A few studies have examined the effects of drug-assisted exposure as a means of reducing anxiety response during CS presentations. In obsessive-compulsive patients, Rachman et al. (1979) evaluated exposure versus relaxation treatments, crossed with clomipramine (antidepressant) versus a placebo administration. The exposure condition was followed by significant improvements in performance and discomfort ratings on an avoidance task, but not in mood changes relative to relaxation controls. The clomipramine group significantly improved in depressed mood relative to placebos; no interaction effect was observed.

In yet a different comparison study, Hackmann and McLearn (1975) compared *in vivo* exposure treatments and thought-stopping techniques in 10 obsessive-compulsive patients in a crossover design. While both were effective in pre–post change in scores on several self-report instruments, no significant differences between treatments were observed despite the authors' claim that "there was a tendency for flooding to be slightly more effective."

In the main, the role of exposure as an effective treatment strategy for obsessive-compulsive disorders has been well documented by the above research (also see Hodgson, Rachman, & Marks, 1972; Rabavilas, Boulougouris, Perissaki, & Stefanis, 1979; Rachman, Marks, & Hodgson, 1973; Shahar & Marks, 1980). The effectiveness of this strategy relative to alternative strategies remains an unanswered question as designs as a whole suffer from a lack of relevant control groups (Foa, Jameson, Turner, & Payne, 1980; Hackmann & McLearn, 1975), a confounding of treatment method by therapist contact (Emmelkamp & Kraanen, 1977), and an absence of behavioral measures. In general, exposure presentations via imagery technique appear to enhance the relative effectiveness of *in vivo* techniques, though this is not consistently the case (i.e., Emmelkamp et al., 1980; Rabavilas et al., 1976). Imagery versus *in vivo* designs suffered from the investigators' ignoring any attempt to equate cue-category content for imaginal versus *in vivo* stimuli. Attempts to guarantee that boundary conditions of the extinction technique have been satisfied (an initial increase followed by a decrease in anxiety concomitant with target behavior change) are virtually absent. Finally, obvious differences between exposure and test stimuli (hence, differential generalization of extinction effects) plus certain inherent stimulus qualities associated with *in vivo* exposure (i.e., stimulus vividness; less potential for escape from the stimulus) build in confounds which are difficult to control experimentally.

Agoraphobic Populations. In total, 16 experimental studies were reviewed using diagnosed agoraphobic patients as subjects. A major shift in emphasis of the recent outcome research with agoraphobics has involved an attempt to evaluate the effects of exposure treatment in the context of a group setting.

Emmelkamp, Knipers, and Eggeraat (1978) successfully exposed groups of agoraphobics to symptom-correlated cues, as did Hafner and Marks (1976) and Zitrin, Klein, and Woerner (1980). While Emmelkamp et al. (1978) included no relevant comparison group (except for their cognitive treatment group), Hafner and Marks (1976) did report a "mildly facilitatory" outcome effect for group exposure relative to their individual therapy subjects. Zitrin et al. (1980) found some effectiveness for group *in vivo* exposure with or without imipramine as a potent facilitator.

Attempts have been made in the context of group therapy to alter the structure of the group to determine whether this mode of treatment can be improved. Hand, Lamontagne, and Marks (1974) met with 25 agoraphobics in either a "structured, cohesive" group or an "unstructured" group. The main variable manipulated appears to be whether the therapist met for a one hour discussion prior to *in vivo* treatment in the context of a group setting (structured, cohesive) or individually (unstructured). The authors reported that the structured group showed greater posttreatment improvement on Behavioral Avoidance Test (BAT) scores and on follow-up, although the latter gains were confounded by supplemental therapy. In a partial replication, Teasdale, Walsh, Lancashire, and Mathews (1977) demonstrated only minimal gains using a structured group setting; however, a comparison with an unstructured group was not made. In both studies nonspecific treatment effects were not assessed.

Sinnott, Jones, Scott-Fordham, and Woodward (1981) attempted to manipulate group structure by establishing agoraphobic patient groups in a cohesive neighborhood (zoned group) versus patients selected from diverse sections of the area (unzoned group). These treatment groups were then compared to a waiting list control group. Both treatment groups relative to the controls improved on the BAT measure while only the zoned subjects showed significant reductions in self-reported anxiety and social range.

Using female agoraphobic outpatients, Jannoun, Munby, Catalan, and Gelder (1980) compared a programed-practice group with a problem-solving group. The programed-practice group entailed each subject going out in her environment for one hour a day with a "partner" to provide encouragement. The problem-solving group discussed their problem with a "partner" who provided encouragement. No significant differences were found on the assessor's ratings or on patient-rating data at the 24-week follow-up, but the programed-practice group was more improved at the 12-week assessment interval. Differences were also not found at the 2- and 6-week posttreatment periods.

In summary, it would appear that group exposure methods can be effective but the degree of effectiveness is unknown. Further, these studies have not been completely successful in isolating potential group variables which may have contributed to this effectiveness.

In vivo exposure methods appear to be particularly effective for agoraphobics, despite procedural limitations of this research. McDonald et al. (1979) observed superior behavioral and subjective rating scores on a self-exposure group of agoraphobics (*in vivo* homework assignments) relate to a nonexposure discussion group. These results are uninterpretable, however, as no pretreatment baseline measures were taken. Foa et al. (1980) presented *in vivo* exposure to 11 agoraphobics in a randomized crossover design, while looking at the relative effects of massed versus spaced *in vivo* exposure. These authors reported a significantly greater effect for massed exposure on assessors' subjective ratings, regardless of the order of presentation. While, as the authors' stated, spaced exposures may allow for spontaneous recovery of symptoms, design problems as a failure to validate assessors' rating independently or an absence of treatment process measures (see Boyd & Levis, 1983) makes evaluation of results limited.

In a comparable study of imaginal versus *in vivo* exposure presentations with agoraphobics, Mathews and his colleagues (Johnston et al., 1976; Mathews et al., 1976) failed to find any significant differences in outcome effects, either alternating imagery and *in vivo* exposure or with combined imagery and *in vivo* exposure. Unfortunately, all subjects were instructed to expose themselves to phobic stimuli in the home, confounding any sure test of *in vivo* versus imagery techniques.

Similar to drug treatment studies with obsessive-compulsive patients, Chambless, Foa, Groves, and Goldstein (1979) compared the relative effectiveness of Brevital (barbiturate) injections with flooding versus flooding alone. The nondrugged flooding group (imaginal exposure) was significantly more improved relative to the drugged group and an attention-control group.

Comparative Therapy Studies. Levis and Hare (1977) have reviewed comparative therapy outcome studies involving both analogue subjects (Barrett, 1969; Borkovec, 1972; Calef & McLean, 1970; Cornish & Dilley, 1973; DeMoor, 1970; Hekmat, 1973; Horne & Matson, 1977; Marshall, Gauthier, Christie, Curry, & Gordon, 1977; Mealiea & Nawas, 1971; Mylan & Clement, 1972; Rachman, 1966; Smith & Nye, 1973; Willis & Edwards, 1969) and patient populations (Boudewyns & Wilson, 1972; Boulougouris et al., 1971; Crowe et al., 1972; Gelder et al., 1973; Hussain, 1971). For almost all of these studies, a comparison was made between extinction-based techniques and systematic desensitization.

Both reviews were highly critical of this research area as consistent methodological flaws were apparent. These are summarized as follows: several studies were cited for (1) a general failure to associate outcome measures with selected target behaviors and inadequacies in dependent measures (e.g., Boudewyns & Wilson, 1972; Calef & McLean, 1970; Hussain, 1971); (2) inadequate subject selection, either selectively biasing one treatment group against another or limiting the generalization of findings to a standard treatment situation (e.g., Boulougouris et al., 1971; DeMoor, 1970; Rachman, 1966; Smith & Nye, 1973; Willis & Edwards, 1969); (3) statistical weaknesses and/or inadequate interpretation of findings (e.g., Barrett, 1969; Horne & Matson, 1977); and (4) failures to equate stimulus material and scene content, exposure duration, and treatment time, as well as inadequate treatment procedures (e.g., Barrett, 1969; Gelder et al., 1973; Hekmat, 1973; Mylan & Clement, 1972). These design problems preclude drawing any conclusions of a comparative nature. This is unfortunate given that both techniques are specific enough to allow critical comparisons.

It should be noted that in their review, Marshall et al. (1979) generally concluded that in comparison to systematic desensitization, extinction-based techniques are more successful if they avoid cues involving "adverse consequences." To support their conclusion they cite two studies (Marshall et al., 1977; Mealiea & Nawas, 1971) which they rated as satisfactorily designed and relevant to issues related to stimulus cue-category content. Unfortunately, we find numerous flaws in both studies, which prevents the drawing of any reasonable conclusions. The serious weaknesses associated with the Mealiea and Nawas (1971) study have already been discussed in the Levis and Hare (1977) review. In the Marshall et al. (1977) study, three analogue experiments, two with snake and one with spider phobics, were conducted. In Experiment III, they compared a flooding scene in which subjects were asked to imagine picking up and stroking the phobic stimulus, with an implosive scene which involved "horrific and somewhat unrealistic images" depicting bodily injury associated with being attacked by the phobic stimulus. They also tested the effects of their three 45-minute, tape-recorded sessions with an immediate or delayed (24 hours) behavioral posttest. The flooding conditions were found to be significantly more effective then implosion on a BAT and subjective rating scale of anxiety. Flooding with immediate posttesting was superior on both measures to the other three treatment conditions. The authors concluded that these results support Bandura's (1969) concern that the use of implosion may confirm the patient's worse fears and potentially exacerbate them.

In critiquing this study, it is important to note that the implosive group did not get worse. In fact, all groups showed decreases on the fear measures, with no differences among flooding-delayed, the pooled implosive groups, and the no-treatment control. "Flooding" as here defined appeared to have had relatively short-lived benefits. Further, the absence of directly measuring the anxiety response to the scene material makes it impossible to assess whether the material produced any anxiety in the implosion group, or whether sufficient exposure was given to results in an extinction effect. The IT model suggests that more exposure would be needed for the more aversive material.

Special attention should also be paid to the issue of changes on outcome being due simply to practice effects resulting from a given treatment stimulus content being similar to the stimulus content of the outcome measure, and to the issue of ensuring that the outcome measures are not administered too close to the last treatment session, which may result in differential carryover effects due to different rates in extinction of fear. Repeated administration of outcome measures is recommended.

The final two studies to be reviewed under this heading compared extinction procedures with variations of cognitive techniques. In the first study, mentioned above, Hackmann and McLearn (1975) compared an *in vivo* exposure plus modeling condition to a thought-stopping procedure with 10 obsessive-compulsive outpatients using a crossover design. Although both treatment procedures resulted in effective pre–post test changes, reliable differences between conditions were not obtained. The authors conclude that "there was a tendency for flooding to be slightly more effective." Unfortunately, the absence of a control comparison group, process measures, cue-category descriptions, control over stimulus duration, and confounding modeling with exposure render the results of this experiment inconclusive. In the second study, Emmelkamp et al. (1978), using a crossover design, compared an *in vivo* exposure procedure with a cognitive relabeling manipulation using agoraphobic patients. Almost all dependent measures showed significant improvements at posttest on both groups combined. Exposure, regardless of order, resulted in significant improvement on most measures (24 out of 30) while the cognitive labeling group resulted in improvement on only 5 of 30 measures. At one-month follow-up, results were essentially the same. In spite of these impressive results, this study suffers from a lack of comparison groups, no process measures, as well as a confound in therapist contact (more apparent contact in the cognitive group).

Overall, the studies cited in this section are supportive of exposure-based treatment approaches. Because of methodological limitations, conclusions regarding the comparative utility with other techniques must await further research.

Other Patient Populations. Despite the theoretical flexibility of the implosive (flooding) treatment approaches, controlled experimental research efforts appear limited for the most part to those populations cited above.

Despite these limitations, two studies to be reviewed involved exposure manipulations conducted on infrequently tested populations. Blakey and Baker (1980) exposed seven alcoholics to cues that "set off drinking." While results are presented in a case study fashion and rely heavily upon patient reports with only a minimal degree of follow-up (zero to nine months), results, nonetheless, point to a degree of success in reported desires to drink and reported drinking behavior. These positive findings are in contrast to Newton and Stein's (1974) reported failure with this population, suggesting that more research is needed.

Finally, Carerra and Elenewski (1980) tested three groups of sleep-disturbed subjects who reported fear of death. The authors manipulated cue areas with Group 1 receiving 45 minutes of taped implosive scenes involving both symptom-contingent cues and death scenes. Group 2 received guided fantasy scenes concerned with loss of control, acting out of various socially forbidden behaviors, and fantasies of becoming psychotic. Group 3 were presented ocean scenes, and Group 4 served as a waiting-list control. All groups improved in terms of time to get to sleep, and no changes were noted on the fear of death scales. The failure to find any effect as a function of cue category is hard to assess without a process measure to operationally determine the effectiveness of the tapes and to evaluate whether extinction effects occurred to the relatively short tape exposure period.

Procedural Variables. The theoretical model associated with implosive (flooding) treatment techniques dictates a number of procedural requirements which must be satisfied in order to meet treatment requirements. Process measures associated with the hypothesized conditioned anxiety response must be monitored during exposure to determine whether or not the hypothesized CS is functionally related to the target symptom. A number of other procedural issues appear to be potentially related to the efficacy of exposure treatments. Because of space limitations, these issues will be highlighted only briefly.

1. *Stimulus content on cue category.* As alluded to in our discussion of the Marshall et al. (1977) study of "flooding" versus "implosion" exposure techniques, a major concern with investigators lies with the type of stimulus content presented to the patient during the exposure sessions. Stampfl and Levis (see Levis & Hare, 1977) have developed this theoretical model and have advanced seven separate types of cue-category content believed to be associated with the patient's symptomatology. As noted earlier, many of these cue content areas have been labeled by others as "horrifying" or "unrealistic." Such value judgments by dimension have no place in the evaluation of a procedure designed to be assessed empirically. Critics like Marshall et al. (1979, p. 225) confuse this issue when they imply that implosive therapy involves "physically injurious" or "adverse" consequences. There is a distinct theoretical and empirical difference between the presentation of the aversive injurious consequences in imagery and in reality. Implosive therapy is an extinction not a punishment procedure.

While a few studies have evaluated the issue of cue-category content, design problems have been significant. Few studies have attempted to evaluate whether or not the stimulus material is even functionally related to the symptom. Without process measures of the subject's reaction to the stimulus material presented, one cannot be certain which sets of stimulus material are more or less aversive, or whether or not the exposure was sufficient to produce an extinction effect. This criticism particularly applies to Fazio (1970), Watson and Marks (1971), Prochaska (1971), Foa et al. (1977), Marshall et al. (1977), and Mathews and Rezin (1977). As a result, no conclusive statements may be presented other than that no evidence points to any danger from the inclusion of hypothesized or aversive imaginal CSs often associated with the implosive technique.

It should be clear that if any definitive conclusions are to be reached in this area, the anxiety response to the stimulus material being presented must be directly monitored. Further, posttesting should not occur until an operational extinction criterion to a given scene content has been reached.

2. *Mode of stimulus presentation.* A number of studies have been conducted evaluating the relative effectiveness of taped versus live therapist presentations (Sherry & Levine, 1980); *in vivo* versus imaginal presentation (Emmelkamp et al., 1980; Foa et al., 1980; Johnston et al., 1976; Mathews et al., 1976); and therapist versus self-directed stimulus presentations (Emmelkamp & Kraanen, 1977; McDonald et al., 1979; O'Brien & Kelly, 1970).

In either case, theory would require that an assessment of the total avoided CS complex be made before a prediction as to the best CS mode of presentation can be generated. In light of this, it would be naive for one to present a general empirical statement as to the best mode of stimulus presentation in all cases. However, it would appear reasonable to determine whether a given mode is more effective for a particular symptom. Further, one might expect that a live therapist may be better able to individualize scene content to a specific patient's needs, and to reduce the chances that the patient will be able to avoid the full effects of the stimulus exposure (see Levis & Hare, 1977). Unfortunately, in every study reviewed in this area, a number of serious methodological confounds were noted, making concrete statements difficult.

3. *Duration of stimulus presentation and session intervals.* A final area of significant concern procedurally is the relative duration of stimulus exposure. Levis and Hare (1977) concluded that durations of 100 or more minutes appeared to be a critical variable in treatment success. Human analogue and outcome studies have only recently begun to address the duration issue, in addition to the issue of massed versus spaced stimulus presentation.

Overall, the data on massed versus spaced presentations is mixed. However, a relative similar effectiveness between massed and spaced procedures was obtained when comparisons were made within a single session (e.g., Grey, Rachman & Sartory, 1981; Parkinson & Rachmkan, 1980; with Mathews & Shaw, 1973, being an exception to this rule); relative superiority for massed exposures was obtained when exposure sessions were carried out over several daily sessions (e.g., Chaplin & Levine, 1981; Foa et al., 1980).

More work on the duration variable is needed and researchers in this area may profit from using the design employed in the infrahuman literature (see Shipley, 1974, for references).

The Issue of Safety

The use of implosive (flooding) therapy has raised concerns of harmful side-effects since the technique first appeared in print. Stampfl in fact waited 10 years before publishing the approach to be sure at a personal level the technique was nonharmful. The first author of this paper also has treated a large number of patients with a wide and diverse range of symptomatology over a 20-year period and has not had a single case in which harmful effects were noted. None of the concerns reported in the literature are based on empirical data or are by individuals trained in the implosive procedure. Rather, they mainly seem to arise from ego psychologists' myth that exposing low-ego-strength patients to direct anxiety-evoking material can elicit a psychotic reaction. No experimental evidence exists to support this hypothesis, and Boudewyns and Levis (1975) have published a study using low-ego-strength subjects which directly argues against the above hypothesis.

Empirical support for the safety of implosive (flooding) procedures can be obtained from two sources of data. The first source is the rather large number of outcome studies using a variety of outpatients and inpatients. Despite methodological difficulties, the vast majority of them reported positive results. Some of these studies have used hypothesized and "dynamic" cues with excellent results (e.g., Boudewyns, 1975; Boudewyns & Wilson, 1972; Hogan, 1966; Levis & Carrera, 1967). Not one of these studies has found an extinction-based approach to produce reliable results worse than the control group.

The second source of support for the safety of extinction-based therapy techniques is a survey conducted by Shipley and Boudewyns (1980). Over 70 therapists who use flooding or implosive therapy responded. Only 6 therapists reported any "serious and negative side-effects." These involved a total of 9 clients out of the 3,493 reviewed (0.26%). The side-effects mainly involved "acute panic reactions," and follow-up indicated that the effects were temporary and were treatable by more CS exposure or by chemotherapy. Twenty-one percent of the therapists reviewed concluded that relative to other treatment approaches, extinction techniques produce fewer side-effects, 66% considered side-effects to be equivalent, and only 13% felt that more negative side-effects occurred. According to the authors, respondents appeared to be equally distributed among "implosive" versus "flooding" techniques differentiated by whether or not hypothesized cues were used.

It has been the authors' experience that patients exposed to high levels of anxiety from the use of the technique are in control in the sense that they are capable of stopping the process at any point. A well-trained therapist can circumvent or directly attack the patient's defense system, but our experience indicates that this cannot be achieved without the patient's cooperation. The only danger we see is the use of the technique by an inexperienced or poorly trained therapist. Once a strong anxiety response is obtained, the technique requires continual CS exposure until a decrease in responding occurs. If the therapist stops the process in midcourse, becomes panicky, and scares the patient about the safety of the approach, the subject may panic and reactivate previously conditioned cues that he or she is "losing control." Such an increase in anxiety may result in increased symptom strength or in the reinforcement of avoidance behavior. Even if this happens, these side-effects should only be temporary. It should be kept in mind that implosive therapy is an extinction approach. Increases in anxiety occur only because conditioned cues previously avoided are exposed. With this exposure, extinction is taking place. The greater the exposure, the greater the extinction effect.

Construct Assessment Design

An overall evaluation of the clinical research using a CS exposure approach suggests such techniques can be powerful tools in modifying human psychopathology. Yet many of the research questions addressed in our review still remain unanswered. Procedural and methodological limitations can be found in most, if not all, of the studies reviewed. Such limitations are not peculiar to research with extinction approaches but can be leveled at any group of clinical studies, regardless of the approach under evaluation. Carefully controlled clinical research is not only difficult to execute but enormously time consuming if all of the appropriate groups are included. Even if this objective is achieved, how can one be certain that the procedures were executed without bias and with competence? Designs can be outlined for clinical research which addresses most of these methodological issues, but such designs would be almost impossible to execute at a patient level. This state of affairs exists in the clinical field as a whole and is why exactly opposite conclusions can be reached on any given set of data, depending on what the reviewer wants arbitrarily to stress.

The fact that clinical research is in a chaotic state is not as disturbing to us as the failure of behavioral researchers to capitalize on the strengths of their discipline in resolving some of these difficult assessment problems. As an approach, behavior therapy has made a critical breakthrough in reducing the difficulty of clinical assessment by operationalizing procedures and by tying theoretical constructs to dependent variables which are different from the outcome variables under study (i.e., symptom behavior). Such a strategy permits an independent assessment of the theoretical propositions as well as providing a concurrent evaluation of whether the technique was properly administered. The advantage and importance of this opportunity cannot be overstressed. It is a strategic breakthrough in evaluation, one not possible in nonbehavioral treatment approaches where constructs are not independently defined. Yet our most consistent criticism of the research reviewed is the failure of the researcher to assess at an individual level whether the boundary conditions of the technique were met.

Clearly, new designs are needed at the applied level that reinforce the feasibility of conducting patient research by increasing the probability that precise conclusions can be reached at the completion of the project. What is needed are designs that permit research on small samples. Levis (1982), in addressing this problem, suggested combining a between-groups design with a within-group analysis design to monitor the treatment process. In the case of an extinction approach like implosive (flooding) therapy, the fear construct would be monitored for each subject. In the case of systematic desensitization, a fear measure plus a relaxation response would be monitored. The between-groups variable involves the treatment group or conditions. The only control needed to assess changes over time is a nontreatment group.

The advantage of monitoring the person's response should be apparent. For example, in the case of an extinction approach, galvanic skin response (GSR) might be used as an index of fear. By monitoring the patient's GSR, one can determine whether or not the therapist's technique affects this response system. Monitoring will also indicate whether sufficient repetition has been given to produce an extinction effect. Such a procedure permits the determination for each subject of whether the boundary conditions of the technique have been met (i.e., the elicitation and extinction of anxiety). When the boundary conditions of the technique are met, symptoms should change. If this does repeatedly occur, then the theory underlying the technique is supported and additional controls can be added. If symptoms change for those subjects for whom the boundary conditions are not met, then the changes which occur are caused by other factors. If this occurs repeatedly, the theory underlying the technique should be modified or abandoned. If the cues introduced fail to produce a fear response, then the cues are incorrect or the technique is inappropriately administered.

In summary, direct assessment of the fear response during treatment can provide answers to the following critical questions: (1) Are the cues introduced eliciting anxiety? (2) Has the number of repetitions or exposure duration required to produce extinction effect for a given patient been provided? (3) Which set of cues produce the most fear? (4) When should termination of treatment occur? (5) Is a given pattern of cues correlated with or related to a given symptom? By directly assessing the boundary conditions of the technique, the therapist's skills in administering the technique are operationalized and directly assessed, as is the appropriateness of the cues introduced and the utility of various fear measures. Such a strategy should greatly reduce the current ambiguity in the literature.

Conclusion

The overriding purpose of this chapter is to stimulate better and more constructive research on the therapeutic use of experimental psychology's strongest documented principle for removing fear and avoidance behavior, the principle of experimental extinction via CS exposure. We attempted to achieve this objective by improving the precision of theoretical statements in this area, by reviewing research issues raised in the literature, and by suggesting a strategy for research which we believe will resolve many of the still unanswered questions. Extinction-based approaches like implosive and flooding therapy have been used with a wide variety of psychopathology, and a growing body of research with patient populations now exists. Supporting data clearly exist for recommending the use of the technique for phobic response including agoraphobia and obsessive-compulsive behaviors. The technique also shows promise for a variety of anxiety-based symptoms and for depression, but controlled studies have yet to be forthcoming. Overall, the bulk of research findings using a CS exposure technique supports the notion that this approach may hold considerable promise for dealing with a variety of symptoms. In fact, we believe the CS exposure technique represents the strongest behavioral approach available in terms of theory, re-

search, and potential. We acknowledge that procedural and methodological limitations exist with most, if not all, of the studies reviewed,
but this statement also applies to any set of clinical outcome data one
desires to review. However, we believe that precision can be greatly
increased in assessing the effectiveness of extinction therapies by
directly measuring each subject's fear response during the course of
treatment. Such an assessment strategy not only provides valuable
feedback to the therapists but operationalizes whether or not the
treatment procedure is being administered effectively. Research
findings also tell us that the duration of CS exposure is a critical
factor and that, despite criticism to the contrary, support for the
safety of the technique is strong.

References

Amsel, A. The role of frustrative nonreward in noncontinuous reward situa-
    tions. *Psychological Bulletin*, 1958, *55*, 102–119.
Amsel, A., & Maltzman, I. The effect upon generalized drive strength of
    emotionality as inferred from the level of consummatory response.
    Journal of Experimental Psychology, 1950, *40*, 563–569.
Ayres, W. A. Implosive therapy: A review. *Psychotherapy: Theory, Research
    and Practice*, 1972, *9*, 242–250.
Bandura, A. *Principles of behavior modification*. New York: Holt, Rinehart &
    Winston, 1969.
Bandura, A. Self-efficacy: Toward a unifying theory of behavioral change.
    Psychological Review, 1977, *84*, 191–215.
Barrett, G. L. Systematic desensitization vs. implosive therapy. *Journal of
    Abnormal Psychology*, 1969, *74*, 587–592.
Baum, M. Extinction of avoidance responding through response prevention
    (flooding). *Psychological Bulletin*, 1970, *70*, 276–284.
Black, A. H. The extinction of avoidance responses under curare. *Journal of
    Comparative and Physiological Psychology*, 1958, *51*, 519–525.
Blakey, R. & Baker, R. An exposure approach to alcohol abuse. *Behavior,
    Research and Therapy*, 1980, *18*, 319–325.
Borkovec, T. D. Effects of expectancy on the outcome of systematic desensi-
    tization and implosive treatment for analogue anxiety. *Behavior Ther-
    apy*, 1972, *3*, 29–40.
Boudewyns, P. A. Implosive therapy and desensitization therapy with inpa-
    tients: A five-year follow-up. *Journal of Abnormal Psychology*, 1975, *84*,
    159–160.
Boudewyns, P. A., & Levis, D. J. Autonomic reactivity of high and low
    ego-strength subjects to repeated anxiety eliciting scenes. *Journal of
    Abnormal Psychology*, 1975, *84*, 682–692.

Boudewyns, P. A., & Wilson, A. E. Implosion therapy and desensitization therapy using free association in treatment of inpatients. *Journal of Abnormal Psychology*, 1972, *79*, 252–268.

Boulougouris, J. C., & Marks, I. M. Implosion (flooding)—A new treatment for phobics. *British Medical Journal*, 1969, *2*, 721–723.

Boulougouris, J. C., Marks, I. M., & Marset, P. Superiority of flooding (implosion) to desensitization for reducing pathological fear. *Behaviour Research and Therapy*, 1971, *2*, 7–16.

Boyd, T. L., & Levis, D. J. The effects of single-component extinction of a three-component serial CS on resistance to extinction of the conditioned avoidance response. *Learning and Motivation*, 1976, *7*, 517–531.

Boyd, T. L., & Levis, D. J. Depression. In R. J. Daitzman (Ed.), *Clinical behavior therapy and behavior modification* (Vol. 1). New York: Garland STPM Press, 1980.

Boyd, T. L., & Levis, D. J. Exposure is a necessary condition for fear reduction: A reply to DeSilva and Rachman. *Behavior Research and Therapy*, 1983, *22*, 143–149.

Brown, J. S. *The motivation of behavior.* New York: McGraw-Hill, 1961.

Brown, J. S., Kalish, H. I., & Farber, I. E. Conditioned fear as revealed by magnitude of startle response to an auditory stimulus. *Journal of Experimental Psychology*, 1951, *41*, 317–328.

Calef, R. A., & McLean, G. D. A comparison of reciprocal inhibition and reactive inhibition therapies in the treatment of speech anxiety. *Behavior Therapy*, 1970, *1*, 51–58.

Carrera, R. N., & Elenewski, J. J. Implosive therapy as a treatment for insomnia. *Journal of Clinical Psychology*, 1980, *36*, 729–734.

Chambless, D. L., Foa, E. B. Groves, G. A., & Goldstein, A. J. Flooding with Brevital in the treatment of agoraphobia: Counteraffective? *Behaviour Research and Therapy*, 1979, *17*, 243–251.

Chaplin, E. W., & Levine, B. A. The effects of total exposure duration and interrupted versus continuous exposure in flooding therapy. *Behavior Therapy*, 1981, *12*, 360–368.

Cornish, R. D., & Dilley, J. S. Comparison of three methods of reducing test anxiety: Systematic desensitization, implosive therapy, and study counseling. *Journal of Consulting Psychology*, 1973, *20*, 499–503.

Crowe, M. J., Marks, I. M., Agras, W. S., & Leitenberg, H. Time-limited desensitization, implosion, and shaping for phobic patients: A cross-over study. *Behaviour Research and Therapy*, 1972, *10*, 319–328.

DeMoor, W. Systematic desensitization vs. prolonged high intensity stimulation (flooding). *Journal of Behavioral Therapy and Experimental Psychiatry*, 1970, *1*, 45–52.

Denny, M. R., Koons, P. B., & Mason, J. E. Extinction of avoidance as a function of the escape situation. *Journal of Comparative and Physiological Psychology*, 1959, *52*, 212–214.

Dollard, J., & Miller, N. E. *Personality and psychotherapy.* New York: McGraw-Hill, 1950.

Dubin, W. J., & Levis, D. J. Influence of similarity of components of a serial CS on conditioned fear in the rat. *Journal of Comparative and Physiological Psychology*, 1973, *85*, 304–312.

Emmelkamp, P. M. G. Self-observation versus flooding in the treatment of agoraphobia. *Behaviour Research and Therapy*, 1974, *12*, 229–237.

Emmelkamp, P. M. G., & Kraanen, J. Therapist-controlled exposure *in vivo* versus self-controlled exposure *in vivo:* A comparison with obsessive-compulsive patients. *Behaviour Research and Therapy*, 1977, *15*, 491–495.

Emmelkamp, P. M. G., Knipers, A. C. N., & Eggeraat, J. B. Cognitive modification versus prolonged exposure *in vivo:* A comparison with agoraphobics as subjects. *Behaviour Research and Therapy*, 1978, *16*, 33–41.

Emmelkamp, P. M. G., Van der Helm, M., van Zanten, B. L., & Plochq, I. Treatment of obsessive-compulsive patients: The contribution of self-instructional training to the effectiveness of exposure. *Behaviour Research and Therapy*, 1980, *18*, 61–66.

Emmelkamp, P. M. G., & Wessels, H. Flooding in imagination versus flooding in vivo: A comparison with agoraphobics. *Behaviour Research and Therapy*, 1975, *13*, 7–15.

Eysenck, H. J. The conditioning model of neurosis. *The Behavioral and Brain Sciences*, 1979, *2*, 155–166.

Fazio, A. F. Treatment components in implosive therapy. *Journal of Abnormal Psychology*, 1970, *76*, 211–219.

Foa, E. B., Blau, J., Prout, M., & Latimer, P. Is horror a necessary component of flooding (implosion)? *Behaviour Research and Therapy*, 1977, *15*, 397–402.

Foa, E. B., Jameson, J. S., Turner, R. M., & Payne, L. L. Massed vs. spaced exposure sessions in the treatment of agoraphobia. *Behaviour Research and Therapy*, 1980, *18*, 333–338.

Foa, E. B., Steketee, G., Turner, R. M., & Fischer, S. C. Effects of imaginal exposure to feared disasters in obsessive compulsive checkers. *Behaviour Research and Therapy*, 1980, *18*, 449–458.

Frankel, A. S. Implosive therapy: A critical review. *Psychotherapy: Theory, Research and Practice*, 1972, *9*, 251–255.

Gelder, M. G., Bancroft, J. H. J., Gath, D. H., Johnston, D. W., Mathews, A. M., & Shaw, P. M. Specific and nonspecific factors in behavior therapy. *British Journal of Psychiatry*, 1973, *123*, 445–462.

Grey, S. J., Rachman, S., & Sartory, G. Return of fear: The role of inhibition. *Behaviour Research and Therapy*, 1981, *19*, 135–143.

Hackmann, A., & McLearn, C. A comparison of flooding and thought stopping in the treatment of obsessional neurosis. *Behaviour Research and Therapy*, 1975, *13*, 263–269.

Hafner, T., & Marks, I. M. Exposure in vivo of agoraphobics: The contributions of diazepam, group exposure and anxiety evocation. *Psychological Medicine*, 1976, *6*, 71–88.

Hand, I., Lamontagne, Y., & Marks, I. M. Group exposure (flooding) in vivo for agoraphobics. *British Journal of Psychiatry,* 1974, *124,* 588–602.

Hare, N., & Levis, D. J. Pervasive ("free-floating") anxiety: A search for a cause and treatment approach. In S. Turner, K. Calhoun, & H. Adams (Eds.), *Handbook of clinical behavior therapy.* New York: Wiley, 1981.

Hekmat, H. Systematic versus semantic desensitization and implosive therapy: A comparable study. *Journal of Consulting and Clinical Psychology,* 1973, *40,* 202–209.

Hodgson, R. J., & Rachman, S. An experimental investigation of the implosion technique. *Behaviour Research and Therapy,* 1970, *8,* 21–27.

Hodgson, R. J., Rachman, S., & Marks, I. M. The treatment of chronic obsessive-compulsive neurosis: Follow-up and further findings. *Behaviour Research and Therapy,* 1972, *10,* 181–189.

Hogan, R. A. Implosive therapy in the short-term treatment of psychotics. *Psychotherapy: Theory, Research, and Practice,* 1966, *3,* 25–31.

Horne, A. M., & Matson, J. L. A comparison of modeling, desensitization, flooding, study skills, and control groups for reducing test anxiety. *Behavior Therapy,* 1977, *8,* 1–8.

Hunt, H. F., Jernberg, P., & Brady, J. V. The effect of electroconvulsive shock (E.C.S.) on a conditioned emotional response: The effects of post-E.C.S. extinction on the reappearance of the response. *Journal of Comparative and Physiological Psychology,* 1952, *45,* 589–599.

Hussain, M. Z. Desensitization and flooding (implosion) in treatment of phobics. *American Journal of Psychiatry,* 1971, *127,* 1509–1514.

Jannoun, L., Munby, M., Catalan, J., & Gelder, M. A home-based program for agoraphobia: Replication and controlled evaluation. *Behavior Therapy,* 1980, *11,* 294–305.

Johnston, D. W., Lancashire, M., Mathews, A. M., Munby, M., Shaw, P. M., & Gelder, M. G. Imaginal flooding and exposure to real phobic situations: Changes during treatment. *British Journal of Psychiatry,* 1976, *129,* 372–377.

Kimble, G. A., & Perlmuter, L. S. The problem of volition. *Psychological Review,* 1970, *77,* 361–384.

Knapp, R. K. Acquisition and extinction of avoidance with similar and different shock and escape situations. *Journal of Comparative and Physiological Psychology,* 1965, *60,* 272–273.

Kostanek, D. J., & Sawrey, J. M. Acquisition and extinction of shuttlebox avoidance with complex stimuli. *Psychonomic Science,* 1965, *3,* 369–370.

Levis, D. J. Effects of serial CS presentation and other characteristics of the CS on the conditioned avoidance response. *Psychological Reports,* 1966, *18,* 755–766.

Levis, D. J. Serial CS presentation and the shuttlebox avoidance conditioning: A further look at the tendency to delay responding. *Psychonomic Society,* 1970, *20,* 145–147.

Levis, D. J. Implosive therapy: A critical analysis of Morganstern's review. *Psychological Bulletin*, 1974, *81*, 155–158.

Levis, D. J. The infrahuman avoidance model of symptom maintenance and implosive therapy. In J. D. Keehn (Ed.), *Psychopathology in animals*. New York: Academic Press, 1979(a).

Levis, D. J. A reconsideration of Eysenck's conditioning model of neurosis. *The Behavioral and Brain Sciences*, 1979(b), *2*, 172–174.

Levis, D. J. Implementing the technique of implosive therapy. In A. Goldstein & E. B. Foa (Eds.), *Handbook of behavioral intervention*. New York: Wiley, 1980(a).

Levis, D. J. The learned helplessness effect: An expectancy, discrimination deficit, or motivational induced persistence? *Journal of Research in Personality*, 1980(b), *14*, 157–169.

Levis, D. J. Extrapolation of two-factor learning theory of infrahuman avoidance behavior to psychopathology. *Neuroscience and Behavioral Review*, 1981, *5*, 355–370.

Levis, D. J. Experimental and theoretical foundations of behavior therapy. In A. S. Bellock, M. Hersen, & A. E. Kazdin (Eds.), *International handbook of behavior modification and therapy*. New York: Plenum, 1982.

Levis, D. J., Bouska, S., Eron, J., & McIlhon, M. Serial CS presentation and one-way avoidance conditioning: A noticeable lack of delayed responding. *Psychonomic Science*, 1970, *20*, 147–149.

Levis, D. J., & Boyd, T. L. Effects of shock intensity on avoidance responding in a shuttlebox to serial CS procedures. *Psychonomic Bulletin*, 1973, *1*, 304–306.

Levis, D. J., & Boyd, T. L. Symptom maintenance: An infrahuman analysis and extension of the conservation of anxiety principle. *Journal of Abnormal Psychology*, 1979, *88*, 107–120.

Levis, D. J., & Carrera, R. Effects of ten hours of implosive therapy in the treatment of outpatients. *Journal of Abnormal Psychology*, 1967, *72*, 504–508.

Levis, D. J., & Dubin, W. J. Some parameters affecting shuttle-box avoidance responding with rats receiving serially presented conditioned stimuli. *Journal of Comparative and Physiological Psychology*, 1973, *82*, 328–344.

Levis, D. J., & Hare, N. A. A review of the theoretical rational and empirical support for the extinction of implosive (flooding) therapy. In M. Hersen, R. M. Eisler, & P. M. Miller (Eds.), *Progress in behavior modification* (Vol. 4). New York: Academic Press, 1977.

Levis, D. J., & Plunkett, W. J. The use of subjective magnitude estimation technique to validate procedures for pre-selecting "phobic" subjects. *Behavioral Assessment*, 1979, *1*, 191–201.

Levis, D. J., & Stampfl, T. G. Effects of serial CS presentation on shuttlebox avoidance responding. *Learning and Motivation*, 1972, *3*, 73–90.

Lowenfeld, J., Rubenfeld, S., & Guthrie, G. M. Verbal inhibition in subception. *Journal of General Psychology*, 1956, *54*, 171–176.

Marshall, W. L., Gautheir, J., Christie, M., Currie, D., & Gordon, A. Flooding therapy: Effectiveness, stimulus characteristics, and the value of brief in vivo exposure. *Behaviour Research and Therapy*, 1977, *15*, 79–87.

Marshall, W. L., Gauthier, J., & Gordon, A. The current status of flooding therapy. In M. Hersen, R. M. Eisler, & P. M. Miller (Eds.), *Progress in behavior modification* (Vol. 7). New York: Academic Press, 1979.

Mathews, A. M., Johnston, D. W., Lancashire, M., Mumby, M., Shaw, P. M., & Gelder, M. G. Imaginal flooding and exposure to real phobic situations: Treatment outcome with agoraphobic patients. *British Journal of Psychiatry*, 1976, *129*, 362–371.

Mathews, A., & Rezin, V. Treatment of dental fears by imaginal flooding and rehearsal of coping behavior. *Behaviour Research and Therapy*, 1977, *15*, 321–328.

Mathews, A. M., & Shaw, P. Emotional arousal and persuasion effects in flooding. *Behaviour Research and Therapy*, 1973, *11*, 587–598.

McDonald, R., Santory, G., Grey, S., Cobb, J., Stern, R., & Marks, I. M. The effects of self-exposure instructions on agoraphobic outpatients. *Behaviour Research and Therapy*, 1979, *17*, 83–85.

McNamara, J. R. Systematic desensitization vs implosive therapy: Issues in outcomes. *Psychotherapy: Theory, Research and Practice*, 1972, *9*, 13–17.

Mealiea, W. L., & Nawas, N. M. The comparative effectiveness of systematic desensitization and implosive therapy in the treatment of snake phobia. *Journal of Behavior Therapy and Experimental Psychiatry*, 1971, *2*, 185–194.

Miller, N. E. Learnable drives and rewards. In S. S. Stevens (Ed.), *Handbook of experimental psychology*. New York: Wiley, 1951.

Miller, N. E., & Kraeling, D. Displacement: Evidence for more generalization of approach than avoidance in an approach-avoidance conflict generalized to a new stimulus situation. Unpublished manuscript, 1950.

Morganstern, K. P. Implosive therapy and flooding procedures: A critical review. *Psychological Bulletin*, 1973, *79*, 318–334.

Mowrer, O. H. On the dual nature of learning—a reinterpretation of "conditioning" and "problem solving." *Harvard Educational Review*, 1947, *17*, 102–148.

Mowrer, O. H. *Learning theory and behavior*. New York: Wiley, 1960.

Mylan, J. L., & Clement, P. W. Prediction and comparison of outcome in systematic desensitization and implosion. *Behaviour Research and Therapy*, 1972, *10*, 235–241.

Newton, J. R., & Stein, L. I. Implosive therapy in alcoholism: Comparison with brief psychotherapy. *Quarterly Journal of Studies on Alcohol*, 1974, *35*, 1256–1265.

O'Brien, T. P., & Kelley, J. E. A comparison of self-directed and therapist-directed practice for fear reduction. *Behaviour Research and Therapy*, 1970, *18*, 573–580.

Parkinson, L., & Rachman, S. Are intrusive thoughts subject to habituation? *Behaviour Research and Therapy*, 1980, *18*, 409–418.

Pavlov, I. P. *Conditioned reflexes*. New York: International Publishers, 1927.

Prochaska, J. O. Symptom and dynamic cues in the implosive treatment of test anxiety. *Journal of Abnormal Psychology*, 1971, *77*, 133–142.

Rabavilas, A. D., Boulougouris, J. C., Perissaki, C., & Stefanis, G. Premorbid personality traits and responsiveness to flooding in obsessive-compulsive patients. *Behaviour Research and Therapy*, 1979, *17*, 575–580.

Rabavilas, A. D., Boulougouris, J. C., & Stefanis, C. Duration of flooding sessions in the treatment of obsessive-compulsive patients. *Behaviour Research and Therapy*, 1976, *14*, 349–355.

Rachman, S. Studies in desensitization. II: Flooding. *Behaviour Research and Therapy*, 1966, *4*, 1–6.

Rachman, S. The passing of the two-stage theory of fear and avoidance: Fresh possibilities. *Behaviour Research and Therapy*, 1976, *14*, 125–131.

Rachman, S., Cobb, J., Grey, S., McDonald, B., Mawson, D., Sartory, G., & Stern, R. The behavioral treatment of obsessional-compulsive disorders, with and without clomipramine. *Behaviour Research and Therapy*, 1979, *17*, 467–478.

Rachman, S., Marks, I. M., & Hodgson, R. The treatment of obsessive-compulsive neurotics by modeling and flooding *in vivo*. *Behaviour Research and Therapy*, 1973, *11*, 463–471.

Seligman, M. E. P. Phobias and preparedness. *Behavior Therapy*, 1971, *2*, 307–321.

Seligman, M. E. P. *Helplessness: On depression, development and death*. San Francisco: W. H. Freeman, 1975.

Seligman, M. E. P., & Johnston, J. C. A cognitive theory of avoidance learning. In F. J. McGuigan & D. B. Lumsden (Eds.), *Contemporary prospectives in learning and conditioning*. Washington: Scripta Press, 1973.

Shahar, A., & Marks, I. M. Habituation during exposure treatment of compulsive rituals. *Behavior Therapy*, 1980, *11*, 397–401.

Shearman, R. W. Response-contingent CS termination in the extinction of avoidance learning. *Behavior Research and Therapy*, 1970, *8*, 227–239.

Sherry, G. S., & Levine, B. A. An examination of procedural variables in flooding therapy. *Behavior Therapy*, 1980, *11*, 148–155.

Shipley, R. H. Extinction of conditioned fear in rats as a function of several parameters of CS exposure. *Journal of Comparative and Physiological Psychology*, 1974, *84*, 699–707.

Shipley, R. H., & Boudewyns, P. A. Flooding and implosive therapy: Are they harmful? *Behavior Therapy*, 1980, *11*, 503–508.

Shipley, R. H., Mock. L. A., & Levis, D. J. Effects of several prevention procedures on activity, avoidance responding, and conditioned fears in rats. *Journal of Comparative and Physiological Psychology*, 1971, *77*, 256–270.

Sinnott, A., Jones, R. B., Scott-Fordham, A., & Woodward, R. Augmentation of *in vivo* exposure treatment for agoraphobia by the formation of neighborhood self-help groups. *Behaviour Research and Therapy*, 1981, *19*, 339–347.

Smith, R. D., Dickson, A. L., & Sheppard, L. Review of flooding procedures in animals and men. *Perceptual and Motor Skills*, Monograph Supplement, 2-U37, 1973.

Smith, R. E., & Nye, S. L. A comparison of implosive therapy and systematic desensitization in the treatment of test anxiety. *Journal of Consulting and Clinical Psychology*, 1973, *44*, 37–42.

Solomon, R. L., & Wynne, L. C. Traumatic avoidance learning: The principle of anxiety conservation and partial irreversibility. *Psychological Review*, 1954, *61*, 353–385.

Stampfl, T. G. Implosive therapy, Part I: The theory. In S. G. Armitage (Ed.), *Behavioral modification techniques in the treatment of emotional disorders*. Battle Creek, MI: V. A. Publications, 1966, pp. 12–21.

Stampfl, T. G. Implosive therapy: An emphasis on covert stimulation. In D. J. Levis (Ed.), *Learning approaches to therapeutic behavior change*. Chicago: Aldine, 1970.

Stampfl, T. G., & Levis, D. J. Essentials of implosive therapy: A learning theory-based psychodynamic behavioral therapy. *Journal of Abnormal Psychology*, 1967, *72*, 496–503.

Stampfl, T. G., & Levis, D. J. Learning theory: An aid to dynamic therapeutic practice. In L. D. Eron & R. Callahan (Ed.), *Relationship of theory to practice in psychotherapy*. Chicago: Aldine, 1969.

Stampfl, T. G., & Levis, D. J. Implosive therapy. In R. M. Jurjevich (Eds.), *Handbook of direct and behavior psychotherapies*. Chapel Hill, NC: U. of North Carolina Press, 1973.

Stampfl, T. G., & Levis, D. J. Implosive therapy: A behavioral therapy. In J. T. Spence, R. C. Carson, & J. W. Thibant (Eds.), *Behavioral approaches to therapy*. Morristown, NJ: General Learning Press, 1976.

Teasdale, J., Walsh, P., Lancashire, M., & Mathews, A. Group exposure for agoraphobics: A replication study. *British Journal of Psychiatry*, 1977, *130*, 186–193.

Wall, H. N., & Guthrie, G. M. Extinction of responses to subceived stimuli. *Journal of General Psychology*, 1959, *60*, 205–210.

Watson, J. P., Gaind, R., & Marks, I. M. Physiological habituation to continuous phobic stimulation. *Behaviour Research and Therapy*, 1972, *10*, 269–275.

Watson, J. P., & Marks, I. M. Relevant and irrelevant fear in flooding: A crossover study of phobic patients. *Behavior Therapy*, 1971, *2*, 275–295.

Watson, J. P., Mullet, G. E., & Pillay, H. The effects of prolonged exposure to phobic situations upon agoraphobic patients treated in groups. *Behaviour Research and Therapy*, 1973, *11*, 531–545.

Weinberger, N. M. Effects of detainment on extinction of avoidance responses. *Journal of Comparative and Physiological Psychology,* 1965, *60,* 135–138.

Willis, W. R., & Edwards, J. A. A study of the comparative effectiveness of systematic desensitization and implosive therapy. *Behaviour Research and Therapy,* 1969, *7,* 387–395.

Zitrin, C. M., Klein, D. F., & Woerner, M. G. Treatment of agoraphobia with group exposure *in vivo* and impramine. *Archives of General Psychiatry,* 1980, *37,* 63–72.

4

The Relaxation Therapies

PAUL M. LEHRER AND ROBERT L. WOOLFOLK

We entitled this chapter "The Relaxation Therapies," in the plural, because there many forms of such therapy and because there are many apparent inconsistencies in the clinical and research literature which resolve only when we distinguish among the various forms. Often "relaxation therapy" is assumed to mean progressive relaxation; but even here, as we will show below, there are several forms of therapy with this label, not all of which produce equivalent results. Other frequently used methods include hypnotic relaxation, autogenic training, biofeedback, the various forms of meditation, and, perhaps the most frequently used of all, such disparate behaviors as engaging in regular prayer, listening to music, jogging, deep breathing, having a good meal, practicing Eastern martial disciplines, watching television, bowling, taking a cruise, having sexual relations, or lying on a beach.

This chapter will concentrate on three of the widely used relaxation therapies whose effects have been well researched: progressive relaxation, autogenic training, and meditation. We will describe the origins and effects of each and their applications to a selected group of problems. In doing so we will compare the relaxation techniques and give some guidelines for their use.

Progressive Relaxation

Progressive relaxation was invented by Edmund Jacobson, a psychologist and physician who was interested in developing a treatment for the psychological and medical problems caused or exacerbated by tension. Jacobson's (1938) relaxation procedure is designed to teach the complete reduction of tonic muscle tension. The trainee learns to recognize very low levels of muscle activity by tensing one muscle at a time until the proprioceptive ("control") sensations produced by muscular activity are recognized. Then the level of tension is progressively reduced, until even the tension produced by *thinking* about tensing the muscle is easily recognized.

Even though this training often takes many months, it is the intensity rather than the length of the training that characterizes Jacobson's work. Although some of Jacobson's cases were trained for 20 or more sessions, Jacobson (1938) published clinical reports about persons treated in only a few sessions. Another hallmark of Jacobson's technique is the strict avoidance of suggestion. Jacobson was concerned that the person's muscles actually be relaxed rather than just feel relaxed to the trainee. He thus refrained from telling his trainees even where in their bodies they should experience control sensations during a contraction. Rather, where possible, he would exert a counterforce to the direction of the movement the trainee was making to render the muscle sensations more obvious. In so doing, Jacobson ensured that the trainee was accurately perceiving the sensations produced by the muscle contractions, rather than imagining such sensations in response to suggestion. For a similar reason, as early as the 1950s, Jacobson had tried and already rejected electromyogram (EMG) biofeedback as an aid in relaxation training. He felt that this procedure would make people reliant on the external stimulus provided by the machine rather than upon their own physiological sensations.

We dwell upon these characteristics of Jacobson's method because they contrast so starkly with the "progressive relaxation" methods that are in common use by behavior therapists (e.g., Bernstein & Borkovec, 1973; Paul, 1966; Wolpe & Lazarus, 1966). The latter methods make extensive use of suggestion, ranging from formal hypnotic inductions to simply telling trainees what sensations they might expect after each contraction. Also, these methods are quite abbreviated, and they emphasize the importance of achieving an overall feeling of deep relaxation quite early in training—something that often is not felt in Jacobson's technique until after quite a few sessions. Indeed, the training emphasis is on immediate psychological, rather than profound physiological, effects. Thus more muscle groups are covered in a single session than in Jacobson's technique. Also various automated procedures, such as tape-recorded training or adjunctive EMG biofeedback, often are employed.

Which form of progressive relaxation is "best" is, obviously, an empirical question—a question that is, for the most part, unanswered at present. Only two comparative studies have thus far been reported (Snow, 1977; Turner, 1978). Turner found marginal advantages to using Jacobson's technique rather than the various modified ones, while Snow found no differences between methods. Both studies, however, used normal college students as subjects, rather than clinical populations, so the clinical implications are, at most, inferential. Indeed, there is some evidence that the physiological effects of having learned a relaxation technique may not be noticeable among a nonanxious population. Lehrer (1978) found marked physiological differences between progressive relaxation and a no-treatment control among anxiety neurotics, but almost no differences among normal subjects.

Despite the lack of clear comparative data differentiating the various progressive relaxation techniques from each other, there are at least some inferential grounds on which to decide which form to use for particular applications. These are taken from studies of various details upon which the techniques differ. In recent literature reviews, Borkovec and Sides (1979), Lehrer (1982), and Lehrer and Woolfolk (1984) found that some components of Jacobson's original technique are critical for achieving physiological results. They account for many of the discrepancies in the empirical outcome literature, which contains studies using a variety of relaxation methods and is, as a whole, approximately equally divided among studies showing significant physiological effects for progressive relaxation and studies finding no such effects. Particularly important is live training. Tape-recorded training does not appear to teach people a relaxation skill that can produce physiological effects outside the treatment session. Also, adjunctive use of EMG biofeedback does not appear to augment the effectiveness of live progressive relaxation training, although it can render taped training clinically effective under some circumstances. Length of training does not appear to be a critical factor for success. The relative effects of muscular skill-oriented training versus suggestion-oriented training have not been systematically assessed, although there is convincing evidence that pure suggestions to relax (i.e., without any training in recognizing muscle sensations) are not effective in teaching relaxation skills that generalize beyond the training session.

In conclusion, then, data on components of various progressive relaxation techniques give us reason to hypothesize that Jacobson's original method probably has stronger physiological effects than the modified progressive relaxation procedures; and, therefore, that the original technique may be more effective for treating various symptoms of somatic tension. On the other hand, conditions that are more closely related to thoughts, beliefs, and perceptions than to physiology (such as anxiety, worry, obsessions) may not be better treated by Jacobson's original method. Indeed, because of their brevity and their emphasis on suggestion and beliefs, the newer techniques may have some advantages. We point out, however, that these are hypotheses, as yet untested.

Autogenic Training

In contrast to Jacobson's progressive relaxation, autogenic training is almost entirely a technique of self-suggestion. Originally devised by the German physician Johannes Schultz, it was modeled upon the experiences reported by persons who experienced states of deep hypnotic relaxation. Strictly speaking, autogenic training is not conceptualized by its proponents exclusively as a relaxation technique. Rather than training people to achieve a state of low arousal, autogenic training aims at a state of psychophysiological equilibrium. Although often this does involve decreasing physiological arousal, autogenic training does not try to produce *complete* relaxation. Such a state is considered to be unnatural. At times autogenic training may, in fact, evoke tears, pain, anxiety, or other forms of emotional and/or physiological arousal; and it may evoke feelings of being energized as well as relaxed. If arousal is increased by the technique, it is assumed that expression of such tension is needed by the body. The procedure, theory, and applications of autogenic training are exhaustively reviewed by Luthe (1969) in a six-volume English-language summary. One volume (Volume IV) is entirely devoted to research, most of it originally reported in languages other than English. This technique is in much wider use in other parts of the world (particularly in German-speaking countries, Eastern Europe, and Japan) than it is in the English-speaking world.

The autogenic method involves assuming an attitude of "passive concentration" on a series of "formulae," or self-suggestions, pertaining to various physical, emotional, and mental sensations. Training generally begins using the following standard formulae (one limb at a time for those relating to the limbs):

1. My arms are heavy.
2. My legs are heavy.
3. My arms are warm.

4. My legs are warm.
5. My forehead is cool.
6. My heartbeat is calm and regular.
7. It breathes me (i.e., my breathing is automatic).
8. My solar plexus is warm.

The individual is encouraged to imagine feelings, sensations, or scenes that may make the sensation more vivid, but is warned not to *try* to make the sensation occur. Concentration on the formula must remain a passive experience, whether or not the sensation is perceived. After mastery of the standard formulae, training is given in the use of individually tailored "organ-specific" and "intentional" formulae, which are tailored to the physical, mental, and emotional problems of the individual.

Although quite voluminous, most of the research on autogenic training tends to be, from a modern behavioral perspective, rather unsystematic. It consists almost exclusively of multiple-case studies. Many of these studies are well documented, and the sheer weight of them (in the thousands) does lend considerable credence to the method; but, until recently, there have been few attempts to compare autogenic training to credible control conditions or otherwise to assess the efficacy of specific components of the autogenic technique. As with progressive relaxation, many variants of autogenic therapy are in common use. Norris and Fahrion (1984) have described a technique of "autogenic feedback training," which consists of combining autogenic-like phrases with biofeedback (usually hand-warming). Some practitioners give all of the autogenic instructions at once (e.g., Norris & Fahrion, 1984), rather than, as in Schultz and Luthe's (1969) technique, giving them gradually over many sessions. Schultz's original technique stresses that the exercises should initially be practiced for very brief periods (30 seconds), in order that traumatic occurrences of "autogenic discharges" (unpleasant emotional or physical reactions) might be kept to a controllable level of comfort. No studies have yet been done comparing the original method with the newer variants.

Some studies have been done, however, comparing autogenic training with progressive relaxation. Because of the different emphases of the two techniques, it is commonly hypothesized that progressive relaxation has relatively greater muscular effects and autogenic training relatively greater autonomic effects. Moreover, although progressive relaxation might be expected to produce more sensations of "relaxation," both techniques might be expected to decrease unpleasant emotions. There is some evidence to support these notions.

Two relevant studies come from our laboratory. One (Shapiro & Lehrer, 1980) was done on normal volunteers and the other (Lehrer, Atthowe, & Weber, 1980) on anxious volunteers. Consistent with our previous findings (Lehrer, 1978) that research on normal subjects is not sensitive to physiological effects of relaxation techniques, the former study found no differences between the two techniques in heart rate and skin conductance, and no differences in these physiological measures between either technique and a no-treatment control. The three groups did, however, differ on self-report measures. Compared to the control group, both methods reduced Symptom Checklist-90 measures of anxiety, depression, and total psychiatric symptoms. Subjects in the autogenic training group also reported more experiences of heaviness and warmth in the limbs than subjects in the progressive relaxation group, and more sensations of breathing deeply. One interpretation of these results is that the strongest difference between the techniques is in perception of the specific kinds of physiological activity that are emphasized in each of the techniques. A harsher interpretation would be that subjects in the autogenic training group merely reported what they had been told to experience—very possibly an effect of the demand characteristics of the experiment. Different amounts of attention from a therapist might also have explained some of the self-reported differences between the treatment groups and the control group, leaving open the possibility that neither treatment had any effect at all.

The Lehrer et al. (1980) study of anxious individuals, however, found between-groups differences that could not so easily be dismissed. At the posttest session, lower heart rates were found among autogenic training subjects than among progressive relaxation subjects, thus verifying our hypothesis of specific autonomic effects for autogenic training. Another finding of interest was that, following introduction to the formula, "My heartbeat is calm and regular," subjects in the autogenic training condition tended to report sensations of cardiac palpitations. The finding that autogenic training produces palpitations and, subsequently, lower heart rate, is certainly consistent with Schultz's theory that such "autogenic discharges" may facilitate homeostasis. Subjects reported practicing progressive relaxation at home more than they practiced autogenic training. Self-reported anxiety decreased more in both treatment groups than in a false-biofeedback placebo group and a no-treatment control.

The findings of our own work are consistent with that done in other laboratories. In a comprehensive literature review (Lehrer & Woolfolk, 1984), we concluded that progressive relaxation has greater muscular effects and autogenic training greater autonomic effects. This review also found evidence that clinical problems associated with skeletal muscle tension (e.g., tension headaches, spasmodic dysmenorrhea) may respond better to progressive relaxation. The converse, however, does not appear to hold. Autonomic problems (vascular headaches, congestive dysmenorrhea, Raynaud's disease, hypertension) do not appear to respond better to autogenic training than to progressive relaxation.

Meditation

Meditation has by far the longest history of the three relaxation therapies reviewed in this chapter. Unlike progressive relaxation and autogenic training, it is not a product of our Western scientific culture. Rather, meditation originates in the religious and spiritual traditions of the East. The forms of meditation that have been systematically examined in controlled empirical investigations derive principally from the Hindu and Buddhist traditions. Various forms of yogic and Zen Buddhist meditation have been especially influential, the former having given rise to Transcendental Meditation (TM) and the latter serving as the prototype for Benson's "relaxation response" (Benson, 1975).

Although methods of meditation differ widely, those that have come to be used by Western science for inducing relaxation or related states have a number of characteristics in common. These include the conscious attempt to focus attention in a nonanalytical way and the avoidance of discursive, ruminating thought (Shapiro, 1982). All varieties of meditation have in common the deployment of attention in a way that is not characteristic of rational thought.

Over the last 15 years meditation has become more accessible to Westerners as its techniques have become removed from their original esoteric contexts. A first step in this direction was the advent of TM, a technique that, although still bearing some vestiges of Hindu ritual in its cultic initiation ceremony and use of a secret mantra, nevertheless has generally been taught with a minimum of Hindu philosophical trappings. The secularization of meditation was accomplished completely in Benson's method, Carrington's "clinically standardized meditation" (1977), and Woolfolk's clinical meditation technique (Woolfolk, Carr-Kaffashan, McNulty, & Lehrer, 1976). Along with TM, these Westernized methods have several commonalities. All require the person to lie or to sit still in a comfortable position, with eyes closed, while concentrating on a repetitive, recurring stimulus, usually a verbal mantra and/or a bodily process.

The research on meditation has yielded a somewhat inconsistent pattern of findings and is, hence, difficult to summarize. Part of the problem is that each study uses a different form of meditation, taught in a different manner (e.g., TM, Zen meditation, yoga; after brief group training or years of intensive training, etc.) Research on highly experienced practitioners of meditation has shown such individuals to be capable of producing profound physiological changes (Benson et al., 1982; Woolfolk, 1975). Studies in which individuals received training as part of the investigation have tended, on the whole, to show stronger meditation effects under two conditions: when subjects received more than very brief training, and either under conditions of experimentally induced stress or when the subject population was composed of individuals who manifested high levels of arousal.

Although the literature is not conclusive, it suggests (Lehrer & Woolfolk, 1984) that meditation may be more motivational for some populations than progressive relaxation. In addition, more regularly than other relaxation techniques, meditation tends to produce changes in EEG rhythms (usually increases in alpha or theta, but sometimes, as in states of meditative ecstacy, increases in beta). Two studies from our laboratory also suggest that meditation augments the cardiac component of the orienting reflex to noxious stimuli (Lehrer, Schoicket, Carrington, & Woolfolk, 1980; Lehrer, Woolfolk, Rooney, McCann, & Carrington, 1984). We have interpreted the latter findings as suggesting that meditation "tunes" the brain to accept environmental stimuli, and not to defend against them— making one react as if the stimuli were, although novel, not noxious. Although Schwartz, Davidson, and Goleman (1978) have interpreted some of their own experimental findings as suggesting that, compared with progressive relaxation, meditation has relatively greater cognitive effects and relaxation tends to have relatively greater somatic effects, our literature review found only marginal other evidence to support this hypothesis (Lehrer & Woolfolk, 1984).

Outcome Studies

Maladaptive Emotions: Excessive Anxiety, Anger, and Depression

Many studies have found significant statistical differences between self-reported emotional effects of various relaxation therapies and the effects of various control conditions. All systematic relaxation techniques produce reliable decreases in self-reported anxiety, an-

ger, and depression (cf. a review of the comparative treatment literature by Lehrer & Woolfolk, 1984.) Although there is some evidence
that combining relaxation therapy with cognitive therapy produces
somewhat stronger effects than either therapy alone, there is no
evidence that the various relaxation therapies differ from each other
in effectiveness.

Few of the studies we reviewed, however, assessed the clinical
significance of the changes in emotions; and most of those that did do
so found that the effects of relaxation therapy on severe emotional
problems are modest at best. Raskin, Johnson, and Rondesvedt
(1973) found that the combination of progressive relaxation training
and frontalis EMG biofeedback failed to stop severe anxiety attacks
among anxiety neurotics. Milder symptoms associated with the problem (e.g., situational anxiety, headaches, insomnia) were improved
by the treatment, however. Similarly LeBoeuf and Lodge (1980)
found that EMG biofeedback and progressive relaxation each had
only marginal effects on anxiety neurosis; and Shoemaker (1977)
found that progressive relaxation had no effect even on self-report
measures of anxiety among anxiety neurotics. We have reviewed
evidence (Lehrer & Woolfolk, 1984) that cognitive therapy is more
effective than relaxation therapy for treatment of test anxiety, and
that exposure therapy is more effective than relaxation therapy for
treatment of phobias. In both cases, the clinical effects of relaxation
therapy alone are marginal; and the value of combining relaxation
therapy with these other treatments is debatable. Relaxation therapy may be slightly more beneficial in treatment of anger, but here
too the effects of relaxation therapy alone are not large. In a study of
chronically angry subjects, Novaco (1976) found that self-report measures of anger and blood pressure levels were both reduced by a
treatment consisting of a combination of relaxation therapy and
cognitive therapy; but that only the self-report index showed improvement when relaxation therapy alone was applied.

Two parametric studies and one study using a single-subject
control methodology had more optimistic results for relaxation therapy. Lavallée, Lamontagne, Pinard, and Annable (1977) showed that
relaxation therapy could have lasting effects in reducing medication
use (as well as in self-reported anxiety) among anxiety neurotics—as
long as subjects had *not* been administered Valium during the eight-
week experimental period. Those who had been administered the
drug tended, over time, to stop using their relaxation skills, and,
instead, to have become relatively more reliant on medication. On
the other hand, a study of depression (Wilson, 1982) found that

depressed subjects given progressive relaxation therapy sought less additional treatment during a one-year follow-up than subjects given minimal treatment. In this case the adjunctive use of medication appeared to be somewhat beneficial. Although combining amitriptyline with relaxation did not change the overall treatment effectiveness, it did speed clinical improvement.

Psychosomatic Disorders: Hypertension, Headaches, and Other Disorders

Relaxation therapies appear to be helpful as primary treatments for a variety of psychosomatic disorders. In this review we will emphasize the two problems that have received the most attention from researchers: hypertension and headaches.

Relaxation therapies appear to be clinically helpful both for tension headaches and for migraine headaches. Blanchard, Andrasik, Ahles, Teders, and O'Keefe (1980) have reviewed the literature for headaches and found that relaxation and biofeedback therapies produce an average of 51 to 70% improvement in tension headaches and 52 to 65% improvement in migraine headaches. The comparable figures for attention-placebo conditions are 34.8% and 16.5%, respectively. In our own review of the literature (Lehrer & Woolfolk, 1984), we have concluded that muscularly oriented relaxation therapy (progressive relaxation, often combined with EMG biofeedback) is more effective than autonomically oriented therapy (autogenic training, often combined with finger temperature biofeedback) for the treatment of tension headaches, but that both kinds of therapy are equally effective for treatment of migraine headache. We also found several studies suggesting that combining cognitive therapy with relaxation therapy yields more powerful therapeutic results than does relaxation therapy alone.

A considerable amount of research has been devoted to evaluating the effect of EMG biofeedback and finger temperature biofeedback (for peripheral warming). Conventionally, tension headaches are treated with EMG biofeedback combined with progressive relaxation, while migraine headaches are treated with finger temperature biofeedback combined with autogenic training. Comparative studies fail to show that either EMG or finger temperature biofeedback adds any incremental effectiveness to autogenic training or progressive relaxation (Lehrer & Woolfolk, 1984). However, an innovative study by Blanchard et al. (1982) using a different methodology did find evidence to support the use of biofeedback in selected cases. In this study biofeedback was administered only to those persons who were not helped by an initial 10-session trial of relaxation therapy. Frontalis EMG biofeedback was administered to sufferers from tension headaches, and finger temperature biofeedback was administered to sufferers from migraine headaches and combined tension and migraine headaches. Significant improvement was noted for all three kinds of headaches, with the greatest improvement found for the combined headache group. Thus biofeedback does appear to be useful for some individuals.

Reviews of the voluminous literature on relaxation treatment for hypertension universally conclude that decreases between 10 and 20 mm Hg can reliably be obtained, usually more with systolic than with diastolic blood pressure (Agras & Jacob, 1979; Frumkin, Nathan, Prout, & Cohen, 1978; Goldstein, 1982; Pinkerton, Hughes, & Wenrich, 1982; Seer, 1979; Tarler-Benlolo, 1978). Most of these reviews also conclude that the various relaxation and biofeedback techniques do not differ from each other in effectiveness, although Pinkerton et al. (1982) comment that, in their opinion, studies of meditation have had less consistent positive effects than studies of progressive relaxation. Although the addition of blood pressure biofeedback to a relaxation therapy has not been found to add incremental effectiveness to the latter, Agras and Jacob (1979) conclude that combinations of relaxation techniques have greater effects than single treatments. Pinkerton et al. (1982), however, remain unconvinced about the value of treating hypertension with combinations of treatment modalities. They argue that subjects in the studies with combined treatments tended to have had higher initial blood pressures than subjects in studies of single treatments. Nevertheless, the most consistently positive findings from studies of relaxation treatment of blood pressure come from the work of Patel (1984), who has described a non-drug treatment of hypertension derived from yoga that has meditative, cognitive, and somatic components, as well as long-term follow-up.

Although there is some evidence that hypertension may be effectively treated with cognitive therapy (cf. review by Pinkerton et al., 1982), we have found no studies comparing the separate or incremental effectiveness of relaxation and cognitive therapies for this problem. One recent study (Southam, Agras, Barr-Taylor, & Kraemer, 1982) found that relaxation-produced decreases in blood pressure were maintained during the work day. This study used newly developed technology for 24-hour ambulatory monitoring of blood pressure.

A number of other psychosomatic disorders also appear to be helped by relaxation therapy. Raynaud's disease may be treated equally well by a variety of relaxation techniques (cf. reviews by Blanchard, 1979; Pinkerton et al., 1982; Sappington, Fiorito, & Brehony, 1979; Surwit, 1982). There also is some indication that various relaxation therapies may be helpful in the treatment of dysmenorrhea, low back pain, asthma, childhood hyperactivity, and childhood attentional disorders (cf. review by Lehrer & Woolfolk, 1984). In most of these cases, however, the number of studies is still too small for us to reach conclusive results.

In conclusion, relaxation therapies appear to be useful in the treatment of a variety of psychosomatic disorders. Some of these disorders are quite debilitating, and the alternative medical or surgical interventions are much more risky, even when they sometimes are more powerful, thus making relaxation therapy a useful alternative for many individuals.

Insomnia

Insomnia is the persistent failure to obtain sleep of adequate quality or duration. It may occur because of retarded sleep onset, frequent arousals, or early awakening (Bootzin & Nicassio, 1978). Many cases of insomnia appear to be unrelated to other identifiable biological, environmental, or psychiatric disturbances. The subjective report of disturbance is common to all complaints of insomnia, but a significant proportion of self-reported insomniacs show no physiological indication of sleep disturbance during electroencephalographic monitoring. Borkovec (1979) has referred to such individuals as "subjective" insomniacs, in contrast with "psychophysiological" insomniacs, whose sleep impairment is corroborated by objective data. Although most treatment studies in the literature have mixed these two subtypes, EEG evaluations have tended to confirm the findings of studies that examined only self-report (Borkovec, 1982). Relaxation therapies have been most effective in reducing latency to sleep onset, averaging approximately 45% improvement on this measure (VanOot, Lane, & Borkovec, in press). Among the treatments found to be effective are progressive relaxation (Borkovec, Grayson, O'Brien, & Weerts, 1979), meditation (Woolfolk et al., 1976), and autogenic training (Nicassio & Bootzin, 1974). Studies that compared various relaxation techniques with each other have found them all to have approximately equivalent therapeutic effects on insomnia (Lehrer & Woolfolk, 1984). The mechanisms underlying this therapeutic effect remain unknown. Although physiological hyperactivity has been hypothesized as a cause of insomnia (Monroe, 1967), improvement in sleep-onset latency has not been found to be correlated with reductions in the autonomic arousal observed during training. Recent research (Borkovec, Lane, & VanOot, 1981; Woolfolk & McNulty, 1983) has lent support to the view that reductions in pre-sleep cognitive activity may mediate the effects of relaxation therapies on sleep-onset insomnia. All relaxation techniques involve focusing on objects or sensations that would direct attention away from worrisome pre-sleep thoughts and images and toward relatively monotonous stimuli that may have direct soporific effects (Bohlin, 1973). Although relatively effective in reducing latency to sleep onset in subjective and psychophysiological insomnia, relaxation therapies have produced relatively weak effects on measures of nocturnal or early morning awakening.

Perhaps the majority of insomnias develop secondarily as a complication to various physical or psychiatric disorders. In such cases treatment of the primary etiological factors is indicated (e.g., depressive disorder, treated by psychotherapy and/or psychoactive medication). When such secondary insomnias are chronic, however, a learned behavioral component may develop, making treatment of the "underlying" condition therapeutically insufficient (Borkovec, 1982). In such instances relaxation-based therapies may be utilized profitably as adjunctive treatments (Borkovec & Boudewyns, 1976).

Clinical Issues in Applying Relaxation Therapies

As we have shown, relaxation techniques alone rarely are sufficient treatment in clinical practice. Clinicians not only must have other methods of intervention at their disposal but also must understand how various individuals' life-styles, their social environments, and their views of the world can create or compound their problems in living. Such factors as the quality and nature of social support and the client's aims in life, attitudes, and values must be evaluated. Often fundamental changes in these areas are required if significant and durable change is to be achieved.

Before embarking on any program of relaxation training, the clinician must answer a number of questions, including:

1. Is the client psychotic?
2. Do the client's difficulties have an organic basis?
3. Does the client have panic attacks?
4. Is the client severely depressed?
5. Is the client troubled by problems in living or located in an environment that would make active participation in relaxation therapy unlikely (e.g., if the client is in the midst of a family or marital crisis, is facing unemployment).

If the answer to any of these questions is "yes," then the client probably has a more pressing need for some form of treatment other than training in relaxation techniques. These other interventions should be prior to or concurrent with any attempt to employ the methods described in this chapter.

Perhaps the thorniest issue in the clinical use of relaxation techniques is that of client noncompliance. Adherence to treatment regimens is a major problem in most forms of behavioral and medical intervention (Dunbar & Stunkard, 1979; Epstein & Cluss, 1982). Although the research literature thus far provides us with little guidance on how to boost client participation in relaxation treatment regimens, our clinical experience has led us to the following hypotheses, which, for now, we use as principles for clinical practice (Woolfolk & Lehrer, 1984):

1. Clients must assume responsibility for active participation in treatment, with special emphasis on home practice.
2. Clients should be trained in a technique that holds some initial appeal for them.
3. Techniques can be modified and tailored for clients.
4. Cooperation of family members should be enlisted.
5. Reasonable expectations should be created.
6. Client and therapist should work out a schedule for home practice, specifying time and place.
7. The therapist should carefully monitor progress.
8. The therapist should use the power of the therapeutic relationship to socially reinforce the therapeutic efforts of the client.

Although some of the appeal of relaxation methods is their standardization and capacity for administration via some programed format, the relationship between client and therapist is a critical factor in the success of these treatments. Both adherence (Dunbar & Stunkard, 1979) and the effects of treatment (cf. reviews by Borkovec & Sides, 1979; Lehrer, 1982; Taub, 1977; Woolfolk, Lehrer, McCann, & Rooney, 1982) are enhanced by training with a live versus an automated therapist and by a therapist who communicates warmth. The therapist-trainer functions in a number of capacities: expert, teacher, role model, and social reinforcer. Although the ability to engage in timely confrontation is as necessary to this form of treatment as it is to others, most often empathy, support, and kindness are called for.

Contraindications

Relaxation techniques are among the most benign of clinical interventions. Nonetheless, occasional problems have been reported in their use. Infrequently the process of relaxation may itself trigger transient symptoms of anxiety. These have been well-described in the autogenic training literature (Schultz & Luthe, 1969) and in the meditation literature (Carrington, 1977), but they are rarely if ever mentioned in the progressive relaxation literature. There is, in fact, some evidence that such "autogenic discharges," "destressing phenomena," or "relaxation-produced anxiety" occur less frequently in progressive relaxation than either in meditation (Carrington et al., 1980; Heidi & Borkovec, 1983; Lehrer et al., 1984), or in autogenic training (Lehrer et al., 1980). The cause of this phenomenon is not known. Schultz and Luthe (1969) consider it to be part of the body's way of attaining the proper equilibrium. Heidi and Borkovec (1983) consider it to result from a combination of cognitive and physiological factors. In our experience, it seems to result partly from the increased sensitivity to bodily processes that often occurs during a state of deep relaxation. Individuals appear to be disturbed by heightened sensitivity to their pulse and by the warm and tingling feelings that often accompany relaxation. Occasionally these sensations have symbolic or conditioned meanings that may produce emotional arousal. The latter experience is illustrated by the case of a young woman who consulted one of us (P.L.) a few years ago. She had been suffering from leukemia for many years, although the disease was then in remission. When she began thinking of the autogenic phrase, "My right arm is warm," she became visibly anxious. Later she revealed that the feelings of warmth in her arm had reminded her of the sensations she had experienced when her disease was active. She found them very anxiety-provoking. This is consistent with the observations of Schultz and Luthe (1969) that autogenic discharges often are related to previous traumatic experiences. Although autogenic discharges usually dissipate within a few minutes, they occasionally do not, necessitating termination of a session. Repeated occurrences usually are managed by shortening the exercises, often to periods of only 30 seconds, and then gradually increasing the length of the exercises as tolerance develops. Carrington (1977) describes a similar procedure for dealing with these experiences during meditation. When such strategies do not work, treatment by these methods must be abandoned.

Special care must also be taken in offering relaxation training to certain vulnerable individuals. Although meditation training is the only form of relaxation that has ever reported to have had beneficial effects on schizophrenics (Glueck & Stroebel, 1975), it also is occasionally known to have precipitated psychotic episodes. Whether this is due to misapplication of meditation in these individuals (e.g., overmeditating in order to avoid social contact) or to special psychobiological vulnerability in these people is not known. We advise, however, that it be applied with care in this population, and discontinued at the first sign of difficulty. Similarly, although autogenic training may have the most powerful beneficial autonomic effects of all relaxation techniques, it is the only technique documented to cause regular increases in blood pressure in some individuals (Schultz & Luthe, 1969). Thus blood pressure among hypertensives must be monitored regularly when this (or any other) technique is applied, and the technique should be discontinued if blood pressure regularly goes up during relaxation. Occasional cases of insulin shock have also been noted among insulin-dependent diabetics during a course of autogenic training, because of a decreased need for insulin produced by relaxation (Schultz & Luthe, 1969). Insulin levels should be monitored regularly in such individuals. Similarly, sufferers from gastric ulcers should avoid the autogenic phrase, "My solar plexus is warm," because of the occasional occurrence of bleeding ulcers reportedly caused by concentration on this formula (Schultz & Luthe, 1969). Depressed individuals also may be specially vulnerable to undesirable side-effects of relaxation. One of the authors (P.L.) once did progressive relaxation instruction with a depressed individual who reported that she was unable to relax unless she imagined a relaxing scene. The scene, she later reported, was of her being dead. Several days after doing this, she telephoned the therapist and reported that she had been a hair's-breath away from killing herself after the relaxation session—because, she reported, she had desensitized herself to the thought of being dead; and her fear of death was, at the time, her main deterrent to suicide. Thus the imagery of depressed individuals should be carefully monitored, and treatment should be discontinued if self-destructive imagery repeatedly occurs.

Despite the above caveats, we maintain that relaxation training is among the safest of treatment techniques. The fact that negative side-effects do occasionaly take place, however, reinforces the notion espoused in nearly all textbooks and manuals on all of these techniques: that they must be administered by skilled and sensitive clinicians; and that competent use of them involves skill in the clinical art as well as in procedural technology.

Methodological Issues

We have already alluded to several of the important methodological issues in relaxation research. Chief among these is adequate specification of the relaxation procedures used (e.g., Jacobson's progressive relaxation vs. modified progressive relaxation procedures, live vs. taped). We also favor studying the most intensive form of relaxation therapy in order to test potential therapeutic uses. Sometimes, however, intensiveness must be traded for motivational qualities in choosing the exact form of a technique for study. Lengthy training may produce greater risk of dropout in some populations, and, for some persons, experience of quick results (as may be achieved more easily through suggestion than through learning a muscular skill) may be necessary because clients may not give the more intensive treatment a chance. In such cases, the choice of technique depends on the question one is asking. Are we interested in knowing whether a particular technique, when properly employed, is effective in treating a particular disorder, regardless of practical difficulties involved in motivating people to do the technique properly? This can, in fact, be a reasonable question for research, and to answer it, we unquestionably should use the more intensive technique and worry about the problem of motivation and dropout later (providing, of course, that the control conditions are adequately matched on these factors). If, on the other hand, we are interested in testing the efficacy of a particular technique in general clinical practice, then such practical matters as motivation must be considered, and a shorter and perhaps less intensive technique might be a better compromise choice.

In addition, studying clinical populations is preferable to studying college students or other groups of normal volunteers. The effects of intervention may be stronger among clinical populations, and the results from normal populations may not tell us how clinical populations will respond. Apropos of this Lehrer (1978) found that progressive relaxation produces increases in EEG alpha among anxiety neurotics, but decreases in that measure among normal volunteers. The way that various populations approach learning relaxation techniques may differ enough to produce quite disparate results (e.g., some groups may practice more than others and generally take the treatment more seriously).

A variety of relevant outcome measures should be sampled. In our recent review of comparative relaxation research (Lehrer & Woolfolk, 1984), we found that various stress-reduction techniques tend to have differential effects on various outcome measures. The empirical research is generally consistent with Davidson and Schwartz's (1976) hypothesis that cognitive, behavioral, and somatic stress-reduction techniques tend to have specifically strong effects on, respectively, cognitive, behavioral, and somatic measures. As mentioned above, progressive relaxation seems to have relatively stronger effects on measures of skeletal muscle tension and autogenic training on autonomic measures.

At least two kinds of outcome measures should be included in studies of relaxation effectiveness: one that functions as a "treatment check," showing that the technique was, in fact, learned; and one that most sensitively measures the extent of the clinical problem that is being treated. A treatment check for a relaxation technique should be measure from the modality at which the technique is ostensibly directed (e.g., muscle tension for progressive relaxation, perception of arm warmth for autogenic training, focus of attention on the mantra during meditation). Such measures should at least be *included* in every study. If no effects are obtained on the treatment check, one might have justifiable cause to question the competence of the therapists, the adequacy of the technique employed in the study, and/or the ability of the subject population to learn the technique. On the other hand, other measures might be *clinically* more important. Thus, measures of behavioral approach may be more important than somatic or cognitive measures in studies of phobias; performance on examinations most important in studies of examination anxiety; self-report of pain intensity and pain-related behavior in studies of chronic pain; respiratory resistance in studies of asthma; blood pressure in studies of hypertension; and so on. In all cases, however, a variety of measures would provide the best overall test.

Perhaps because of a floor effect among normal subjects, psychophysiological studies of relaxation have shown the greatest relaxation effects when experimental stressors were used, or when subjects were chosen because they naturally manifested the effects of anxiety or stress. Thus Lehrer (1978) and Lehrer et al. (1984) found the strongest physiological differences between relaxation and control groups during anxious subjects' responses to various psychological stressors; and Lehrer, Hochron, McCann, Swartzman, and Reba (1983) reported stronger relaxation effects on respiratory resistance after subjects had inhaled a standardized dilution of methacholine (a drug that produces a bronchial spasms) than under standard rest conditions among asthmatics. Lehrer (1978) reported significant reductions in physiological arousal among anxiety neurotic patients, but not among nonpatients, and Fenwick et al. (1977) reported greater physiological changes among tense individuals than among others in response to meditation. Shapiro and Lehrer (1980) found no physiological differences between either progressive relaxation or autogenic training and a no-treatment control group in a study of normal volunteers, whereas Lehrer, Atthowe, and Weber (1980), using very similar training and testing methods, found pronounced heart rate effects for autogenic training among anxious individuals.

Choice of Control Groups

Choice of control group is a major consideration in all clinical research. In fact, there is no "perfect" control group, and the choice of control group should be determined by the particular question the investigator wishes to answer. Such questions may include:

1. Does relaxation therapy produce therapeutic benefits (for whatever reason)?
2. Does specific training in relaxation produce greater benefits than nonspecific attention from a therapist or than simply being told to relax more regularly?
3. Is relaxation therapy more or less effective than other commonly used therapies? Each of these legitimate questions requires a different kind of control group.

If we are interested only in measuring whether relaxation therapy is an effective therapy, and we do not care about the reason for its
effectiveness, then a no-treatment or waiting-list control group is
adequate, as long as subjects are placed randomly into this group and
the treatment group and the two groups are otherwise tested in an
equivalent manner. It would be desirable, however, for treatment to
be carried out at a different site from physiological testing sessions,
because it is well known that people show lower levels of physiological arousal and reactivity after repeated exposure to testing in a
particular laboratory. For the same reason, and also in order to
minimize experimenter bias, it is preferable that testing be done by
individuals other than those involved in providing treatment and
that those who carry out the testing sessions be unaware of the group
to which each subject belongs. Finally, it is important for most purposes that instruction in relaxation not be offered to subjects during a
testing session. As we have shown elsewhere (Lehrer, 1982; Lehrer &
Woolfolk, 1984), techniques that do show physiological effects during
a training session might not do so when testing is done at a separate
session. It is obvious that any technique whose effects fail to generalize beyond the training session would be clinically useless. It is
therefore essential to show that a relaxation technique has effects
throughout each day and that these effects endure after treatment is
ended. Thus provision for frequent assessment and long-term follow-
up is essential. Simple daily questionnaires during treatment and
during selected weeks after treatment is over may suffice for some
purposes. At other times, daily, hourly, or even continuous measurement of one or more physiological variables may be desirable. It is
now technologically feasible to do this for most physiological measures (cf. the study of blood pressure by Southam et al., 1982), and it is
rapidly becoming economically feasible, as the cost of equipment
decreases.

   If we wish to know whether training in relaxation per se is the
effective ingredient in the treatment program, or whether the therapeutic effects of a technique are produced by such "placebo" variables as the client's expectancies or contact with a warm and sympathetic therapist, then special controls should be used for these
variables. Research methods for studying the problem from this
perspective are discussed in detail by Borkovec, Johnson, and Block
(1984). A common solution is to use a pseudotreatment control. The
problem with this solution, however, is that many of these pseudotreatments may actually teach some form of effective relaxation
skill, while some, on the other hand, may produce frustration and

heightened arousal. Virtually all pseudotreatments suffer one of these drawbacks. When such a control is employed, it would be scientifically more cautious to err on the side of using a technique that actually might work (e.g., listening to music or to sounds of nature) than one that often causes arousal because of frustration (e.g., false biofeedback). Expectancies may be manipulated as a separate variable. Thus some studies have used separate expectancy groups, with one group given positive and others given no expectancies (cf. Borkovec, Grayson, & Cooper, 1978) or negative expectancies (Beiman, 1976). The problem with giving negative expectancies is that subjects in this condition tend not to practice their techniques very much, thus biasing the outcome in favor of the active treatment with positive expectancies. Lewis, Biglan, and Steinbock (1978) found that subjects high in internal locus of control tended to have higher expectancies for the success of relaxation therapy as well, and that these subjects practiced their relaxation instructions more at home and, consequently, showed a greater reduction in trait anxiety than externally oriented subjects. Borkovec and his colleagues (cf. Borkovec & Hennings, 1978) have designed an ingenious method of "counterdemand" instructions. They tell their subjects that they should not expect to feel any therapeutic effects until after the fourth or fifth session. They then test the subjects before, as well as after, the point at which the subjects are led to believe they will experience therapeutic effects. In all of these designs, it is critically important that subjects' expectancies be measured throughout the study. Despite the attention given in the literature to the importance of expectancies, manipulation of expectancies does not always influence therapeutic results (e.g., Woolfolk & Rooney, 1981).

The self-relaxation group is a frequently used method of controlling for the effects of simple (uninstructed) relaxation. This procedure simply involves telling subjects to relax on a regularly scheduled basis, at approximately the same intervals as recommended for the relaxation group. Although this method tests the necessity of the specific training offered in relaxation procedures, it does not control for the effects of coming to a clinic for therapy, interpersonal contact with a therapist, and so on.

Comparative treatment designs can control for placebo effects, while they simultaneously allow us to study the relative effects of various treatments. We have used this method extensively in our own research (Lehrer, Atthowe, & Weber, 1980; Lehrer, Schoicket, Carrington, & Woolfolk, 1980; Lehrer et al., 1984; Shapiro & Lehrer, 1980; Woolfolk, Carr-Kaffashan, McNulty & Lehrer, 1976; Woolfolk et al., 1982). The advantage of this method is that it reveals the effects that are specific to each treatment and eliminates the problem of interpreting whether a given placebo is or is not effective in its own right as a relaxation strategy. Usually, however, this method should be accompanied by one of the other controls listed above, in the event that the various active treatments are found not to differ from each other. We would then want to know whether they are equally effective or equally ineffective. Finally, it is particularly important in comparative treatment designs that "process" variables be accurately measured: subjects' beliefs about and enthusiasm for each treatment; subjects' perceptions of the competence and personality of the therapist; the amount of time spent practicing and applying each method; therapeutic and countertherapeutic effects at each stage of treatment; and the like. Finally, measures should be included that are expected to be differentially sensitive to the two techniques. Such careful measurement is necessary in order to determine the reason for the various differences between techniques that might occur.

In summary, we have outlined considerations that we deem to be most important in choosing relaxation methods, subject population, testing procedures, and control groups. Most important is the nature of the questions we wish to ask. There are few simple rules that apply to all situations, but in general we advise using the most intensive possible relaxation techniques on clinical populations, with a broad array of outcome measures that are both sensitive to the strengths of the particular measures employed and relevant to the kinds of clinical problems being studied.

Summary, Conclusions, and Directions for Further Research

There are many varieties of relaxation training, and many procedural variations within each method. Each variation may have unique effects that are measurably, and sometimes clinically, distinct from others. The research methodologies that we use in studying these techniques should be directed at answering particular questions. Just as there is no single relaxation therapy that is most useful in all situations, there is no single "best" research design, control group, and so forth. We have reviewed the empirical literature on three of the best researched relaxation methods and on applications of these techniques to several clinical problems that have been well studied.

We have pointed out that these techniques are rarely useful in isolation and that they must be used within the context of sensitive and sophisticated clinical practice.

Despite some inherent limitations in parametric research as a method for determining clinical practice (which is, after all, as much an art as it is the application of psychotechnology), additional research could provide useful guidance to the clinician. Few studies have employed intensive clinical trials with multiple and continuous outcome measures and long-term follow-up. Furthermore, there are few studies of the incremental effectiveness of relaxation therapy combined with other forms of therapy (cognitive therapy, family therapy, psychoanalytic therapy, drug therapy, etc.). This latter consideration is critical, because relaxation therapies are almost never used in isolation. Finally, there are numerous emotional and psychosomatic problems on which *any* kind of research is, thus far, rather sparse. This is an area of immense promise and opportunity for research.

References

Agras, S., & Jacob, R. Hypertension. In O. F. Pomerleau & J. P. Brady (Eds.), *Behavioral medicine: Theory and practice*. Baltimore: Williams & Wilkins, 1979.

Beiman, I. The effects of instructional set on physiological response to stressful imagery. *Behaviour Research and Therapy*, 1976, *14*, 175–179.

Benson, H. *The relaxation response*. New York: Morrow, 1975.

Benson, H., Lehmann, J. W., Malhotra, M. S., Goldman, R. F., Hopkins, J., & Epstein, M. D. Body temperature changes during the practice of g Tum-Mo Yoga. *Nature*, 1982, *225*, 234–236.

Bernstein, D., & Borkovec, T. D. *Progressive relaxation training: A manual for the helping professions*. Champaign, IL: Research Press, 1973.

Blanchard, E. B. Biofeedback: A selective review of clinical applications in behavioral medicine. In R. McNamara (Ed.), *Behavioral approaches to medicine: Application and analysis*. New York: Plenum, 1979, pp. 131–190.

Blanchard, E. B., Andrasik, F., Ahles, T. A., Teders, S. J., & O'Keefe, D. Migraine and tension headache: A meta-analytic review. *Behavior Therapy*, 1980, *11*, 613–631.

Blanchard, E. B., Andrasik, F., Neff, D. F., Teders, S. J., Pallmeyer, T. P., Arena, J. G., Jurish, S. E.,, Saunders, N. L., Ahles, T. A., & Rodichok, L. D. Sequential comparisons of relaxation training and biofeedback in the treatment of three kinds of chronic headaches, or, the machines may be necessary some of the time. *Behaviour Research and Therapy*, 1982, *20*, 469–482.

Bohlin, G. Interaction of arousal and habituation in the development of sleep during monotonous stimulation. *Biological Psychology*, 1973, *1*, 99–114.

Bootzin, R. R., & Nicassio, P. M. Behavioral treatments for insomnia. In M. Hersen, R. Eisler, & P. Miller (Eds.), *Progress in behavior modification*. New York: Academic Press, 1978.

Borkovec, T. D. Pseudo (experimental)-insomnia and idiopathic (objective) insomnia: Theoretical and therapeutic issues. In H. J. Eysenck & S. Rachman (Eds.), *Advances in behaviour research and therapy* (Vol. 2). London: Pergamon Press, 1979, pp. 27–55.

Borkovec, T. D. Insomnia. *Journal of Consulting and Clinical Psychology*, 1982, *50*, 880–895.

Borkovec, T. D., & Boudewyns, P. A. Treatment of insomnia by stimulus control and progressive relaxation methods. In J. Krumbholtz & C. E. Thoresen (Eds.), *Behavioral counseling methods*. New York: Holt, Rinehart, & Winston, 1976.

Borkovec, T. D., Grayson, J. B., & Cooper, K. M. Treatment of general tension: Subjective and physiological effects of progressive relaxation. *Journal of Consulting and Clinical Psychology*, 1978, *46*, 518–528.

Borkovec, T. D., Grayson, J. B., O'Brien, G. T., & Weerts, T. C. Relaxation treatment of pseudoinsomnia and idiopathic insomnia: An electroencephalographic evaluation. *Journal of Applied Behavior Analysis*, 1979, *12*, 37–54.

Borkovec, T. D., & Hennings, B. L. The role of physiological attention-focusing in the relaxation treatment of sleep disturbance, general tension, and specific stress reaction. *Behaviour Research and Therapy*, 1978, *16*, 7–19.

Borkovec, T. D., Johnson, M. C., & Block, D. L. Evaluating experimental designs in relaxation research. In R. L. Woolfolk & P. M. Lehrer (Eds.), *Principles and practices of stress management*. New York, Guilford Press, 1984.

Borkovec, T. D., Lane, T. W., & VanOot, P. H. Phenomenology of sleep among insomniacs and good sleepers: Wakefulness experience when cortically asleep. *Journal of Abnormal Psychology*, 1981, *90*, 607–609

Borkovec, T. D., & Sides, K. Critical procedural variables related to the physiological effects of progressive relaxation: A review. *Behaviour Research and Therapy*, 1979, *17*, 119–126.

Carrington, P. *Freedom in meditation*. New York: Doubleday, 1977.

Carrington, P., Collings, G. H., Jr., Benson, H., Robinson, H., Wood, L. W., Lehrer, P. M., Woolfolk, R. L., & Cole, J. W. The use of meditation-relaxation techniques for the management of stress in a working population. *Journal of Occupational Medicine*, 1980, *22*, 221–231.

Davidson, R. J., & Schwartz, G. E. Psychobiology of relaxation and related states. In D. Mostofsky (Ed.), *Behavior modification and control of physiological activity*. Engelwood Cliffs, NJ: Prentice-Hall, 1976.

Dunbar, J. M., & Stunkard, A. J. Adherence to medical regimen. In R. Levy, B. Rifkind, B. Dennis, & N. Ernst (Eds.), *Nutrition, lipids, and coronary heart disease.* New York: Raven, 1979.

Epstein, L. H., & Cluss, L. S. A behavioral medicine perspective on adherence to long-term medical regimens. *Journal of Consulting and Clinical Psychology,* 1982, *50,* 950–971.

Fenwick, P. B., Donaldson, S., Gillis, L., Bushman, J., Finton, G. W., Perry, I., Tilsley & Serafinowicz, H. Metabolic and EEG changes during transcendental meditation: An explanation. *Biological Psychology,* 1977, *5,* 101–118.

Frumkin, K., Nathan, R. J., Prout, M. F., & Cohen, M. C. Nonpharmacological control of essential hypertension in man: A critical review of the experimental literature. *Psychosomatic Medicine,* 1978, *40,* 294–320.

Glueck, B. C., & Stroebel, C. F. Biofeedback and meditation in the treatment of psychiatric illness. *Comprehensive Psychiatry,* 1975, *16,* 303–321.

Goldstein, I. B. Biofeedback in the treatment of hypertension. In L. White & B. Tursky, *Clinical biofeedback: Efficacy and mechanisms.* New York: Guilford Press, 1982.

Heidi, F. J., & Borkovec, T. D. Relaxation-induced anxiety: Paradoxical anxiety-enhancement due to relaxation training. *Journal of Consulting and Clinical Psychology,* 1983, *51,* 171–182.

Jacobson, E. *Progressive relaxation.* Chicago: University of Chicago Press, 1938.

Lavallée, Y. J., Lamontagne, G., Pinard, G., Annable, L., & Tétreault, L. Effects of EMG biofeedback, diazepam and their combination on chronic anxiety. *Journal of Psychosomatic Research,* 1977, *21,* 65–71.

LeBoeuf, A., & Lodge, J. A comparison of frontalis EMG feedback training and progressive relaxation in the treatment of chronic anxiety. *British Journal of Psychiatry,* 1980, *137,* 279–284.

Lehrer, P. M. Psychophysiological effects of progressive relaxation in anxiety neurotic patients and of progressive relaxation and alpha feedback in nonpatients. *Journal of Consulting and Clinical Psychology,* 1978, *46,* 389–404.

Lehrer, P. M. How to relax and how not to relax: A re-evaluation of the work of Edmund Jacobson: I. *Behaviour Research and Therapy,* 1982, *20,* 417–428.

Lehrer, P. M., Atthowe, J. M., Weber, E. S. P. Effects of progressive relaxation and autogenic training on anxiety and physiological measures, with some data on hypnotizability. In F. J. McGuigan, W. Sime, & J. M. Wallace (Eds.), *Stress and tension control.* New York: Plenum, 1980.

Lehrer, P. M., Hochron, S., McCann, B., Swartzman, L., & Reba, P. *The effect of progressive relaxation on a non effort-dependent measure of pulmonary function in asthmatics.* Paper presented at the annual meeting of the Association for the Advancement of Behavior Therapy, Washington, DC, December, 1983.

Lehrer, P. M., Schoicket, S., Carrington, P., & Woolfolk, R. L. Psychophysiological and cognitive responses to stressful stimuli in subjects practicing progressive relaxation and clinically standardized meditation. *Behaviour Research and Therapy,* 1980, *18,* 293–303.

Lehrer, P. M., & Woolfolk, R. L. Are all stress-reduction techniques interchangeable, or do they have specific effects? A review of the comparative empirical literature. In R. L. Woolfolk & P. M. Lehrer (Eds.), *Principles and practices of stress management.* New York: Guilford Press, 1984.

Lehrer, P. M., Woolfolk, R. L., Rooney, A. J., McCann, B., & Carrington, P. Progressive relaxation and meditation: A study of psychophysiological and therapeutic differences between two techniques. *Behaviour Research and Therapy,* 1984, *22.*

Lewis, C. E., Biglan, A., & Steinbock, E. Self-administered relaxation training and money deposits in the treatment of recurrent anxiety. *Journal of Consulting and Clinical Psychology,* 1978, *46,* 1274–1283.

Luthe, W. *Autogenic therapy* (Vols. 1–6). New York: Grune & Stratton, 1969.

Monroe, L. Psychological and physiological differences between good and poor sleepers. *Journal of Abnormal Psychology,* 1967, *72,* 255–264.

Nicassio, P., & Bootzin, R. A comparison of progressive relaxation and autogenic training as treatments for insomnia. *Journal of Abnormal Psychology,* 1974, *83,* 253–260.

Norris, P. A., & Fahrion, S. L. Autogenic biofeedback in psychophysiologic therapy and stress management. In R. L. Woolfolk & P. M. Lehrer (Eds.), *Principles and practices of stress management.* New York: Guilford Press, 1984.

Novaco, R. W. Treatment of chronic anger through cognitive and relaxation controls. *Journal of Consulting and Clinical Psychology,* 1976, *44,* 681.

Patel, C. Yogic therapy. In R. L. Woolfolk & P. M. Lehrer (Eds.), *Principles and practices of stress management.* New York: Guilford Press, 1984.

Paul, G. *Insight vs. desensitization in psychotherapy.* Stanford: Stanford University Press, 1966.

Pinkerton, S., Hughes, H., & Wenrich, W. W. *Behavioral medicine: Clinical applications.* New York: Wiley, 1982.

Raskin, M., Johnson, G., & Rondesvedt, J. W. Chronic anxiety treated by feedback-induced muscle relaxation. *Archives of General Psychiatry,* 1973, *28,* 263–267.

Sappington, J. T., Fiorito, E. M., & Brehony, K. A. Biofeedback as therapy in Raynaud's disease. *Biofeedback and Self-Regulation,* 1979, *4,* 155–169.

Schultz, J. H., & Luthe, W. Autogenic methods. In W. Luthe (Ed.), *Autogenic therapy* (Vol. I). New York: Grune & Stratton, 1969.

Schwartz, G. E., Davidson, R. J., & Goleman, D. J. Patterning of cognitive and somatic processes in the self-regulation of anxiety: Effects of meditation versus exercise. *Psychosomatic Medicine,* 1978, *40,* 321–328.

Seer, P. Psychological control of essential hypertension: Review of the literature and methodological critique. *Psychological Bulletin,* 1979, *86,* 1015–1043.

Shapiro, D. H., Jr. Overview: clinical and physiological comparison of meditation with other self-control strategies. *American Journal of Psychiatry,* 1982, *139,* 267–274.

Shapiro, S., & Lehrer, P. M. Psychophysiological effects of autogenic training and progressive relaxation. *Biofeedback and Self-Regulation,* 1980, *5,* 249–255.

Shoemaker, J. *Treatments for anxiety neurosis.* Unpublished doctoral dissertation, Colorado State University, 1976. *Dissertations Abstracts International,* 1977, *37B,* 5377. University Microfilms order no. 77-6813.

Snow, W. G. *The physiological and subjective effects of several brief relaxation training procedures.* Unpublished PhD dissertation, York University (Canada), 1977. *Dissertations Abstracts International,* 1978, *38B,* 3417.

Southam, M. A. Agras, W. S., Barr-Taylor, C., & Kraemer, H. C. Relaxation training: Blood pressure lowering during the working day. *Archives of General Psychiatry,* 1982, *39,* 715–717.

Surwit, R. S. Biofeedback and the behavioral treatment of Raynaud's disease. In L. White & B. Tursky (Eds.), *Clinical biofeedback: Efficacy and mechanisms.* New York: Guilford Press, 1982.

Tarler-Benlolo, L. The role of relaxation in biofeedback training: A critical review of the literature. *Psychological Bulletin,* 1978, *85,* 727–755.

Taub, E. Self-regulation of human tissue temperature. In G. E. Schwartz & J. Beatty (Eds.), *Biofeedback: Theory and research.* New York, Academic Press, 1977.

Turner, P. E. *A psychophysiological assessment of selected relaxation strategies.* Unpublished PhD dissertation, University of Mississippi, 1978. *Dissertations Abstracts International,* 1978, *39B,* 3010.

Wilson, P. H. Combined pharmacological and behavioural treatment of depression. *Behaviour Research and Therapy,* 1982, *20,* 173–184.

Wolpe, J., & Lazarus, A. A. *Behavior therapy techniques.* New York: Pergamon, 1966.

Woolfolk, R. L. Psychophysiological correlates of meditation. *Archives of General Psychiatry,* 1975, *32,* 1326–1333.

Woolfolk, R. L., Carr-Kaffashan, L., McNulty, T. F., & Lehrer, P. M. Meditation training as a treatment for insomnia. *Behavior Therapy,* 1976, *7,* 359–365.

Woolfolk, R. L., & Lehrer, P. M. Clinical issues in stress-reduction therapies. In R. L. Woolfolk & P. M. Lehrer (Eds.), *Principles and practices of stress management.* New York: Guilford Press, 1984.

Woolfolk, R. L., Lehrer, P. M., McCann, B. S., & Rooney, A. J. Effects of progressive relaxation and meditation on cognitive and somatic manifestations of daily stress. *Behaviour Research and Therapy,* 1982, *20,* 461–467.

Woolfolk, R. L., & McNulty, T. F. Treatment of insomnia: A component analysis. *Journal of Consulting and Clinical Psychology,* 1983, *51,* 495–503.

Woolfolk, R. L., & Rooney, A. J. The effect of explicit expectations on initial meditation experiences. *Biofeedback and Self-regulation,* 1981, *6,* 483–491.

5

Social Skills Therapy: A Model and a Treatment

JAMES P. CURRAN

Introduction

Social skills therapy is a direct and systematic attempt to teach interpersonal skills and strategies to individuals with the intention of improving their individual interpersonal competency in specific types of social situations. The premises underlying social skills training as a therapy approach are relatively straightforward and evident. These premises are: (1) interpersonal relationships are important to psychological development and functioning; (2) interpersonal disharmony can contribute or lead to psychological distress and dysfunction; (3) certain interpersonal styles and strategies are more adaptive than other styles and strategies for specific types of social encounters; (4) these interpersonal styles and strategies can be specified and taught; (5) once learned, these styles and strategies will improve competence in these specific situations; (6) improved interpersonal competence can contribute or lead to improvement in psychological functioning.

There appear to be many influences which have led to the emergence of social skills training as a therapy approach. In the following section we will examine some of the influences which converged to produce social skills therapy. These influences have been grouped under three major headings, although it must be admitted that the boundaries between these branches are quite arbitrary and permeable.

Origins of Social Skills Therapy

Theoretical Influences

Numerous theoretical systems have emphasized the importance of interpersonal relationships and interpersonal competence in personality development, in psychological functioning, and as a mechanism for behavioral change. Although seldom acknowledged in the social skills literature, many neo-Freudian and ego-psychologists stressed the role of interpersonal competence and the learning of interpersonal skills in their systems. These neo-Freudian and ego-psychologists objected to Freud's emphasises on biological instincts as being paramount in personality development and instead favored a more interpersonal model of development. Although many of these theorists (Adler, 1935; Hartmann, 1958; Horney, 1939) stressed the importance of interpersonal competency in psychological functioning, the writings of Harry Stack Sullivan (1953) and Robert White (1960) are particularly germane to the topic of social skills therapy.

For Sullivan, personality was a hypothetical construct which could not be studied apart from interpersonal situations. Personality is organized around interpersonal events rather than intrapsychic events. For Sullivan (1953), personality is the relatively enduring pattern of recurrent interpersonal situations and the coping strategies developed to meet these situations. Anxiety is socially produced and is a result of faulty interpersonal relations. According to Sullivan, the self-system develops in order to guard the person from anxiety. That is, in order to avoid and minimize anxiety individuals adapt various interpersonal strategies, some of which Sullivan said are more adaptive than others. Sullivan saw some strategies being particularly maladaptive and as interfering with an individual's ability to live constructively with others. Clearly, Sullivan's writings are consistent with the premises of social skills therapy. He emphasized the importance of interpersonal relationships, felt that personality was a reflection of the interpersonal skills and styles developed to cope with interpersonal events, and further stressed that some strategies which developed were less adaptive than others and interfered with constructive psychological functioning.

White (1960) rejected Freud's notion of instincts and drives as the sole basis for man's learning to cope with the environment. White saw man as much more active and predicated an "effective motive" to explain man's active encounters with the environment. For White,

satisfaction with one's accomplishments stems from the ego-
enhancing effects of a sense of competence gained through satisfaction of the effectance motive. The cumulative result of a long and
successful series of interactions with the environment is referred to
as a state of competence. For White, one of the most crucial components of a general sense of competence was interpersonal competence
or the ability to sustain effective transactions with people. Again,
White stressed the importance of interpersonal encounters and the
role of various skills and strategies in these encounters. In addition,
he developed a hypothetical construct which is in some ways similar
to Bandura's notion of self-efficacy to help explain man's actions.

Although early S-R theorists eschewed cognitive mediational
constructs, social learning theorists such as Mischel (1973) and Bandura (1977) have made such constructs once again fashionable in the
behavioral literature. While both theorists have emphasized the role
of interpersonal competency, more importantly they have also
evolved constructs stressing the role of man as an active organism
which are useful in the implementation of social skills therapy.

Bandura developed the pivotal construct of "self-efficacy" as an
attempt to explain the discrepancy between our theoretical notions
and the empirical data regarding treatment outcome. This construct
attempts to explain behavioral change in cognitive terms, yet most of
the successful treatments involved performance enactments. "Self-
efficacy" was seen as a mediational construct wherein performance
accomplishments effect self-efficacy and self-efficacy mediates performance. Bandura distinguishes between efficacy expectancies and
outcome expectancies stating that the former consists of an individual's belief that he can produce certain responses as opposed to the
expectation that particular consequences would proceed from the
responses. The feeling of self-efficacy determines the extent to which
an individual initiates certain responses, the amount of effort ex-
pended in performing the responses, and the maintenance of the
effort. For Bandura, as for White (1960), an individual's self-efficacy
is based upon a history of performance accomplishments mediated by
cognitive events. Whether an individual attempts a task and over-
comes obstacles to his goal is not only a function of skills but a belief
in one's capabilities. Bandura's notion of self-efficacy is an important
construct to bear in mind for conducting social skills therapy. Anyone
who has conducted social skills training could attest to the importance of convincing the trainees that they have the capabilities to
emit skilled responses with practice. It is important to program

performance enactments in such a way as to build up a trainee's notion of self-efficacy.

Mischel's (1973) constructs are also useful to incorporate when conducting social skills therapy. Mischel stresses an individual's ability to acquire information about the world and his potential to generate vast repertoires of organized behavior including, among other things, social rules and conventions that guide conduct. He feels that it is important to assess a subject's expectancies regarding the consequences of different behavioral possibilities. These include awareness of reinforcing contingencies and outcome relations wherein an individual learns that certain events predict other events or outcomes. Mischel also postulates a self-regulatory system wherein persons set performance goals for themselves and react with self-criticism or self-satisfaction to their behavior depending on how well it matches the expectations and criteria. When conducting social skills therapy, it is critical to assess trainee's knowledge of social rules, their grasp of the linkage between consequences, and behavioral possibilities and their personal goals in each setting.

Phillips (1978) proposed the most ambitious model for social skills therapy. He sees the social skills model as a replacement for the medical model of psychopathology. For Phillips, psychopathology is the result of the organism's inability to solve problems, resolve conflicts, and reach goals. The organism's lack of requisite skills results in maladaptive behavioral strategies and negative emotional states. Phillips (1978, p. 15) states that "the viewpoint preferred here posits the lack of social skills as the essential behavioral deficit, owning to conflictual person–environmental conditions, and sets out to promote change through better understanding of, and alterations in, the environmental contingencies regulating behavior." Phillips' model is a useful way to view psychological problems and is often helpful in developing therapeutic strategies. In fact, in a later section we will demonstrate how the use of such a conceptual system might alter the course of treatment. However, I feel strongly that Phillips' model is only one of many conceptualizations regarding psychopathology that should be utilized in developing treatment strategies.

In this section I have indicated both seeds of thought of earlier theoretical systems which are consistent with social skills therapy and also the importance of the constructs developed by modern-day theorists like Bandura and Mischel to conducting social skills therapy. Now let us turn our attention to a set of data which appears to have influenced the development of social skills.

The Linkage Between Social
Competency and Psychopathology

In addition to the decidedly social nature of "mental illness," an association has been established between general indicators of social competency and various parameters of psychiatric disturbance including incidence, age at first admission, length of hospitalization stay, chronicity, posthospital adjustment, quality of interpersonal life, and recidivism rate. Melnick and Shulsinger (1968) found that high-risk children who subsequently had schizophrenic breaks were distinguished by their social behavior at school. Their teachers had rated them as being more aggressive, domineering, and disturbing to other children. They were also seen as less popular with peers and appeared to remain upset for longer periods of time if frustrated. Barthell and Holmes (1968), using high school year books to measure social activity, found that high school graduates later diagnosed as schizophrenics had participated in significantly fewer social activities in high school than did normal control subjects. Davidson and Neale (1974) indicated that schizophrenics are more likely to have been rated as disagreeable by their teachers and also appear more delinquent and withdrawn.

Socially withdrawn patients, when compared with active patients, have been found to be hospitalized at an early age, to spend more time in a hospital during each admission, and to be lower in their premorbid adjustment (Depue & Dubicki, 1974). A study by Curran, Miller, Zwick, Monti, and Stout (1980) indicated that the patients labeled as having social skills deficits had longer psychiatric hospitalization stays and less adequate function after discharge. A patient's social behavior on a ward appears to predict the extent of chronicity (Nuttall & Soloman, 1965). Jenkins and Gurel (1959) found that social behavior was identified as a more crucial determinant of duration of hospitalization than was severity of symptoms.

A number of studies conducted by Zigler and Phillips (Phillips & Zigler, 1961; Zigler & Levine, 1973; Zigler & Phillips, 1960, 1962, 1972) demonstrated that the level of premorbid social competence in a hospitalized psychiatric patient was the best predictor of posthospital adjustment. This relationship was not affected by either the patient's diagnostic label or treatment received during the course of hospitalization. Paul (1969) noted that the biggest single deficit found in chronic psychiatric patients was a lack of instrumental role functioning. Paul and Lentz (1977) found that one of the best predictors for discharge and posthospital functioning among a group of chronic mental patients was their degree of social competency. Strauss and Carpenter (1971) reported that premorbid levels of instrumental role behavior and skill were important predictors in subsequent social adjustment, clinical outcome, and quality of interpersonal life for schizophrenic patients.

Whether discharged patients have a successful stay in the community or not is related to some extent to their degree of social activity. Patients remaining in the community have greater participation and membership in social groups than those who return to the hospital (Freedman & Simmons, 1963). Freedman and Simmons also found that patients remaining in the community had relatives who placed more demands on them for instrumental role performances, that is, having them engage in occupational, social, and household activities.

It should be remembered that the evidence presented is associational in nature and does not imply a direct cause-and-effect relationship. Several different interpretations of the established associations are possible. Social inadequacy could be viewed as a factor which predisposes individuals to develop a range of psychological disorders; or alternatively social inadequacies could be viewed as a consequence or symptom of psychopathology. Another interpretation would be that both psychopathology and social incompetency could be regarded as handicaps which might have quite separate etiologies. Psychopathology and social incompetency could also have a cyclical relationship with each other. That is, they could have a reciprocal maintaining and exacerbating effect on each other. For example, a pathological state of high arousal might lead to social withdrawal or avoidance, which if prolonged could lead to social isolation and limit the opportunity to develop skills, thus making the person less able to cope with social situations, produce failures, and increase social anxiety, and so on. A final possibility exists, and that is that neither one has any causal effect on the other but rather both are related to a third yet undetermined factor. The exact interrelationship between social incompetency and psychopathology is of more than academic interest. If social incompetency predisposes, maintains, or exacerbates an individual's psychological disorder, then it is quite obviously a major target for treatment. If social incompetency is unrelated to psychopathology (and I feel this is quite unlikely), it still may be a worthwhile treatment target behavior because it is distressing to the individual.

Clinical Practice Develops a
Response-Acquisition Approach to Treatment

It can be argued that the single most influential impetus for the development of a social skills training was the theoretical and practical work of Wolpe and Lazarus (1969). These theorists were concerned with distressed emotional states and developed a procedure called assertion training as a means of treating these distressed states. Assertion training was seen as a procedure for helping people overcome distressful emotional states which were felt to inhibit effective performance. Assertion training was seen as especially useful in helping individuals overcome anxiety in social encounters. Initially, the emphasis in assertion training was on teaching individuals how to release feelings such as resentment and anger that they experienced when they allowed themselves to be intimidated by others in social encounters. It was felt that by teaching individuals how to express their anger appropriately, the disabling effects of the anxiety would gradually be overcomed by a process called reciprocal inhibition. Reductions in anxiety would then lead to more effective interpersonal behavior. Assertion training was directed at reducing a hypothesized emotional state. It was assumed that once the anxiety was removed, the natural adaptive responses in the patient's repertoire would surface.

Kanfer and Phillips (1970) saw that assertion training might have utility beyond merely a procedure for anxiety reduction. They stressed the importance of learning new skills and labeled such an approach *replication therapy*. They attributed the success of replication therapy not only to the fact that anxiety is reduced in the problem situations but also to the fact that new behaviors are observed and practiced in settings designed to facilitate learning. McFall and Twentyman (1973) called this type of treatment a response-acquisition approach to treatment. Maladapted behaviors are construed in terms of the absence of specific response skills. The objective to a response-acquisition approach to treatment is to provide direct training in precisely those skills deemed lacking. In a response-acquisition approach, little attention is given to eliminating existing maladapted behaviors. It is assumed that once skillful adapted behaviors are acquired, maladapted responses will be displaced and disappear. A response-acquisition approach to treatment is a direct and systematic attempt to teach those skills required in problematic situations. It is thought that once an individual can handle problematic situations more appropriately, then better psychological functioning will occur. If the skills taught are interpersonal in nature, then this training is called social skills therapy. I wish to emphasize that a response-acquisition approach to treatment is a generic term which applies to any treatment approach wherein the therapist specifically and directly attempts to teach a skill.

A responsive-acquisition approach to treatment emphasizing the educational aspects of psychotherapy is a relatively new way of thinking about the process of therapy. Therapists need to ask themselves, "What skills can I teach my client that will enable him or her to handle problematic situations?" These skills may not be obvious. For example, I once had a case of a man with a presenting complaint of impotence. The man had been married for several years and had a satisfactory marriage. He had not previously experienced any sexual difficulties. Upon detailed questioning, it was learned that several months prior to his sexual difficulties, the client had a significant and dramatic increase in his amount of alcohol intake. Increased alcohol intake was interfering with his sexual functioning. Next we explored the cause of the sudden and dramatic increase in alcohol intake. The increased intake was a result of a career change. That is, the man moved from a nonadministrative position to an administrative position which he was not handling well. He was using the alcohol to cover his own disappointment created by his knowledge that he was not performing adequately in his administrative position. He liked many aspects of his new position, especially the increased monetary reward. He did not want to go back to his old position. Treatment centered on helping the client learn administrative skills such as keeping accurate appointment calendars and so on. As the client became more successful, his alcohol intake decreased and his sexual difficulties were resolved. Here, the skills taught were mostly administrative and bureaucratic and not particularly social, but it does illustrate how a response-acquisition conceptualization of treatment can affect the course of treatment.

Although the major impetus for a response-acquisition approach to treatment stems from work on assertion training, it should be noted that a response-acquisition approach to treatment was being increasingly used for many different problems. Skills taught range from Masters and Johnson (1966, 1979) teaching sexual skills to Sarason (1957) teaching students how to study for examinations and note-taking procedures as a treatment strategy for test anxiety. To underscore my point that the emergence of a response-acquisition approach to treatment was a broad-based movement, I would like to comment briefly on a conference held at the National Institute of

Mental Health in 1965. The conference was attended by a selected group of mental health professionals who met to discuss and explore ways in which clinical interventions might be facilitated through greater emphasis upon improving the social competence of persons who seek or need professional help in dealing with emotional or adjustment problems. As impetus for this conference was the dissatisfaction of these practitioners with the then current emphasis in treatment on the resolution of inner conflicts. As Gladwin (1967, p. 31) stated:

> It can be questioned whether understanding and insight regarding maladaptive behaviors can be maximally useful, unless more adaptive, alternative behaviors are taught. Put another way, the person seeking help must learn useful and effective ways of acting to supplement those which are being replaced.

The members of the conference were able to agree on the following premises (Gladwin, 1967, p. 37):

> One is that in order to become effective the psychologically inadequate person not only needs to relieve his anxieties and correct his maladaptive behaviors, but also to learn alternative success oriented ways of behaving in society. A second is that when a person grows in social competence and achievement, he also grows in general psychological strength, so that he can then by himself cope with formerly serious emotional problems. Third, social competence is most effectively achieved when intervention is directed toward an ecological unit, consisting of a person and his immediate social environment, rather than towards the person alone. Fourth, the ecological unit can range in definition from the immediate context of treatment to the total society. But throughout it is clear that there must be equal concern with a person's competence and with the design of a social pathway through which he will travel and which he will learn.

In this section on the origins of social skills training I have traced the converging influences on its development. The greatest impact and the most direct lineage is the work of Wolpe and Lazarus (1969). However, as I have demonstrated, a very eclectic band of practitioners and scholars were becoming increasingly more dissatisfied with insight-oriented approaches to treatment. The dissatisfaction helped bring about the development of a response-acquisition approach to treatment for many types of disorders. The focus on teaching social skills in a response-acquisition format is not surprising given the data relating social incompetency and psychopathology and the various theoretical conceptualizations emphasizing the importance of social competency and psychological functioning. Now I would like to turn our attention toward a definition of social skills therapy and its implications.

Social Skills Therapy: Treatment and Outcome

A Definition of Social Skills Therapy

The most widely used definition of social skills therapy was proposed by Goldsmith and McFall (1975, p. 51), who described social skills training as:

> . . . a general therapy approach aimed at increasing performance competence in critical life situations. In contrast to the therapies aimed primarily at the elimination of maladaptive behaviors, skills training emphasizes the positive educational aspects of treatment. It assumes that each individual always does the best he can, given his physical limitations and unique learning history in every situation. Thus, when individual's best effort is judged to be maladaptive, this indicates the presence of a situation specific skill deficit in the individual's repertoire . . . whatever the origin of this deficit (e.g., lack of experience, faulty learning, biological dysfunction), it often may be overcomed or paritally compensated through appropriate training in more skill response alternatives.

I would like to make several points regarding this definition. First of all, because Goldsmith and McFall did not restrict themselves to social events, their definition is really a definition of the more generic response-acquisition approach to treatment. McFall (1982) himself restricts the terms *social skills training* to behavior viewed from a social perspective. The frame of reference is social in nature, and we are most interested in the social implications of the behavior. Second, skills training emphasizes positive educational aspects of treatment and not the elimination of maladaptive behavior. Third, the assessment of social skill deficit revolves around a judgment regarding the subject's performance. An individual's performance is judged as inadequate or maladaptive presumably by someone who is competent to make this judgment. In Goldsmith and

McFall's definition, it is assumed that the faulty performance is due to a specific skills deficit and not to other factors (motivational, emotional, cognitive, etc.) which could interfere in performance. A point which will be made shortly is that, theoretically, although social skills therapy is most suited to treat specific skills deficits, it *may* also be a useful procedure for treating interfering factors even when the person possesses the requisite skills. Fourth, Goldsmith and McFall's definition stresses the fact that whatever the origin of the deficit, it may be overcome or partially compensated for by skills training. Indeed, much as eyeglasses help correct poor eyesight caused by a number of different conditions, skills training may be a useful procedure regardless of the etiology of the problem.

Social Skills Therapy Training Procedures

Social skills therapy may be individually based or in a group format. While the content of the training program varies, as we soon shall see, the procedures used in the training appear to have a more widespread acceptance and can be found in most training programs. Most skills therapy programs use some, if not all, of the following procedures: (1) instruction and discussion, (2) modeling, (3) behavior rehearsal, (4) performance feedback, (5) reinforcement and shaping procedures, and (6) transfer-inducing procedures.

Information is imparted and exchanged via instruction and discussion. The therapist often describes general strategies for optimizing interpersonal effectiveness and may summarize rules for the implementation of these strategies. The rules are often discussed in the context of the goals, both short and long term, of the situation. A discussion of various alternative strategies and the likely outcomes of each of these strategies are also usually topics of discussion. During these discussions, inhibiting thought processes may also be brought up and disputed. Usually, some form of modeling is made use of to introduce the skills to be taught. The model often is the therapist. Some training programs make use of videotape models. In some cases, inappropriate and appropriate strategies are modeled in order to contrast these styles and demonstrate the likely consequences of each strategy.

Behavioral rehearsal is the most characteristic feature of social skills therapy. It is here that subjects attempt to rehearse, during the treatment session, behaviors which are taught as part of the program. Subjects get to practice these skills in a relatively nonthreatening situation, either with each other or with the therapists. Several rehearsal attempts may be made in order to allow the subject time to master the skills. In some cases, subjects may be asked to do role reversals and the therapists or another member of the group portrays the subject while the subject himself may role-play the protagonist in the situation. After the rehearsal, the subjects receive constructive criticism and/or praise for their attempts.

The performance feedback provided after the rehearsal is typically done by both therapists and other group members. In some skills therapy programs subjects may view a videotape reenactment of their rehearsal. Performance feedback is a very delicate matter. Subjects must be given constructive criticism, but in such a way that they do not become distressed at their own inadequacy. Often, it is useful to have individuals with whom the subjects interact in the role-play provide feedback. As mentioned previously, subjects often do several rehearsals in the context of any treatment session. Behaviors which are the goals of the lesson are gradually shaped by the therapists via group reinforcement.

Transfer-inducing procedures are integral parts of skills therapy programs. That is, procedures are instituted as part of the training the intention of which is to promote the transfer of skills learned in the group to the subject's natural environment. One of the more common techniques used is the assignment of homework tasks. Assignments are programed into each treatment session wherein subjects are requested to perform certain tasks involving a newly learned skill in their natural environment. Often these tasks are ordered in a gradient fashion from easy to hard with the easier assignments coming first. Typically, each homework assignment is reviewed and discussed in the following treatment sessions. Other transfer-inducing procedures include a "buddy" system in which two subjects are yoked together in order to practice with each other in the natural environment.

Social Skills Therapy Training Content

The content of social skills therapy varies depending upon a host of factors including the goals of the treatment program, the types of tasks targeted for treatment, the diagnostic categories of the subjects being treated, the individual needs and deficits of the individuals in the program, and so on. The content issue of social skills therapy programs is controversial in several aspects. First, in most programs the content skills to be taught are based on the intuition of the investigator or therapist and not on any empirical data. Consequently, even if these skills are learned, there is no guarantee that the subject's performance will be any more competent than it was before in that targeted situation. This issue will be addressed more thoroughly in the section on research methodology.

Second, some skills training programs include, as content components, procedures which are regarded as treatment procedures in their own right, for example, relaxation training. Often these ancillary components are taught in a much briefer fashion than they are usually taught, and hence, it is questionable whether they are taught adequately. The inclusion of these ancillary procedures appears to be a result of the difficulty in diagnosing whether a skill deficit actually exists or whether inadequate performance is due to interfering mechanisms. Therapists include them in their skills training programs because, it would seem, they feel that these are necessary components at least for some of their subjects. The inclusion of such procedures obviously makes it difficult to attribute the results of these social skills therapy programs just to skills training. My own preference is not to regard these ancillary components as part of social skills training, but as treatment procedures in and of themselves. It also appears to me that these procedures should be given sufficient time during training so that they may be adequately learned. These ancillary components should also be evaluated by themselves and in conjunction with social skills therapy with special emphasis on how they interact with various diagnosed individuals.

A third area of controversy regarding the content skills therapy programs regards both the level of the behaviors to be taught and the nature of the behaviors to be taught (Trower, 1982). At the onset of social skills therapy, the goals of most programs seemed to be aimed at teaching very discrete specific behavioral components such as eye contacts, decreasing speech latency, and other very molecular behavioral components. The utility of limiting social skills therapy to such discrete response training was questioned (McFall, 1982; Trower, 1982). In addition, it was felt that more than specific discrete motoric responses were actually being taught in these programs, albeit unsystematically (McFall, 1982; Trower, 1982). Skills training programs do indeed teach more than motoric responses. Most skills programs establish goals, provide feedback regarding perceptions, increase self-efficacy, discuss outcome expectations, disprove illogical thoughts and irrational beliefs, and so on. In fact, as Trower (1982) has stated, these other components fit a more generative model of social skills than do discrete behavioral components. We need to acknowledge that these other components are taught, build a more comprehensive model to include these components, and determine how best to teach them. We will briefly address this issue again in the section on research methodology.

Effectiveness of Social Skills Therapy

One of the problems in evaluating the effectiveness of social skills training is its appeal as a panacea. Taking the position of Phillips (1978) for the moment, if the lack of social skills is the major psychological deficit, then social skills therapy would be the therapy of choice for *all* forms of psychopathology. Psychopathology for Phillips results because the organism does not have the requisite skills to solve problems, resolve conflicts, and reach goals. Negative emotional states and maladaptive cognitions occur in lieu of social solutions to problems. Lack of social competency leads to faulty problem solving, emotional distress, and psychopathology.

While I certainly do not feel that social skills therapy is a panacea, there can be no denying its broad-based appeal as an adjunct treatment or as a therapy of choice for many types of disorder behaviors. As Bandura (1977) has noted, the most effective forms of treatment are ones that are performance based. From a conceptual point of view, it certainly makes sense to adequately assess a person's skill level vis-à-vis those situations which are problematic and distressing to the individual. If deficits are determined it is entirely appropriate to teach those skills required in those situations as part of a broad-based comprehensive treatment plan.

Because of its appealing quality, social skills therapy has been used as a treatment procedure for just about every major form of psychopathology and for many other types of disorder behaviors. Several recent books (Bellack & Hersen, 1979; Curran & Monti, 1982; Eisler & Frederiksen, 1980; Kelley, 1982; Wine & Smye, 1981) have examined the effectiveness of social skills therapy with many types of populations including chronic schizophrenics, bipolar depressive patients, distressed marital couples, unassertive females, alcoholics, the mentally retarded, isolated and withdrawn children, dating-anxious college students, job interviewees, and so on. It is obviously impossible to review in this chapter the treatment effectiveness of social skills therapy with each and every population on which it has been implemented. Let it suffice for me to make some general observations regarding its treatment effectiveness and make some suggestions for future research and treatment.

I will limit my observations to the following:

1. In many studies an increase in social effectiveness is demonstrated immediately after treatment with some "fall-off" at follow-up assessment. However, this demonstrated increase effectiveness is usually based on assessment measures, which are for the most part laboratory simulations or paper-and-pencil tests. Social skills therapy has not looked nearly so effective on measures of transfer to the subject's natural environment.

2. In many studies social skills therapy is given in conjunction with other forms of treatment in such a way as to confound interpretation of the results.

3. In most studies the ultimate goal of treatment is not merely a change in the social adequacy level of the subjects, but rather a change in the disordered behavior (e.g., alcohol abuse). What one finds in some studies is that even with changes in social adequacy level, there are no concomitant changes in the targeted behaviors. However, in all fairness, it should be remembered that many factors may be maintaining the disordered behavior, some of which have nothing to do with the subject's adequacy level.

4. In many studies, the application of social skills therapy does not appear to me to be well thought out. Let me be more specific. In many studies, there is no attempt to (a) determine whether a skills deficit exists, (b) if a deficit exists whether there is any relationship between the deficit and targeted behaviors, or (c) if a deficit exists and if it is related to the disordered behaviors, what skills including cognitive skills are needed to make for more adequate functioning.

5. It appears to me that social skills therapy should be well thought out and researched. In many cases, it should be used in conjunction with other treatment strategies as part of a comprehensive and systematic treatment plan.

Combination with Other Treatments

It is already apparent that social skills therapy can be used in conjunction with other types of treatment. When applying social skills therapy, one goal of the treatment is quite obviously to increase the adequacy of social performance. Other motivational, cognitive, and emotional factors may also be interfering with adequate social performance. Any and all treatments which may eliminate these interfering mechanisms could be implemented as part of a comprehensive treatment package. For example, medication and social skills training can be seen as mutually facilitating. Certain medications can be prescribed which will decrease feelings of subjective distress, high levels of which may be interfering with adequate social performance. Other types of medications may be prescribed that will make it easier for a patient to think more clearly, which in turn will facilitate the patient's mastery of the skills taught as part of a social skills therapy program. Treatment procedures that are often given in conjunction with skills training include anxiety-reducing procedures such as a systematic desensitization and various forms of cognitive therapy aimed at eliminating irrational thoughts and assumptions which may be interfering with effective interpersonal functioning. These and other techniques appear to dovetail nicely with social skills therapy and can be seen as complementing each other.

Contraindications

Very few contraindications for social skills therapy exist if indeed it appears to be the treatment choice. The only contraindications would be the following: (1) The subject's present environment would not tolerate change in the social competency level of subject and would work to sabotage such change. (2) More efficient procedures exist which could more easily and readily produce changes in subjects social competency level. (3) A subject's intellectual ability or motivational level is such that he or she would not profit greatly from social skills therapy.

Methodological Issues

As I see it, there are four major methodological issues which must be resolved if social skills therapy is to make advancements as a treatment modality. These issues involve diagnosis, a determination of skillfulness, the adequacy of the assessment procedures, and the development of a comprehensive model of social skills. All of these issues are interrelated and interdependent. In the following sections each of these issues will be examined more closely.

Diagnosis

As has already been mentioned, an inadequate performance may or may not reflect a skill deficit. Theoretically, social skills therapy should prove most effective for those individuals experiencing a skills deficit, and consequently our ability to diagnose such a deficit in an issue. Figure 5.1 was taken from Curran and Wessberg (1982) and contains a model illustrating factors involved in competent and incompetent performance. Individuals in Cell A are viewed as performing competently in the criterion situation. They have adequate skills and their performance is not interfered with by other factors. Individuals in Cell B are also regarded as having adequate behavioral repertoires; however, their performance is judged as inadequate because it is being interfered with by other factors. Individuals in Cell B are also regarded as having adequate behavioral repertoires; however, their performance is judged as inadequate because it is being interfered with by other factors. Factors interfering with adequate performance could be emotional, motivational, cognitive, and so on. For example, and individual may not perform well in a situation because he or she is anxious because of some previous conditioning, or may not be motivated to perform well because the reward for adequate performance has a low or even negative valence, or because the person possesses a faulty cognitive set which incorrectly links competent performance with punishment. Individuals in Cells C and D do not possess the response capabilities required in the criterion situation. Individuals in Cell D, besides having inadequate behavioral repertoires, also experience interference from other factors. For example, a lack of skills leads to poor social performance and negative consequences. The individual engages in negative self-evaluations, develops failure-oriented cognitions, and anticipates anxiety when confronted with situations that are similar. As a consequence, these individuals may decrease attempts to handle these problematic situations and begin to avoid these situations at the expense of forgoing possible reinforcers found in those situations. In this case, inadequate skills lead to distressing cognitive and emotional states. In such a model as outlined in Figure 5.1, individuals in Cells C and D appear to be most efficaciously treated by response-acquisition approaches to treatment, while it would appear that individuals in Cell B might benefit from other types of approaches such as anxiety-reduction or cognitive-modification procedures. Hence, it is important when diagnosing skills deficit to assess a subject's motivational, cognitive, and emotional states.

Social Skills Repertoire

		Adequate	Inadequate
Interference Mechanisms	Absent	**Cell A** Adequate Skills/ No Interference	**Cell C** Inadequate Skills/ No Interference
	Present	**Cell B** Adequate Skills/ Interference	**Cell D** Inadequate Skills/ Interference

FIGURE 5.1. Mini-model of social skills performance.

After carefully stressing the importance of an adequate diagnosis, let me appear to contradict myself. It may be found that social skills therapy is a useful approach even with individuals with relatively competent repertoires but whose performance is judged inadequate because of other interfering mechanisms. This hypothesis is based on my observation that in many social skills therapy programs mechanisms exist which appear to be directed at changing cognitions and emotional states. On the cognitive level, many social skills therapy programs involve the acquiring of social knowledge, strategies for developing plans and goals, logical disputing and empirical disputing of invalid inferences and negative evaluations, and so on. With respect to altering emotional states, many skills programs are group based, and hence, subject's attempt to master these skills in a nonthreatening atmosphere with a fairly supportive group of individuals, which may lead to overall anxiety reduction. As Bandura (1977) has noted, performance-based treatment programs seem to be the most effective. It could be that the best way to change faulty cognitions and distressed emotional states is by means of performance-based treatments.

One study by Trower, Yardley, Bryant, and Shaw (1978) suggests that skills training may be a useful procedure regardless of whether the inadequate performance is due to skills deficits or to interfering factors. Trower et al. (1978) made a distinction between a skill deficit versus interference interpretations of inadequate performance. They labeled this distinction as primary versus secondary social failure. Primary social failure was defined as a result of faulty socializations or lack of social experience. Secondary social failure was attributed to other kinds of psychopathology resulting from biological, cognitive, or dynamic disturbances. Patients from both groups were assigned to one of two types of treatment: social skills versus desensitization. It was hypothesized that patients suffering from primary social failure would benefit only from a skills training approach, and patients suffering from secondary social failure would benefit only from a desensitization approach. The result indicated that both the primary and secondary social failures benefited from the skills training approach, while only patients suffering from secondary social failure benefited from the desensitization approach. Of course, the results of one study are only suggestive at best. However, it appears that there may be procedures within a comprehensive social skills training approach which might be beneficial in treating these interfering factors. Likewise, these factors may be more efficaciously treated by other procedures. Confirmation of either alternative is awaiting empirical support.

Determining Skillfulness

The skills to be taught in most social skills therapy programs are often merely intuited and not based on any empirical justification. It obviously is of little therapeutic benefit if the skills taught in the social skills therapy programs are not relevant to the criterion situation. Merely guessing at what skills might be important in a particular criterion situation is, at best, an approximation to the requisite skills.

In addressing this problem, McFall (1982) proposed conducting a thorough task analysis of the criterion situation. He suggested utilizing the behavior-analytic methodology for empirically developing component behaviors. McFall and his colleagues (Freedman, Rosenthal, Donahue, Schlundt, & McFall, 1978; Goldsmith & McFall, 1975), as well as others (Conger & Conger, 1982; MacDonald, 1978; Perri & Richards, 1979), have detailed requisite skills for a number of criterion situations.

As an illustration of the strategies that may be adopted in conducting these skills analyses and also to convey the enormity of the task, I would like to briefly review here the work of Conger and Conger (1982). In a series of studies, the Congers' detailed the requisite heterosocial skills required of college-age males during conversational interactions with opposite-sex peers. In their first study

(Kulich & Conger, 1978), they requested subjects from an Introductory Psychology subject pool to list problems they encountered when interacting on dates. They were also asked to identify those situations which they found to be most problematic. The 740 subjects generated over 2,200 responses. These responses were grouped into various categories. This information was then used to construct questionnaires to investigate differences between high- and low-frequency daters and among different demographic groups with respect to the occurrence of specific problems, how dates were made, what was done on dates, and so forth. The results from this study led the Congers to focus on conversational interactions, particularly those involved in initial heterosocial peer interactions. At this point, the Congers initiated two alternative and complementary strategies for determining the important components in conversational interactions. One strategy involved relating the frequency and duration of potential important behaviors to global ratings of social competence. The second strategy involved having peers of the interactees specify what they considered to be performance strengths and weaknesses.

In a series of studies, the Congers had peer judges review videotapes of both high and low skilled males and asked them to generate component behaviors. Thus, they had the potential recipient of the interaction stipulate what would influence their judgment. These peers were asked to provide, in their own words, specific characteristics and/or behaviors that they used to make judgments of competence. These peers generated over 900 cues on which the Congers imposed a four level inclusive hierarchial structure. Cues that were generated by the peers were later operationalized and rated and found to significantly differentiate groups of competent and incompetent males. Clearly, the specifying of the requisite skills demanded in the criterion situation is a laborious and time consuming but very necessary task.

Assessment

Numerous investigators (Bellack, 1979; Curran & Mariotto, 1980; McFall, 1982) have repeatedly called for more studies examining the validity of our assessment measures of social competency. It is trite to say that if we do not have valid assessment measures we are quite likely building a house of cards. Again, the task is enormous. We need to develop instruments which will differentiate both component skills and other factors which may be contributing to inadequate performance. We need to develop assessment procedures that will reflect the myriad skills that go into a successful performance. As we can see from the work of Conger and Conger (1982), a host of component behaviors can be found in the mosiac of competent performance. In addition, competent performance is more than just emitting a list of component behaviors; rather, it evolves a generative process which must be also assessed.

A Generative Model of Social Skills

Trower (1982) recently has criticized social skills therapy programs that teach just a list of component behaviors. He feels that such programs are doomed to failure because there will be little generalizability gained from such attempts. Trower believes that we should be teaching a generative model of social skills. The generation of skill behavior according to Trower requires that an individual draw on his or her repertoire of component behaviors, organizing them into new sequences according to discourse and situational rules and his or her own goals and subgoals. This process may often involve learning new components or scripts. Trower feels that we need to assess and teach individuals monitoring capabilities of both external and internal events, performance capabilities, goals or standards, and cognitive representations of logical functions. In treating a subject we must know his purpose, perceptions, inferences, and evaluation processes. We need to know the norms and rules of social behavior and understand the structure and function of social discourse and social situations. According to Trower, we need to monitor and logically dispute invalid inferences and the negative evaluations of our subjects.

There is no doubt that our earlier models of skills training were overtly simplistic. It's to early to foresee how our final model of social skills therapy will evolve. It is my belief that Trower's (1982) model provides an impetus in the right direction.

References

Adler, A. Individual psychotherapy. In C. Murcheson (Ed.), *Psychologies of 1930,* Worcester, MA: Clark University Press 1935.
Bandura, A. Self-efficacy and toward a unifying theory of behavioral change. *Psychological Review,* 1977, *84,* 191–215.

Barthall, C. N., & Holmes, D. S. High school yearbooks: A nonreactive measure of social isolation in graduates who later became schizophrenic. *Journal of Abnormal Psychology*, 1968, *73*, 313–316.

Bellack, A. S. A critical appraisal of strategies for assessing social skill. *Behavioral Assessment*, 1979, *1*, 157–176.

Bellack, A. S., & Hersen, K. *Research and practice in social skills training*. New York: Plenum Press, 1979.

Conger, J. C., & Conger, A. J. Components of heterosocial competence. In J. P. Curran & P. M. Monti (Eds.), *Social skills training: A practical handbook for assessment and treatment*. New York: Guilford Press, 1982.

Curran, J. P., & Mariotto, M. J. A conceptual structure for the assessment of social skills. In M. Hersen, R. M. Eisler, & P. M. Miller (Eds.), *Progress in behavior modification* (Vol. 9), New York: Academic Press, 1980.

Curran, J. P., Miller, I. W., Zwick, W. R., Monti, P. M., & Stout, R. L. The socially inadequate patient: Incidence rate, demographic and clinical features, hospital and post-hospital functioning. *Journal of Consulting and Clinical Psychology*, 1980, *48*, 375–382.

Curran, J. P., & Monti, P. M. *Social skills training: A practical handbook for assessment and treatment*. New York: Guilford Press, 1982.

Curran, J. P., & Wessberg, H. W. The assessment of social inadequacy. In D. H. Barlow (Ed.), *Behavioral assessment of adult disorders*. New York: Guilford Press, 1982.

Davidson, G. C., & Neale, J. M. The effects of single-noise similarity on visual information processing of schizophrenics. *Journal of Abnormal Psychology*, 1974, *83*, 683–686.

Depue, R. A., & Dubicki, M. D. Hospitalization and premorbid characteristics of withdrawn and active schizophrenics. *Journal of Consulting and Clinical Psychology*, 1974, *42*, 628–632.

Eisler, R. M., & Frederiksen, L. W. *Perfecting social skills*. New York: Plenum Press, 1980.

Freedman, H. E., & Simmons, O. G. *The mental patient comes home*. New York: Wiley, 1963.

Freedman, B. J., Rosenthal, L., Donahue, C. P., Jr., Schlundt, D. G., & McFall, R. M. A social-behavioral analysis of skill deficits in delinquent and nondelinquent adolescent boys. *Journal of Consulting and Clinical Psychology*, 1978, *46*, 1448–1462.

Gladwin, T. Social competence and clinical practice. *Psychiatry*, 1977, *40*, 30–38.

Goldsmith, J. B., & McFall, R. M. Development and evaluation of an interpersonal skill-training program for psychiatric inpatients. *Journal of Abnormal Psychology*, 1975, *84*, 51–58.

Hartmann, H. *Ego psychology and the problem of adaption* (Trans. by D. Rapaport). New York: International University Press, 1958.

Horney, K. *New ways in psychoanalysis*. New York: Norton, 1939.

Jenkins, R. G., & Gurel, L. Predictive factors in early release. *Mental Hospital*, 1959, *10*, 11–14.

Kanfer, R. H., & Phillips, J. S. *Learning foundations of behavior therapy*. New York: Wiley, 1970.

Kelley, J. A. *Social-skills training*. New York: Springer, 1982.

Kulich, R., & Conger, J. A step toward a behavior analytic assessment of heterosocial skills. Paper presented at the meeting of the Association for the Advancement of Behavior Therapy, Chicago, 1978.

MacDonald, M. L. Measuring assertion: A model and method. *Behavior Therapy*, 1978, *9*, 889–899.

Masters, W., & Johnson, V. *Human sexual response*. Boston: Little, Brown, 1966.

Masters, W., & Johnson, V. *Human sexual inadequacy*. Boston: Little, Brown, 1970.

McFall, R. M. A review and reformulation of the concept of social skills. *Behavioral Assessment*, 1982, *4*, 1–33.

McFall, R. M., & Twentyman, C. T. Four experiments on the relative contributions of rehearsal, modeling and coaching to assertion training. *Journal of Abnormal Psychology*, 1973, *81*, 199–218.

Melnick, S. A., & Schulsinger, F. Some premorbid characteristics related to the breakdown of children with schizophrenic mothers. In D. Rosenthal & S. S. Kety (Eds.), *The transmission of schizophrenia*. New York: Pergamon, 1968.

Mischel, W. Toward a cognitive social learning reconceptualization of personality. *Psychological Review*, 1973, *80*, 252–283.

Nuttall, R., & Solomon, L. Factorial structure and prognostic significance of premorbid adjustment in schizophrenia. *Journal of Consulting Psychology*, 1965, *29*, 362–372.

Paul, G. L. Behavior modification research: Design and tactics. In C. M. Franks (Ed.), *Behavior therapy: Appraisal and status*. New York: McGraw-Hill, 1969.

Paul, G. L., & Lentz, R. J. *Psychosocial treatment of chronic mental patients: Mileau vs. social learning program*. Cambridge: Harvard University Press, 1977.

Perri, M., & Richards, C. S. Assessment of heterosocial skills in male college students: Empirical development of a behavioral role-playing test. *Behavior Modification*, 1979, *3*, 337–354.

Phillips, E. L. *The social skills basis of psychopathology: Alternative to abnormal psychology and psychiatry*. New York: Grune & Stratton, 1978.

Phillips, E. L., & Zigler, E. Social competence: The action-thought parameter and vicariousness in normal and pathological behaviors. *Journal of Abnormal and Social Psychology*, 1961, *63*, 137–146.

Sarason, I. Test anxiety, general anxiety and intellectual performance. *Journal of Consulting Psychology*, 1957, *21*, 485–490.

Strauss, J. S., & Carpenter, W. T. The prediction of outcome in schizophrenia:

I. Characteristics of outcome. *Archives of General Psychiatry,* 1972, *21,* 739–746.

Sullivan, H. S. *The interpersonal theory of psychiatry.* New York: Norton, 1953.

Trower, P. Toward a generative model of social skills: A critique and synthesis. In J. P. Curran & P. M. Monti (Eds.), *Social skills training: A practical handbook for assessment and treatment.* New York: Guilford Press, 1982.

Trower, P., Yardley, K., Bryant, B. M., & Shaw, P. The treatment of social failure: A comparison of anxiety reduction and skill-acquisition procedures on two social problems. *Behavior Modification,* 1978, *2,* 41–60.

White, R. Competence and the psychosexual stages of development. In M. R. Jones (Ed.), *Nebraska symposium on motivation.* Lincoln, Ne: University of Nebraska Press, 1960.

Wine, J. D., & Smye, M. D. *Social competence.* New York: Guilford Press, 1981.

Wolpe, J., & Lazarus, A. A. *Behavior therapy techniques.* New York: Pergamon Press, 1969.

Zigler, E., & Phillips, L. Social effectiveness and symptomatic behaviors. *Journal of Abnormal and Social Psychology,* 1960, *62,* 231–238.

Zigler, E., & Phillips, L. Social competence and the process-reactive distinction in psycholopathology. *Journal of Abnormal and Social Psychology,* 1962, *65,* 215–222.

Zigler, E., & Levine, J. Premorbid adjustment and paranoid-non-paranoid status in schizophrenia: A further investigation. *Journal of Abnormal Psychology,* 1973, *82,* 189–199.

6

Beck's Cognitive Therapy of Depression: Treatment and Outcome

KAREN M. SIMON AND BARBARA M. FLEMING

The past two decades have seen a burgeoning of interest in the role of cognition in human functioning (e.g., Neisser, 1967). This interest has been especially fruitful in the field of psychotherapy. Any number of cognitive therapies have been introduced in the recent past. Although psychodynamically oriented theorists have long asserted that cognition should be considered a factor in psychotherapy, it was not until the pioneering work of Kelly (1955), Ellis (1962), and Beck (1967; 1976; Beck, Rush, Shaw, & Emery, 1979), that a central position was ascribed to cognition. Their approach to therapy can be summed up in the words of *Hamlet* (Act 2, Scene 2), "Nothing in this world is either good or bad, but thinking makes it so."

In the cognitive model of psychotherapy, the primary focus is on the individual's thoughts and images, rather than on his emotions or behavior. The rationale for this has been that distressing emotions and dysfunctional behaviors can be effectively treated by altering the individual's cognitive appraisal of problematic situations. Although cognitive therapy appeals to common sense and currently enjoys great popularity among therapists, the appropriate test of the value of a therapeutic model lies in its effectiveness as a treatment. The purpose of the present chapter is to determine whether cognitive therapy has fulfilled its promise as an effective treatment. This will be done, first, by presenting an introduction to the practice to cognitive therapy and then by reviewing the outcome research reported since the review article of Beck and Rush (1978).

The first major dilemma one confronts when setting out to evaluate the efficacy of cognitive therapy is defining what is to be included in the term *cognitive therapy*. Despite the fact the cognitive therapy is a relatively new model of psychotherapy, there are already a wide variety of "cognitive therapies." Furthermore, it is almost impossible to make general statements about the efficacy of cognitive therapy as a whole because of the vast differences among cognitive approaches.

Despite Kiesler's (1966) warning to avoid the myth of therapist uniformity, many researchers continue to write as if they were studying one consistent model of cognitive therapy. The most widely known and well-established of the cognitive therapies—Beck's Cognitive Therapy,[1] Ellis' Rational-Emotive Therapy, and Meichenbaum's Self-instructional Training—differ from each other in clinically significant ways.

The present chapter will focus primarily on Beck's Cognitive Therapy because Beck and his colleagues have presented a comprehensive therapeutic model with clear guidelines for its clinical practice (Beck et al., 1979). This model has generated a substantial empirical literature and has been shown to be applicable to a wide variety of clinical disorders (for example, depression, anxiety, and substance abuse).

Beck's Cognitive Therapy is an active and directive short-term model of psychotherapy. In this model, the patient and therapist work collaboratively to identify and reality-test the patient's dysfunctional and distorted thinking (Beck et al., 1979; Freeman, 1983). This is done by strategically applying cognitive and behavioral interventions, some of which are described in the following section.

The application of Cognitive Therapy with depressed patients is based on Beck's Theory of Depression, which has three basic components. First, Beck asserts that the thinking of depressed persons is characterized by the *cognitive triad:* They have a negative view of themselves (e.g., "I'm a loser."), of the world (e.g., "No one cares about me,"), and of the future (e.g., "It will never change").

Second, Beck states that the negative thinking of depressed individuals is often the product of *cognitive distortions.* For example, after ending a 10-minute conversation with a friend, a depressed person may pick out the one vaguely critical remark made by the friend and dwell upon it. The person may conclude that the supposed friend really has a very low opinion of him. Such distortions are hypothesized by Beck to promote depressed mood.

The third basic concept in Beck's Theory of Depression is that

---

[1]In order to minimize confusion without giving the impression that all cognitive therapies are the same, Beck's version of cognitive therapy will be referred to here as Cognitive Therapy. When cognitive therapies in general are being referred to, lower-case letters will be used.

these distorted thoughts are generated by the depressive's *under-lying assumptions*. These assumptions, or "rules of life," are seen as determining the meaning people give to their experiences. A person who suffers from depression is believed to have depressogenic assumptions. For example, a commonly held rule of life among depressives is, "If I'm not perfect, no one will value me." Since no one is perfect, the individual who holds this belief is likely to feel lonely and unlovable whenever his or her imperfections become evident. Beck argues that in order for long-term success to be gained from therapy, it is important to teach patients to challenge their underlying assumptions as well as their distorted cognitions.

Cognitive therapy cannot be applied correctly to a particular problem without an adequate conceptualization of that problem. Depending upon the diagnosis, cognitive distortionism, and underlying assumptions, the strategies and techniques chosen by the therapist may differ greatly.

How does the practice of Beck's model differ from that of other cognitive therapies? Cognitive Therapy differs most clearly from Ellis' Rational-Emotive Therapy in its use of collaboration and the Socratic method. Beck's approach is to gently question the patient, guiding him to make therapeutic discoveries and changes in cognition himself. Ellis, on the other hand, relies much more heavily on the use of confrontation. He is more likely to tell the patient how she is distorting reality, rather than guiding her to make her own realizations. This difference may be important for several reasons. First, because the collaborative approach may be experienced as less threatening to certain types of patients than the confrontational approach, a higher percentage of patients may stay in treatment long enough to be helped. Second, there is less likelihood of "resistance" with the collaborative approach, since the changes in cognition seem to originate in the patient rather than being imposed by the therapist. Third, the collaborative approach may give the patient a greater expectation of self-efficacy (Bandura, 1977a) than does confrontation. Self-efficacy is a person's level of confidence in his own ability to cope with a particular type of problematic situation. Since in Cognitive Therapy the patient discovers important information himself rather than being told by the therapist, he may develop the confidence to think things out for himself. Changes in self-efficacy have been shown to reliably predict progress in therapy (Bandura, 1977a). Thus, this difference between the approaches of Beck and Ellis may be very significant clinically. Finally, since Cognitive Therapy relies on testing beliefs against experience more than on logical refutation, it may have a different impact from the more philosophical Rational-Emotive approach.

Cognitive Therapy differs from Meichenbaum's Self-instructional Training in that Cognitive Therapy involves challenging the specific dysfunctional thoughts of each patient. Meichenbaum's approach, on the other hand, is to teach the patient a list of coping self-statements with which she can replace her dysfunctional self-statements in problematic situations. Thus, in Cognitive Therapy, patients learn more than just to follow the therapist's instructions and to substitute thoughts relevant to a particular situation. They learn a process of evaluating their thoughts—a process that they may be able to use in a variety of situations in the future. It is possible that because of this difference, the effects of Cognitive Therapy may be more resistant to relapse than those of Self-instructional Training.

Cognitive Therapy is also different from the "power of positive thinking" approach to therapy. Cognitive Therapy seeks to teach the patient to think more rationally and realistically, as well as more positively. Unrealistic positive thinking can sometimes be as dysfunctional as unrealistic negative thinking. An extreme example of this would be the grandiose thinking of people with mania. Because realistic thinking is likely to be validated more often than unrealistic thinking of any sort, it is likely to be more believable to the individual and, hence, more enduring.

Although it has not yet been empirically demonstrated that the variations among the different approaches are clinically significant, it is very likely that such results will be found for the reasons given above. Until the equivalence of various cognitive and cognitive-behavioral therapies has been demonstrated, it will be important to consider the effects of each separately.

Strategies and Techniques in Cognitive Therapy

As in the practice of any model of psychotherapy, attention must initially be paid to establishing a good working relationship with the patient. This is especially important in Cognitive Therapy, which requires the active collaboration of both participants in promoting change. Another important characteristic of the practice of Cognitive Therapy, which differentiates it from many other models, is the role of structure, both in individual sessions and over the course of therapy. Therapist and patient develop a list of problems the patient would like to resolve during therapy and choose specific items from that list as their agenda for a particular treatment session. This enables patient and therapist to monitor progress as well as teaching the patient to be systematic in his or her approach to life problems.

It may be a platitude to assert that patients make more progress when they know what is expected of them than when they do not. However, this point is often overlooked by therapists. Beginning in the first session, Cognitive Therapy patients receive socialization in the basics of the cognitive model; experience leads to emotion through the intervening process of cognition. Wherever possible, the therapist uses examples from the patient's own history to show how thoughts influence mood and, therefore, how changing thoughts can lead to changed emotions.

The next step in Cognitive Therapy is to teach patients to identify their dysfunctional thoughts. These thoughts are often called "automatic" because they come to mind effortlessly and automatically in a given situation. These thoughts are the primary focus of therapy because they tend to be experienced as being unequivocally true. As a result, negative automatic thoughts can produce much emotional misery. For example, if upon coming to pick up his girlfriend for a date, the boyfriend finds her not at home, he may have the following stream of thoughts, "She hates me. She wants to get rid of me. It's all over. I must have done something wrong. I always screw up. This always happens to me. I'll never have anyone to love." Such automatic thoughts are likely to result in his feeling hurt and depressed. It is the relationship between automatic thoughts and their accompanying distressing emotions that patients are first taught to monitor.

Challenging Automatic Thoughts

This is the core of Cognitive Therapy. There is little value in simply being able to identify automatic thoughts. The patient must also be able to respond to them in a realistic, emotionally helpful way in order to benefit from Cognitive Therapy. There are a variety of ways to help patients challenge their automatic thoughts, a few of which are described below.

A valuable intervention is to lead the patient to *question the evidence* for her dysfunctional thoughts. After identifying a problematic automatic thought, the patient is asked to examine the objective evidence that supports the thought. She is then asked to weigh the supporting evidence against the objective evidence that disconfirms the thought. This may allow the patient to realize that her automatic thought is more false than true according to objective evidence. The patient may then modify her evaluation of the situation to be more accurate and less upsetting. As an illustration, consider the boyfriend in the example above. As a result of questioning the evidence for his automatic thoughts, he may develop the following rational responses:

> "Hold on a minute. I don't know for sure that she hates me. She probably wouldn't have gone out with me eight times in the past month unless she was interested in me.
> "And it isn't like Peggy to end a relationship by standing the guy up. She's fairly assertive and I think she'd tell me instead.
> "In thinking back to our last date, I can't think of anything horrible that I might have done. In fact, she seemed to be having a good time.
> "It's not true that this always happens to me. With Janice, I was the one who ended the relationship."

It is frequently the case that an automatic thought will contain a distorted, negative attribution, for example, "She stood me up because she hates me." When this occurs, it is often helpful to ask the patient to consider other causal attributions. By introducing the possibility of a nondistressing explanation, the therapist is often able to help the patient through this *reattribution* process. If the boyfriend in the above example used this technique, he might generate the following automatic responses:

> "Maybe Peggy's not showing up for our date isn't intentional on her part. Maybe she forgot, or thought our date was for Saturday, not Friday night. Maybe she had a last minute emergency with one of her clients and couldn't get to a phone.
> "If she did try to call me, she probably would have had trouble getting through because I was on the phone up until the time I left.
> "Even if she did stand me up to get rid of me, it doesn't mean I did something wrong. A person who'd do something like that has problems of her own.
> "In any case, I won't know until I ask her."

People often have automatic thoughts to the effect that they are trapped, helpless, or have only one, intolerable course of action open to them. In these instances, it is helpful to guide the patient to generate options for action. The knowledge that patients have alternatives can help them to feel better and cope with their problems more effectively. If the man in our example utilized this strategy, he might develop the following rational responses:

> "Even if I have made a mistake and she wants to end it, I may be able to make it up to her. Maybe I can change her mind.
> "Even if I can't change her mind, I have options: My married friends are always offering to fix me up with single women they know. I could call up a friend and go to a nightclub—that's how I met Peggy in the first place. I could join a single's club or take a cooking class.
> "Losing Peggy wouldn't be the end of the world."

Patients frequently tell themselves that something so catastrophic is going to happen that they will be devastated. When this happens, they are likely to feel panicky and helpless. In this situation, the therapist might guide the patient to describe and examine the hypothesized "catastrophe." The patient is then asked what she could do to cope with it. In most cases, the patient is able to see that even if the worst happened, she would still have options and coping strategies. This process of *decatastrophizing* can be applied to the automatic thoughts in our example, with the following results:

> "Let's say she does hate me and wants to get rid of me; it's not the end of the world. I still have my career.
> "It doesn't mean I'll never have another relationship. There have been women in the past who have loved me. So there's no reason to think there won't be someone in the future.
> "Even if it is over, I'll be hurt and upset for awhile, but I'll survive."

Thus, patients learn how to respond to their dysfunctional automatic thoughts using a variety of cognitive strategies.

Behavioral Techniques in Cognitive Therapy

Behavioral interventions are an integral part of Cognitive Therapy. They are often the quickest and most effective way of promoting cognitive change and of improving functioning. Some of the behavioral techniques most often employed in Cognitive Therapy are described below.

It is often the case that patients have automatic thoughts about which they have little or no objective evidence, for example, "I would never go to a single's bar because everybody there is a loser." When such thoughts occur, it is often helpful to have the patient design an *experiment* to empirically test them. This can be a powerful way of disconfirming an assumption. Conducting an experiment is also a good way for patients to try a new behavior about which they have reservations. For example, patients may be willing to go to a single's bar and talk to strangers "in order to gather data," when they would not consider doing so otherwise. Of course, this technique is most appropriate when the therapist expects the resulting data to be therapeutic.

For patients whose automatic thoughts revolve around their being completely unproductive or anhedonic, it can be helpful to have them explicitly predict the level of mastery or pleasure they expect to derive from a particular activity. The patient then compares her actual level of mastery or pleasure to her prediction. Patients are frequently startled to discover that there is quite a discrepancy between the two. Knowledge that they have a tendency to underestimate mastery and pleasure can aid patients' willingness to engage in activities in which they would not ordinarily participate.

Activity scheduling is frequently used in conjunction with mastery and pleasure predicting. The severely depressed or procrastinating patient is given a blank schedule for the following week, which is divided into one-hour blocks. The patient is then asked to commit himself to engaging in a particular therapeutic task by entering it on the schedule. This tends to increase the probability that the patient will actually perform the activity. Discrepancies between planned and completed schedules can be discussed and resolved in subsequent sessions.

Many times, a patient's goal in therapy is to make substantial changes in his level of functioning or in his life-style. Whenever big changes are called for, the patient is likely to experience a great deal of anxiety and indecision. It is usually necessary in such cases to request that the patient make small successive steps toward his goal. This tends to lead to less anxiety and avoidance, while providing the patient with mastery experiences.

Role-playing performs an important function in Cognitive Therapy. When the patient gives voice to her irrational thoughts and the therapist takes the role of rational responder, this technique can be used to teach the patient to generate her own rational responses. When these roles are reversed, this technique can be used to give the patient practice in being rational as well as giving the therapist an indication of the patient's level of mastery of this skill.

Patients who have difficulty making decisions can be taught a technique to aid them. They are instructed to identify the choices available to them. For each choice they are asked to write down all the relevant advantages and disadvantages. When they compare the lists, two possibilities remain. If one option clearly has more or fewer disadvantages than the others, the decision is obvious. If no one option stands out, all are probably about equally good and the patient can choose at random, if he wishes.

Patients who ruminate a great deal about upsetting events can benefit greatly from techniques designed to reduce their ruminating. In thought stopping, the patient is asked to picture a large red stop sign in her mind's eye while yelling, "STOP!" to herself (mentally) whenever she notices herself ruminating on a problematic issue. She is then asked to distract herself by refocusing her attention on some predetermined topic or activity to prevent her from resuming her rumination.

Thus, a variety of behavioral strategies play an important role in the practice of Beck's Cognitive Therapy.

Contraindications

There are no contraindications which would absolutely rule out the skilled use of cognitive therapy techniques. This is certainly true as long as the therapist has a clear conceptualization of the case and tailors the treatment according to the needs of the individual patient. However, there are certain types of patients for whom Cognitive Therapy is unlikely to be helpful unless the standard model is modified.

The practice of Cognitive Therapy should always take account of the abilities and disabilities of the patient. With retarded or brain-damaged individuals, it is appropriate to emphasize behavioral over cognitive reconstructive techniques. These patients learn more quickly and with less frustration through experiencing actual outcomes than through verbal means.

Often, a patient will be referred for Cognitive Therapy without having much information about its principles. Once it is explained, most patients have no objections to trying it. Some, however, may want a different model of therapy; others may be unwilling to tolerate a structured approach. Whatever their reasons, patients who are not willing to try Cognitive Therapy should be referred to a competent therapist who practices the preferred model of psychotherapy. Cognitive Therapy requires collaboration between the participants. Without this, there is little value in attempting treatment.

There are quite a few conditions which produce symptoms identical to psychological depression. Among these are hypothyroidism and congestive heart disease. It is obvious that even an expert Cognitive Therapist will be ineffective in treating a depression caused by a vitamin or hormone deficiency. For this reason, whenever the possibility of organic disease exists, or whenever the individual has not had a complete physical exam within one year of beginning therapy, a medical consult should be arranged. Even if the results of such an exam are positive, Cognitive Therapy may be an appropriate adjunct to medical treatment. If the patient is not complying with a necessary medical regimen, or is having difficulty coping with the effects of the illness or the drugs, Cognitive Therapy can be very helpful.

A small number of extremely perfectionistic patients become self-critical upon discovering that they have dysfunctional automatic thoughts. They may obsess upon this "failing" to the point of becoming suicidal. If the therapist cannot teach these patients to challenge their perfectionistic, self-critical thoughts fairly quickly, the standard Cognitive Therapy approach may be countertherapeutic. It is necessary in this situation to employ strategies that circumnavigate the patient's self-critical tendency, possibly by emphasizing skill-building and problem-solving strategies.

With actively psychotic patients, the Cognitive Therapist must be careful to discriminate between delusional and nondelusional automatic thoughts. By its very definition, a delusional thought is not amenable to reality testing. Thus, there is little value in trying to teach psychotic patients that their delusions are unsubstantiated. At best, the therapist is wasting her time; at worst, the patient will feel threatened and refuse therapy. In Cognitive Therapy with psychotics, it is best to focus on the neurotic, nondelusional automatic thoughts, which they have in abundance (Greenwood, 1983). There is no evidence that psychosis can be cured through Cognitive Therapy alone. However, it is possible that by helping psychotic patients to function more effectively and with less stress, they may have fewer psychotic episodes. Clinical experience suggests that Cognitive Therapy, in conjunction with appropriate medication, can be quite helpful in some cases.

One area in which psychotic processes may be addressed directly is with regard to "command" hallucinations. In these hallucinations, patients may hear voices telling them to kill themselves or others or to perform other dysfunctional acts. A strategy that can be useful is to teach the patient to respond assertively to the voices, saying, "I don't want to and I don't have to." When the patient realizes that he has the option of refusing commands, he is able to exercise more effective control over his behavior.

Combination with Other Treatments

Any model of psychotherapy has elements in common with other models, and Cognitive Therapy is no exception. Since research has validated various therapeutic techniques without regard to their theoretical basis, it would be poor therapy to exclude techniques solely because of their noncognitive origin. However, all techniques that are employed in Cognitive Therapy are used because of their ability to foster cognitive change.

There is a considerable body of research showing that therapist characteristics of genuineness, warmth, and accurate empathy may be necessary for therapeutic progress to take place (e.g., Traux & Mitchell, 1971). The Cognitive Therapist realizes that developing and maintaining a trusting, collaborative relationship is essential to effective therapy and often will make use of some of the principles emphasized by Rogerian therapists.

Behavioral strategies have been an integral component of Cognitive Therapy since its inception. Any behavioral technique may be used when appropriate; however, some are more commonly used than others (see the section on Strategies and Techniques in Cognitive Therapy). However, in Cognitive Therapy behavioral interventions are not used as an end in themselves, but in order to facilitate cognitive reappraisal.

Social learning techniques, such as enactive, covert, and participant modeling (Bandura, 1977b), are also an integral part of Cognitive Therapy. Such techniques are imperative whenever therapeutic progress requires exposure to feared and avoided people and situations. Furthermore, as in any form of psychotherapy, the therapist serves as a model of rational adjustment for the patient.

From the psychodynamic therapist the Cognitive Therapist has learned to attend to therapeutic interactions. Although the Cognitive Therapist and the psychodynamic therapist do not conceptualize transference and countertransference in the same way, they agree that the interactions between the patient and therapist can provide valuable information regarding their assumptions. In Cognitive Therapy, transference is reconceptualized as the automatic thoughts of the patient regarding therapy and the therapist. In order to identify these, the therapist may consider how the patient behaves toward the therapist, what demands the patient makes, and how the patient views the therapist. Answers to such questions may serve as material for discovering the adaptiveness of the patient's characteristic interpersonal expectations. They may also help to identify beliefs that interfere with the therapeutic process. Similarly, therapists often react to patients in ways that may have more to do with their own underlying assumptions than with the behavior of their patients (e.g., "Patients should be appreciative of their therapists."). In these situations, it is important for therapists to be able to identify and test the reality of their own expectations.

There are certain patients for whom Cognitive Therapy is unlikely to work without chemotherapy. For example, active schizophrenics and manic-depressives should, in almost all cases, be on appropriate medication. While medication is an option, as well, for unipolar depressives, most Cognitive Therapists prefer to teach such patients to gain control over their distressing moods without it. However, if this is not possible or if the suffering is prolonged and severe, medication should be considered. When Cognitive Therapy is used in conjunction with antidepressant medication, it is important to monitor the patient's attributions about the medication. It is generally recommended that the medications be gradually discontinued while the patient is still in treatment. This will allow any cognitions such as, "I'm only getting better because of the pills," and, "I'll get depressed again if I don't take them," to be challenged.

Thus far, the basics of Beck's Cognitive Therapy have been presented, along with some important differences and commonalities between the most prominent forms of cognitive therapy. Issues regarding the appropriateness of Cognitive Therapy with various populations have also been considered. However, the question remains as to whether Cognitive Therapy is effective in the treatment of unipolar depression. It is to that question that we now turn.

Efficacy of Cognitive Therapy

Beck originally developed Cognitive Therapy specifically for the treatment of depression, and depression remains the problem area where the clearest and most complete guidelines for the application of Cognitive Therapy have been provided (Beck et al., 1979). It is therefore not surprising that the majority of outcome studies of Beck's Cognitive Therapy have involved the treatment of depression. A number of case studies and studies using within-subjects designs have demonstrated that depressed individuals become less depressed during treatment with Cognitive Therapy (Bartholow, 1980; deJong, Henrich, & Ferstl, 1981; Fennell & Teasdale, 1982; Hamilton & Waldman, 1983; Leizer, 1980; Rush, Khatami, & Beck, 1975; Schmickley, 1976).

There have also been many outcome studies of Cognitive Therapy of depression using experimental designs.[2] Most of the outcome studies comparing Cognitive Therapy of depression to a waiting-list or no-treatment control group have shown Cognitive Therapy to be superior as measured by both self-report measures and clinician ratings. Cognitive Therapy has been found to be significantly more effective in reducing depression than no treatment in studies of community volunteers (Besyner, 1978; Carrington, 1979; Wilson, Goldin, & Charbonneau-Powis, 1983), low SES and unemployed Puerto Rican women (Comas-Diaz, 1981), undergraduate students (Shaw, 1977; Taylor & Marshall, 1977), and a mixed sample of depressed outpatients and community volunteers (Magers, 1977).

Other combinations of cognitive and behavioral interventions have also been shown to result in a significantly greater reduction in depression than waiting-list controls. Such combinations have included Beck's Cognitive Therapy and the Kelly fixed-role therapy (Zeiss, Lewinsohn, & Munoz, 1979), Rehm's Self-control Therapy (Fuchs & Rehm, 1977; Rehm et al., 1981), a cognitive modification treatment with an interpersonal group focus (Hodgson, 1981), a multimodal treatment (Schmidt, 1980), an imagery-modification procedure (Jarvinen & Gold, 1981), and Meichenbaum's Self-instructional Training (Morris, 1975). A study by Harpin, Liberman, Marks, Stern, and Bohannon (1982) did not show statistically significant differences between the treatment group (a conjoint cognitive-behavioral treatment package) and waiting list, although the treatment group

---

[2]Thirty-five outcome studies were reviewed for this chapter. Their characteristics were as follows: (1) Seven experimental studies using a complete version of Beck's Cognitive Therapy of depression, 6 of which used clinical populations; (2) 9 experimental studies using a modified version of Beck's Cognitive Therapy of depression, 2 of which used clinical populations; (3) 19 experimental studies using cognitive-behavioral approaches to depression other than Beck's approach, 5 of which used clinical populations. Tabular summaries of these studies may be obtained from the first author.

showed significant pre–post treatment differences on depressive symptomatology while the waiting-list group showed no such differences. The lack of significant differences in this study seems most likely to be a result of the extremely small number of subjects (six in each condition). In the other two outcome studies which found no significant differences between the cognitive-behavioral treatment and waiting list (Kirkpatrick, 1977; Munoz, 1977), the treatments were conducted in a time-frame that was unrealistic as well as unrepresentative of the general practice of cognitive-behavioral therapies. On the whole, however, Beck's Cognitive Therapy and other approaches to cognitive-behavior modification appear to be consistently more effective than no treatment in reducing depression.

Comparisons with Antidepressant Medications

The most important tests of the efficacy of Cognitive Therapy for the treatment of depression have been comparisons between Cognitive Therapy and tricyclic antidepressant medication, which is accepted by many (e.g., Berger, 1977) as the most effective treatment for clinical depression. In the first major comparative outcome study of Cognitive Therapy of depression (Rush, Beck, Kovacs, & Hollon, 1977), researchers at the Center for Cognitive Therapy at the University of Pennsylvania compared Cognitive Therapy to imipramine, one of the most popularly used tricyclic medications. The 41 subjects (15 males and 26 females) in this study comprised a clinically depressed sample. Most of the subjects had multiple prior depressive episodes, and the mean period of time since the onset of the first depressive episode was 8.8 years. When they entered the study, 75% of the sample reported suicidal thoughts, 12.2% had a history of previous suicide attempts, and 22% had previous psychiatric hospitalizations. Their MMPI profiles indicated substantial psychopathology, and each subject had a Beck Depression Inventory score of at least 20, a Hamilton Rating Scale for Depression score of at least 14, and a definite depressive syndrome diagnosis according to the criteria of Feighner et al. (1972).

Subjects were randomly assigned to either Cognitive Therapy or pharmacotherapy (imipramine hydrochloride). Patients in the Cognitive Therapy condition were seen individually for a maximum of 20 50-minute sessions over a 12-week period, with an average of 15 sessions over 10.9 weeks. Patients in the pharmacotherapy condition were seen individually for not more than 12 weekly 20-minute sessions. The doses started at 75 mg at bedtime, and increased flexibly up to 250 mg to obtain optimum clinical response. The last 2 weeks of treatment were used to taper off and discontinue medication. Eighteen therapists, including 11 psychiatric residents, 2 postdoctoral and 2 predoctoral clinical psychologists, and 3 psychiatrists, participated in the study. Most of the therapists were committed to a psychodynamic orientation and had little experience in Cognitive Therapy, whereas the 14 residents and psychiatrists in the group had substantial training and expertise with the pharmacotherapy of depression.

Subjects in both treatments showed a significant reduction in depressive symptomatology as measured by both self-report measures and clinician ratings. Cognitive Therapy, however, produced significantly greater improvement than did pharmacotherapy and had a significantly lower dropout rate over the course of the study. The lower dropout rate in Cognitive Therapy is an important finding, since these patients showed a substantial suicide risk and losing patients from therapy could have serious consequences.

Since analysis of group data may reflect small but consistent between-group differences with little clinical relevance, Rush et al. (1977) also analyzed their data by determining how many subjects in each condition showed marked or complete clinical improvement. They found that 78.9% of the Cognitive Therapy patients showed marked clinical improvement or complete remission of symptoms (Beck Depression Inventory [BDI] levels of 9 or less) as compared to only 22.7% of the pharmacotherapy patients. On most measures, the same patterns of results were maintained at a one-year follow-up (Kovacs, Rush, Beck, & Hollon, 1981). In a later analysis of the data by Rush, Kovacs, Beck, Weissenburger, and Hollon (1981), cross-lagged panel analyses were used to evaluate the temporal relationships among changes in symptoms during the first four weeks of the treatment. During the course of Cognitive Therapy, improvements in hopelessness, views of the self, and mood generally preceded changes in vegetative and motivational symptoms, as would be predicted by Beck's cognitive theory of depression. Contrary to expectations, however, no consistent pattern of change was associated with pharmacotherapy.

Since tricyclic antidepressants have been widely viewed as the treatment of choice for depression and the results obtained with pharmacotherapy in the Rush et al. (1977) study are comparable to previous findings with antidepressant medications, the apparent superiority of Cognitive Therapy to pharmacotherapy is an exciting finding and gives strong evidence of the efficacy of Cognitive Therapy in the treatment of depression. However, critics of this study have argued that the drug treatment was not administered for a satisfactory period of time and therefore was not representative of the way tricyclic antidepressants are actually used in clinical practice.

Blackburn, Bishop, Glen, Whalley, and Christie (1981) have conducted an extensive outcome study that addresses criticism against the Rush et al. (1977) study. To make their pharmacotherapy condition more representative of current clinical practice, the prescribing physicians were allowed maximum flexibility, provided that they administered medications in recognized therapeutic doses. Subjects were depressed outpatients who had been referred from two sources: hospital outpatient clinics and a general practice clinic in a largely working-class area of Edinburgh. To be included in the study, patients had to satisfy the criteria for primary major depressive disorder on Spitzer's Research Diagnostic Criteria (Spitzer, Endicott, & Robins, 1978) and have a score of at least 14 on the BDI according to the British norms (Metcalfe & Goldman, 1965). A total of 64 patients completed treatment, 40 from the hospital and 24 from general practice. In the hospital sample 33% of the subjects were male and mean age was 44.5, while in the general practice sample 20% of the subjects were male and mean age was 41.3. In the hospital sample 55% of the subjects had suicidal thoughts, and in the general practice group 45% reported suicidal ideation. In both samples the majority of subjects had endogenous symptoms according to the criteria of Spitzer et al. (1978).

Subjects were randomly assigned to one of three therapy conditions: Cognitive Therapy, drug of choice (usually amitriptyline or clomipramine, 150 mg daily), or a combination of Cognitive Therapy and medication. Subjects were seen for approximately 12 weeks in all conditions. In the two Cognitive Therapy conditions, hospital patients were seen for an average of 17 sessions, while general practice patients were seen for an average of 12 sessions. Subjects in the medication-only condition were seen according to the current clinical practice of the prescribing physician. Treatment was administered by experienced clinical psychologists and psychiatrists, with the medications in general practice being administered by general practitioners after consultation with psychiatrists.

Different patterns of results were found for the general practice sample and the hospital outpatient sample. In the general practice sample, both the Cognitive Therapy condition and the combination condition were significantly more effective than the medication-only condition, with no significant differences between the Cognitive Therapy alone and the combination groups. In the hospital outpatient sample, however, the combination condition was significantly more effective in reducing depression than either Cognitive Therapy or medication alone. There was little difference between the Cognitive Therapy and the medication groups for the hospital sample, except on self-reported anxiety where Cognitive Therapy was more effective. When the results from both clinical samples were viewed, Blackburn et al. (1981) concluded that a combination of cognitive therapy and medication is more effective than Cognitive Therapy alone and that Cognitive Therapy alone is more effective than medication alone.

In her dissertation Simons (1982) found support for the equivalence of Cognitive Therapy and pharmacotherapy, but no evidence of any superiority of Cognitive Therapy over medication. Depressed outpatients (23 women and 5 men) were randomly assigned to either Cognitive Therapy alone or to nortriptyline (from 50 mg to 150 mg for a 12-week period.) The therapists included eight psychiatrists (ranging from second-year residency to postresidency), one psychologist who had completed his PhD, and one psychologist who had completed all doctoral requirements except the dissertation. The results showed both treatments to be effective in reducing both self-report and interviewer ratings of depression, with no significant differences between the groups at termination or at a one-month follow-up.

Two studies compared Cognitive Therapy to a combination of Cognitive Therapy and medication in the treatment of depressed outpatients. In a study reported by Beck et al. (1979), the effects of Cognitive Therapy alone were compared with the effects of the combination of Cognitive Therapy and amitriptyline, prescribed according to a flexible dosage schedule. A study by Rush and Watkins (1981) compared Cognitive Therapy to Cognitive Therapy plus antidepressant medication (as chosen by the treating physician as being most indicated for each individual patient). In these two studies, both the Cognitive Therapy and the combination conditions showed highly significant and clinically substantial improvements on self-report and clinician-rated measures of depression. Neither study found any significant differences between the two groups at the termination of therapy. The Beck et al. (1979) study also showed no significant difference between treatments at the end of a six-month follow-up period. Thus, the addition of medication to Cognitive Therapy was not shown to significantly enhance the efficacy of Cognitive Therapy in these two studies of depressed outpatients.

Three other studies have compared cognitive-behavioral treatments for depression with medication. Although these treatments did not specifically follow the procedures for Cognitive Therapy, they did include several cognitive techniques in addition to behavioral procedures. In their study of 154 depressed outpatients, McLean and Hakstien (1979) found their cognitive-behavior modification package to be significantly more effective in reducing self-reported depression than amitriptyline (increased gradually up to doses of 150 mg). Dunn (1979) found that a combination of his version of cognitive-behavioral therapy and tricyclic antidepressants (less than 125 mg) was significantly more effective than similar levels of medication and weekly support sessions. The results were maintained at a six-month follow-up. Finally, in a study of depressed community volunteers, Roth, Bielski, Jones, Parker, and Osborn (1982) found that Rehm's self-control training and self-control training combined with desipramine hydrochloride (gradually increased to 150 or 200 mg) showed no significant differences at termination or at a three-month follow-up.

One argument that could be leveled against most of these studies comparing Cognitive Therapy with pharmacotherapy is that the Cognitive Therapy patients received more actual time with the therapist than the medication patients, giving an advantage to Cognitive Therapy. Since the studies that had originally established the efficacy of pharmacotherapy for depression used a weekly, minimal-contact design and the intention of these studies was to compare Cognitive Therapy with the existing practice of pharmacotherapy, it was not seen as necessary or even appropriate to equate the treatments on length of therapy time. It seems unlikely that the additional amount of time spent with the therapist was solely responsible for the effectiveness of Cognitive Therapy, since in studies of other treatment approaches (such as Covi, Lipman, Derogatis, Smith, & Pattison, 1974; Friedman, 1975; Klerman, DiMascio, Weissman, Prusoff, & Paykel, 1974) the psychotherapy patients received more time yet showed less symptomatic relief than the pharmacotherapy patients.

To summarize the results of the studies comparing cognitive therapy with tricyclic antidepressants, Cognitive Therapy has been consistently shown to be at least as effective as treatment with medication and often superior. Studies comparing Cognitive Therapy to combinations of Cognitive Therapy and medication do not generally indicate that the addition of medication significantly enhances the efficacy of the Cognitive Therapy. As pointed out by Beck et al.

(1979), these findings do not preclude the possibility that for specific individuals, the addition of an antidepressant medication might have an important additive effect to the Cognitive Therapy. In fact, finding useful ways to match patients to the most appropriate treatment or combination of treatments is an important goal for future research.

Comparisons with Other Psychotherapy Approaches

Comparisons of Cognitive Therapy of depression to other psychotherapy approaches show results that are much more difficult to interpret than the comparisons with pharmacotherapy. Several studies have compared exclusively cognitive therapies to exclusively behavioral therapies, with varying results. It is unclear how meaningful these comparisons are, however, since the major proponents of the most popular cognitive therapies (Ellis, Beck, and Meichenbaum) all explicitly include behavioral interventions as an important part of their therapy. One cannot, therefore, legitimately compare a purely cognitive version of Cognitive Therapy, for example, with behavioral techniques since Cognitive Therapy itself includes those same behavioral techniques. The studies that claim to be comparing cognitive therapies to behavioral therapies are actually comparing some of the more cognitive components of treatment with some of the more behavioral components of treatment. Comparisons of the various components of a treatment package can be important and useful research as long as it is clearly framed in that way. Unfortunately, researchers often claim that they are comparing Cognitive Therapy to behavior therapy rather than realizing that both cognitive and behavioral techniques are important components of Cognitive Therapy (Beck et al., 1979).

Regardless of the treatment approach used for comparison (behavioral interventions, interpersonal skills training, insight-oriented treatment, or nonspecific discussion), some studies have shown cognitive approaches to be more effective than the alternative treatment and other studies have found no significant differences. Only one study (Hodgson, 1981) found any alternative treatment to be significantly more effective in treating depression than cognitive approaches; in all other studies, the cognitive approaches were at least as effective in reducing depression as the alternative treatments, and often more effective. Under the circumstances, it cannot definitely be said that Cognitive Therapy is superior to other forms of psychotherapy. However, it does seem that where one form of therapy is shown to be more effective than another, Cognitive Therapy is likely to be the superior one.

The first major step in establishing the efficacy of any treatment program is to determine whether the program is effective at accomplishing its goals. Cognitive Therapy has clearly completed this step for the treatment of depression. In virtually every outcome study, it showed a significant reduction in depression following Cognitive Therapy. In addition, Cognitive Therapy has been shown to compare favorably to other available treatments, including tricyclic antidepressant medication, which is, for many, the treatment of choice for depression.

Methodological Issues

Methodological differences make comparisons across outcome studies quite difficult. Some researchers have tried to compare studies by using a box score analysis (Ledwidge, 1978) or meta-analysis (Dush, 1981; Miller & Berman, 1981), giving studies equal weight regardless of the merits of the study or the specific techniques being used. The use of meta-analysis has evoked much controversy (see the special section of the February 1983 issue of the *Journal of Consulting and Clinical Psychology*). However, it does seem clear that these types of comparisons are limited in usefulness when the studies involved vary so widely in methodologies as well as in precisely what they are calling Cognitive Therapy.

Obviously, the more closely the study resembles actual clinical practice, the more external validity it has. The outcome studies of Cognitive Therapy of depression vary widely in how closely they approximate the realities of clinical practice. Many studies use nonclinical populations, including undergraduate students and volunteers who respond to media announcements of treatment availability. In fact, since many of the studies of Cognitive Therapy have been conducted on nonclinical samples, some authors have hypothesized that this treatment is effective only on very mildly depressed, nonclinical samples. If anything, however, it is the studies of Cognitive Therapy with clinical populations that have shown the strongest support for Cognitive Therapy. Out of 12 studies on clinical populations, 7 have shown Cognitive Therapy to be significantly more effective than the comparison conditions, while the other 5 studies have shown them to be equally effective.

The vast majority of outcome studies have employed inexperienced therapists who have not yet completed their clinical training. The inexperience of the therapists may reduce the efficacy of all of the therapies involved and minimize differences between treatment. Only four of the outcome studies reviewed here used experienced therapists and one additional study (Rush et al., 1977) used a mix of experienced and inexperienced therapists. These studies also all involve clinical samples. Out of these five studies, four showed Cognitive Therapy to be more effective than the alternative treatments and one showed the two treatments to be equivalent.

Another aspect of outcome studies that is often unrepresentative of clinical practice is the length of therapy and the number of sessions. The treatments used in outcome studies range from 1.5 hours within 3 weeks' time (Jarvinen & Gold, 1981) to 30 hours over 12 weeks (Rush & Watkins, 1981). Clearly, these lengths of treatment are not at all comparable. Beck's manual for the Cognitive Therapy of depression (Beck et al., 1979) specifies that the typical course of Cognitive Therapy is between 15 and 25 sessions. Therefore, treatments lasting only a few hours or consolidated into one or two weeks would not be expected to achieve similar results or to be a very powerful test of the Cognitive Therapy of depression.

Since many studies have found no significant differences among treatment conditions, it has been hypothesized (Zeiss et al., 1979) that these treatments are all useful not because they are effective at modifying the targeted behaviors but because of nonspecific effects of the therapies. It is possible, however, that methodological limitations could also help explain the lack of differences. In studies where the treatment is unrepresentative of the actual clinical practice of Cognitive Therapy (for example, using inexperienced therapists, extremely brief time frames, or a very limited range of interventions), perhaps nonspecific factors do account for most of the results. Distinctions among treatments may become evident only once the therapists involved achieve a higher degree of skill, or when the treatment is an accurate representation of the therapy being studied.

Furthermore, when one is comparing treatments, each of which has been based on sound theoretical and clinical grounds, it would take a fairly powerful study with reliable outcome measures to be able to detect the subtle differences among treatments. Most of the outcome studies discussed have quite small sample sizes, and as a result the power of these studies is very limited. Thus, the probability of a Type II error is generally high, making it quite possible that no difference between treatments would be found even when one, in fact, exists.

Beck's Cognitive Therapy of depression was originally developed as an individual therapy and his manual (Beck et al., 1979) focuses primarily on the treatment of depressed patients as seen individually. In most of the outcome studies of Cognitive Therapy, however, the therapy has been conducted in groups rather than individually. Two studies using clinical samples and experienced therapists have compared individual with group Cognitive Therapy and obtained differing patterns of results.

Rush and Watkins (1981) found that both individual Cognitive Therapy and group Cognitive Therapy led to significant decreases in depressive symptomatology. However, the group Cognitive Therapy resulted in significantly poorer results as compared to individual treatment both with and without medication. On the other hand, Shaffer, Shapiro, Sank, and Coghlan (1981) found that their version of cognitive-behavioral therapy as conducted in a group format and in an individual format led to a significant reduction in depression, state anxiety, and trait anxiety, and a significant increase in assertion by the end of treatment. No significant differences were found between treatment modalities.

The apparent equivalence between group and individual cognitive therapy found by Shaffer et al. (1981) is in direct contrast to the findings of Rush and Watkins (1981). Some important differences in the designs of these two studies may help to explain this discrepancy of results. Subjects in the Rush and Watkins (1981) study were depressed outpatients who met the definite depressive syndrome diagnosis according to the criteria of Feighner et al. (1972) and had a minimum score of 20 on the BDI and a minimum score of 14 on the Hamilton Rating Scale for Depression. The subjects in the Shaffer et al. (1981) study were members of a health maintenance organization (HMO) who were referred by their physicians for treatment of anxiety, depression, or both, and could also be said to constitute a clinical sample. However, there was no minimum level of depression required for admission into this study. As a result some patients scored in the nonclinical range for depression. The mean BDI scores during the evaluation period for subjects in the Shaffer et al. (1981) study ranged from 8 to 16 (all below the level of depression that was required for inclusion in the Rush and Watkins study). These two studies may indicate that for mild levels of depression, group Cognitive Therapy is as effective as individual, but that for patients with more severe depressions an individual therapy is preferable. Until group methods have been clearly shown to be comparable to individual treatments, it may be wise to keep in mind that outcome studies comparing group Cognitive Therapy to other types of treatments may not be making the most powerful use of Cognitive Therapy.

The outcome studies of Cognitive Therapy of depression are subject to the same methodological problems that plague outcome studies in general. For example, clinicians are clearly most interested in differences among treatments that are maintained over time. However, most of the studies have either no follow-up or very brief periods of follow-up. Several of the studies that do have follow-ups show changes in the patterns of results, emphasizing the need to look at treatments over time before definite conclusions are drawn. Many of these studies are also subject to bias from the fact that the experimenter is the therapist or one of the therapists and is fully aware of the experimental hypotheses. Also, in many of the studies, the demand characteristics are strong and no check has been made to determine whether the treatments being compared are equally credible.

Perhaps the two biggest methodological problems in the outcome studies of Cognitive Therapy of depression are the lack of specificity of the treatment procedures used and the absence of any check on the quality and consistency with which the interventions are administered. It has often been said that we need to study what we actually do in therapy, not just what we say we do. This is especially important when investigating the efficacy of cognitive approaches to treatment because such a wide variety of treatments have been subsumed under the title of cognitive therapy. Treatments which are considered cognitive range from the implementation of one brief procedure designed to modify daydreams (Jarvinen & Gold, 1981) to a comprehensive version of Cognitive Therapy (Rush et al., 1977). Also, just because an outcome study is conducted using a particular type of cognitive-behavioral treatment, that does not ensure that the therapists involved are competent to administer that treatment. Most of the therapists conducting the therapy in the outcome studies of the Cognitive Therapy of depression had not been trained at any of the major training centers for Cognitive Therapy and in most cases there were no checks on the quality and appropriateness of the interventions used.

Although the research on the efficacy of Cognitive Therapy has its full share of methodological problems, cognitive therapists are actively working to overcome many of these problems. Kendall and Hollon (1983) emphasize the problem of differential quality of interventions limiting the ability to compare the effects of treatment across studies and suggest that therapy outcome researchers archive and make available audio or audiovisual tapes of the therapy as implemented in their published studies. The researchers affiliated with Beck's Center for Cognitive Therapy are already taking steps in this direction and have made sample therapy tapes available, as well as analyzing and giving feedback on tapes submitted by other researchers. Young (1980) is taking additional steps toward quality control through the development of the Cognitive Therapy Scale, a measure that is used to rate samples of therapy sessions to assess the quality with which Cognitive Therapy is practiced. This measure clearly delineates the factors that are considered the most crucial aspects of Cognitive Therapy, and thus is one step toward the goal of clearly specifying treatment techniques. Future outcome studies where the therapists follow the procedures in Beck's manuals and where representative therapy samples are rated by experienced professionals on the Cognitive Therapy Scale will allow much more valid comparisons.

Directions for Further Study

In addition to the methodological issues raised in previous sections, there are at least three major areas that need to be addressed empirically. These are (1) the Cognitive Therapist's handling of the problem of depressive relapse, (2) the refinement of outcome research to determine which Cognitive Therapy approach or strategy is best for which type of depressed patient, and (3) the efficacy of Cognitive Therapy with disorders other than depression.

Depressive Relapse

Clinical experience has shown that a time of crucial importance in determining the long-term outcome of Cognitive Therapy is the time of the first relapse. Depression tends to be a recurrent problem for individuals who have experienced it. Cognitive Therapy may help individuals to be more resistant to relapse and may make relapses shorter and less severe, but it cannot completely protect a patient against any future feelings of depression. Relapse may confirm the patient's hopelessness and may result in termination of therapy before the patient learns how to deal with the return of depression. Because of this, it seems that a necessary direction for future research would be to examine the effectiveness of various ways of handling the first relapse.

The authors propose the following treatment package, which constitutes their current practice, as a sample approach for empirical testing: First, the patient is taught early in therapy to *expect* relapse. Almost all people who have had one depressive episode will have a second. This is the case whether they have had therapy or not. It is countertherapeutic to withhold this information from patients. Next, the patient is taught to *decatastrophize* relapse. They are asked to consider the worst possible thing that could happen and how they could deal with it. This reduces the patient's fear of depression and gives him a sense of control. Beyond this, however, the patient is presented with the idea that he might even *welcome* relapse. Relapse can be seen as an opportunity to experience a sense of mastery over a difficult problem. It can also be seen as an unequivocal way of demonstrating to the patient that the skills acquired in therapy can be relied upon to resolve future depressive episodes quickly and effectively.

Because individuals who are experiencing depression often do not remember to rationally respond to their automatic thoughts without assistance, it is also important to teach the patient to decatastrophize contacting the therapist after termination of therapy if necessary. The patient can be told that this is commonly done by individuals who have received therapy and that she can expect to need "booster" sessions on occasion. It is important to convey the message that this does not signify a failure of therapy, but that it means the patient has learned a variety of strategies for coping with problems.

It is also important for patients who might fail to seek help until they are severely depressed to be taught how to monitor their depression level. The therapist might give the patient a supply of Beck Depression Inventories (Beck, 1978) for the patient to self-administer at regular intervals. The patient and therapist can decide in advance which depression score will prompt the patient to contact the therapist.

Inherent in all the strategies described above for dealing with relapse is the necessity of preparing the patient for likely automatic thoughts regarding relapse and how to respond to them. Some common thoughts are: "I am really hopeless." "My therapy (or therapist) really did not help me after all." "It would be too embarrassing to let my therapist know I've failed." Such automatic thoughts and their responses can be written out and stored by the patient for future use. Finally, if at all possible, therapy should be continued until the resolution of the first depressive relapse. Doing so tends to increase the patient's confidence in her ability to cope effectively with relapse and to increase the likelihood that the cognitive strategies acquired during therapy will be utilized afterward.

The authors think that this approach to dealing with depressive relapse has the potential for making a significant impact on treatment outcome. However, only carefully controlled research can determine whether or not this is the case, and if so, which components are the most important.

Matching Patients to Treatments

Since Cognitive Therapy, as a package, has shown itself to be an effective treatment for depression, it might be useful to attempt to match specific types of depressed patients to specific types of interventions. There are many hypotheses as to which categories of individuals would benefit most from which treatments. For example, Beck et al. (1979) hypothesize that behavioral methods are most useful with severely depressed patients in the early stages of treatment when they are displaying many vegetative symptoms. Later in the treatment, however, they hypothesize that cognitive techniques become more important. If research validates these hypotheses, treatment could be made more reliable and more effective.

Freeman et al. (in press) have proposed a great number of modifications of the standard model of Cognitive Therapy described here and by Beck et al. (1979). For example, they present the idea that obsessional depressives should be treated differently from nonobsessional depressives. The obsessional patient is hypothesized to require more active and consistent structuring of therapy sessions for improvement to take place. The idea is also presented that when treating obsessional individuals, the therapist might emphasize self-instructional techniques, rather than rational responding, in order to minimize the possibility of promoting obsessional rumination. These are empirical questions which, when answered, could lead to more sophisticated conceptualizations of treatment than do more basic questions as to which treatment is best.

Cognitive Therapy with Anxiety and Other Disorders

Cognitive Therapy has been used in the treatment of a wide variety of disorders, ranging from anxiety to obesity, unassertiveness to tension headache, and drug addiction to ulcers. Although clinicians have developed their own applications of Cognitive Therapy to a full range of psychological problems, Beck and his colleagues have written formal treatment manuals only for the treatment of depression (Beck et al., 1979) anxiety and phobic disorders (Beck & Emery, 1979), and substance abuse (Beck & Emery, 1977). The manuals for the treatment of anxiety and of substance abuse have not received wide circulation, being available only through Beck's Center for Cognitive Therapy. Therefore, most of the outcome studies that have been conducted investigating cognitive and behavioral approaches to the treatment of disorders besides depression use approaches other than Beck's specific model of Cognitive Therapy.

The majority of cognitive-behavioral outcome studies for problems other than depression have involved treatments of test anxiety, public speaking anxiety, social anxiety, and unassertiveness, using samples of college students or volunteers (see summaries by Barrios & Shigetomi, 1979; Rachman & Wilson, 1980). The results of these studies are encouraging and indicate that cognitive-behavioral approaches are superior to waiting-list controls and are at least as effective and often more effective than alternative treatments.

Outcome studies of cognitive-behavioral therapy with clinical samples, however, are quite rare. Studies of treatment for stuttering (Moleski & Tosi, 1976), chronic low back pain (Turner, 1982), duodenal ulcer (Brooks & Richardson, 1980), generalized anxiety (Woodward & Jones, 1980), and multiple "neurotic" disorders (Lipsky, Kassinove, & Miller, 1980) have provided initial support for the efficacy of cognitive-behavioral approaches.

In a series of studies of agoraphobics, however, the results have been less clear. Emmelkamp, Kuipers, and Eggeraat (1978) found prolonged exposure *in vivo* to be significantly more effective in reducing anxiety and avoidance than their version of cognitive restructuring (which primarily involved the use of coping self-statements). This study has been criticized (by Albert Ellis, 1979, among others) as being unrepresentative of cognitive approaches, since none of the major proponents of cognitive therapies advocate a solely cognitive treatment for phobias or for most other disorders. *In vivo* exposure is as much a part of cognitive therapies for phobias as it is a part of behavioral therapies.

In a later study, Emmelkamp and Mersh (1982) compared agoraphobics assigned to cognitive restructuring, prolonged exposure *in vivo*, or a combination of components, each conducted in eight sessions over the course of three weeks. This study differed from the earlier study in that it used a cognitive restructuring approach that placed much more emphasis on insight into unproductive thinking, rather than focusing solely on the learning of coping self-statements. At posttest, prolonged exposure alone and the combination treatment were both significantly more effective at reducing phobic anxiety and avoidance than cognitive restructuring. In another study of agoraphobics (Williams & Rappoport, 1983) as well as in a study of obsessive-compulsive patients (Emmelkamp, van de Helm, van Zanten, & Plochq, 1980), no significant differences were found between exposure alone and a combination of exposure and self-instructional training.

It is important to note, however, that the results of the Emmelkamp and Mersh (1982) study changed over time. At a one-month follow-up, the differences between treatments were no longer statistically significant. This was due to a continuing improvement in the cognitive restructuring condition and a slight relapse in the prolonged exposure condition. It would be interesting to see a later follow-up to determine whether the conditions continued to diverge. It was also discovered at follow-up that only cognitive restructuring had led to significant improvement at follow-up in depression, locus of control, and assertiveness. It may be that cognitive restructuring leads not only to change in the target behaviors but also to generalized behavior changes.

The treatment used in the Emmelkamp and Meresh (1982) study was a somewhat more sophisticated version of cognitive treatment, coming closer to Beck's model of Cognitive Therapy than earlier studies, which were limited to a self-instructional model. Self-instructional training has been shown to be useful in treating a variety of disorders, but it may be that for treating more severe anxiety disorders, such as agoraphobia and obsessive-compulsive disorders, a more comprehensive version of cognitive treatment is necessary. The Cognitive Therapy manual for anxiety and phobic disorders (Beck & Emery, 1979) places much emphasis on the use of imagery procedures in the treatment of clinical anxiety, based on the finding that 90% of anxious patients studied reported visual images of being in danger prior to, and concomitant with, their anxiety (Beck, Laude, & Bohnert, 1974). Perhaps as this manual becomes more readily available to clinicians, empirical tests of Beck's Cognitive Therapy with anxiety will be conducted to determine whether a more comprehensive cognitive-behavioral treatment will receive stronger support in the treatment of clinical anxiety than did earlier cognitive-behavioral approaches.

Conclusion

Cognitive Therapy seems to have lived up to its promise as an important new model of psychotherapy. The outcome literature reviewed here demonstrates that Beck's Cognitive Therapy is an effective treatment for unipolar depression. This approach appears to have considerable potential as a treatment for other clinical disorders, as well. However, clear treatment guidelines are needed for the application of Cognitive Therapy to the treatment of disorders besides depression, and further research evaluating the efficacy of Cognitive Therapy with a variety of psychological problems is needed as well.

References

Bandura, A. Self-efficacy: Towards a unifying theory of behavioral change. *Psychological Review*, 1977, *84*, 191–215. (a)

Bandura, A. *Social learning theory*. Englewood Cliffs, NJ: Prentice-Hall, 1977. (b)

Barrios, B. A., & Shigetomi, C. C. Coping-skills training for the management of anxiety: A critical review. *Behavior Therapy*, 1979, *10*, 491–522.

Bartholow, J. S. *Processes of cognitive behavioral therapy of depression: Reductions in dysfunctional attitudes and negative self-statements*. Unpublished doctoral dissertation, California School of Professional Psychology, San Diego, 1980.

Beck, A. T. *Depression: Clinical, experimental, and theoretical spects*. New York: Harper and Row, 1967.

Beck, A. T. *Cognitive therapy and the emotional disorders*. New York: International University Press, 1976.

Beck, A. T. *Depression inventory*. Philadelphia: Center for Cognitive Therapy, 1978.

Beck, A. T., & Emery, G. D. *Individual treatment manual for cognitive behavioral psychotherapy of drug abuse*. Philadelphia: Center for Cognitive Therapy, 1977.

Beck, A. T., & Emery, G. *Cognitive therapy of anxiety and phobic disorders*. Philadelphia: Center for Cognitive Therapy, 1979.

Beck, A. T., Laude, R., & Bohnert, M. Ideational components of anxiety neurosis. *Archives of General Psychiatry*, 1974, *31*, 319–325.

Beck, A. T., & Rush, A. J. Cognitive approaches to depression and suicide. In G. Sraban (Ed.), *Cognitive Deficits in the Development of Mental Illness.* New York: Brunner Mazel, 1978.

Beck, A. T., Rush, A. J., Shaw, B. F., & Emery, G. *Cognitive therapy of depression.* New York: Guilford Press, 1979.

Berger, P. A. Antidepressant medications and the treatment of depression. In J. D. Barchas, P. A. Berger, R. D. Ciaranello, & G. R. Elliott (Eds.), *Psychopharmacology: From theory to practice.* New York: Oxford University Press, 1977.

Besyner, J. K. *The comparative efficacy of cognitive and behavioral treatments of depression: A multi-assessment approach.* Unpublished doctoral dissertation, Texas Tech University, 1978.

Blackburn, I. M., Bishop, S., Glen, A. I. M., Whalley, L. J., & Christie, J. E. The efficacy of cognitive therapy in depression: A treatment trial using cognitive therapy and pharmacotherapy, each alone and in combination. *British Journal of Psychiatry,* 1981, *139*, 181–189.

Brooks, G. R., & Richardson, F. C. Emotional skills training: A treatment program for duodenal ulcer. *Behavior Therapy,* 1980, *11*, 198–207.

Carrington, C. H. *A comparison of cognitive and analytically oriented brief treatment approaches to depression in black women.* Unpublished doctoral dissertation, University of Maryland, 1979.

Covi, L., Lipman, R. S., Derogatis, L. R., Smith, J. E., & Pattison, J. H. Drugs and group psychotherapy in neurotic depression. *American Journal of Psychiatry,* 1974, *131*, 191–198.

deJong, R., Henrich, G., & Ferstl, R. A behavioral treatment program for neurotic depression. *Behavior Analysis and Modification,* 1981, *4*, 275–287.

Dunn, R. J. Cognitive modification with depression-prone psychiatric patients. *Cognitive Therapy and Research,* 1979, *3*, 307–317.

Dush, D. M. *A meta-analysis of cognitive restructuring therapy.* Unpublished doctoral dissertation, Kent State University, 1981.

Ellis, A. *Reason and emotion in psychotherapy.* New York: Lyle Stuart, 1962.

Ellis, A. A note on the treatment of agoraphobics with cognitive modification versus prolonged exposure in vivo. *Behaviour Research and Therapy,* 1979, *17*, 162–164.

Emmelkamp, P. M. G., Kuipers, A. C. M., & Eggeraat, J. B. Cognitive modification versus prolonged exposure in vivo: A comparison with agoraphobics as subjects. *Behaviour Research and Therapy,* 1978, *16*, 33–41.

Emmelkamp, P. M. G., & Mersh, P. P. Cognition and exposure in vivo in the treatment of agoraphobia: Short-term and delayed effects. *Cognitive Therapy and Research,* 1982, *6*, 77–88.

Emmelkamp, P. M. G., van der Helm, M., van Zanten, B. L., & Plochq, I. Treatment of obsessive-compulsive patients: The contribution of self-instructional training to the effectiveness of exposure. *Behaviour Research and Therapy*, 1980, *18*, 61–66.

Feighner, J. P., Robins, E., Guze, S. B., Woodruffe, R. A., Winokur, G., & Munoz, R. Diagnostic criteria for use in psychiatric research. *Archives of General Psychiatry*, 1972, *47*, 310–316.

Fennell, M. J. V., & Teasdale, J. D. Cognitive therapy with chronic, drug-refractory depressed outpatients: A note of caution. *Cognitive Therapy and Research*, 1982, *6*, 455–460.

Freeman, A. (Ed.), *Cognitive therapy with couples and groups*. New York: Plenum, 1983.

Freeman, A., Simon, K. M., Fleming, B. M., & Pretzer, J. *The clinical application of cognitive therapy*. New York: Plenum, in press.

Friedman, A. Interaction of drug therapy with marital therapy in depressed patients. *Archives of General Psychiatry*, 1975, *32*, 619–637.

Fuchs, C. Z., & Rehm, L. P. A self-control behavior therapy program for depression. *Journal of Consulting and Clinical Psychology*, 1977, *45*, 206–215.

Greenwood, V. B. Cognitive therapy with the young adult chronic patient. In A. Freeman (Ed.), *Cognitive therapy with couples and groups*. New York: Plenum, 1983.

Hamilton, S. B., & Waldman, D. A. Self-modification of depression via cognitive-behavioral intervention strategies: A time-series analysis. *Cognitive Therapy and Research*, 1983, *7*, 99–105.

Harpin, R. E., Liberman, R. P., Marks, I., Stern, R., & Bohannon, W. E. Cognitive-behavior therapy for chronically depressed patients: A controlled pilot study. *Journal of Nervous and Mental Disease*, 1982, *170*, 295–301.

Hodgson, J. W. Cognitive versus behavioral-interpersonal approaches to the group treatment of depressed college students. *Journal of Counseling Psychology*, 1981, *28*, 243–249.

Jarvinen, P. J., & Gold, S. R. Imagery as an aid in reducing depression. *Journal of Clinical Psychology*, 1981, *37*, 523–529.

Kelly, G. A. *The psychology of personal constructs (Vols. 1 & 2)*. New York: Norton, 1955.

Kendall, P. C., & Hollon, S. D. Calibrating the quality of therapy: Collaborative archiving of tape samples for therapy outcome trials. *Cognitive Therapy and Research*, 1983, *7*, 199–204.

Kiesler, D. J. Some myths of psychotherapy research and the search for a paradigm. *Psychological Bulletin*, 1966, *65*, 110–136.

Kirkpatrick, P. W. *The efficacy of cognitive behavior modification in the treatment of depression*. Unpublished doctoral dissertation, University of Texas at Austin, 1977.

Klerman, G. L., DiMascio, A., Weissman, M., Prusoff, B., & Paykel, E. S. Treatment of depression by drugs and psychotherapy. *American Journal of Psychiatry*, 1974, *131*, 186–191.

Kovacs, M., Rush, A. J., Beck, A. T., & Hollon, S. D. Depressed outpatients treated with cognitive therapy or pharmacotherapy: A one-year follow-up. *Archives of General Psychiatry*, 1981, *38*, 33–39.

Ledwidge, B. Cognitive behavior modification: A step in the wrong direction? *Psychological Bulletin*, 1978, *85*, 353–375.

Leizer, H. S. *Negative view of the future as a factor in the maintenance of depression: Changes in verbalization of depressives during cognitive/ behavioral intervention.* Unpublished doctoral dissertation, California School of Professional Psychology, San Diego, 1980.

Lipsky, M. J., Kassinove, H., & Miller, N. J. Effects of rational-emotive therapy, rational role reversal, and rational-emotive imagery on the emotional adjustment of community mental health center patients. *Journal of Consulting and Clinical Psychology*, 1980, *48*, 366–374.

Magers, B. D. *Cognitive-behavioral short-term group therapy with depressed women.* Unpublished doctoral dissertation, California School of Professional Psychology, San Francisco, 1977.

McLean, P. D., & Hakstien, A. R. Clinical depression: Comparative efficacy of outpatient treatments. *Journal of Consulting and Clinical Psychology*, 1979, *47*, 818–836.

Metcalfe, M., & Goldman, E. Validation of an inventory for measuring depression. *British Journal of Psychiatry*, 1965, *111*, 240–242.

Miller, R. C., & Berman, J. S. *The efficacy of cognitive-behavior therapy: A quantitative review of the research evidence.* Presented at the meeting of the American Psychological Association, Los Angeles, 1981.

Moleski, R., & Tosi, D. J. Comparative psychotherapy: Rational-emotive therapy versus systematic desensitization in the treatment of stuttering. *Journal of Consulting and Clinical Psychology*, 1976, *44*, 309–311.

Morris, N. E. *A group self-instruction method for the treatment of depressed outpatients.* Unpublished doctoral dissertation, University of Toronto, 1975.

Munoz, R. F. *A cognitive approach to the assessment and treatment of depression.* Unpublished doctoral dissertation, University of Oregon, 1977.

Neisser, U. *Cognitive psychology.* New York: Appleton-Century-Crofts, 1967.

Rachman, S. J., & Wilson, G. T. *The effects of psychological therapy* (2nd ed.). New York: Pergamon, 1980.

Rehm, L. P., Kornblith, S. J., O'Hara, M. W., Lamparski, D. M., Romano, J. M., & Volkin, J. I. An evaluation of major components in a self-control therapy program for depression. *Behavior Modification*, 1981, *5*, 459–489.

Roth, D., Bielski, R., Jones, M., Parker, W., & Osborn, G. A comparison of self-control therapy and combined self-control therapy and antidepressant medication in the treatment of depression. *Behavior Therapy*, 1982, *13*, 133–144.

Rush, A. J., Beck, A. T., Kovacs, M., & Hollon, S. D. Comparative efficacy of cognitive therapy and pharmacotherapy in the treatment of depressed outpatients. *Cognitive Therapy and Research,* 1977, *1,* 17–37.

Rush, A. J., Khatami, M., & Beck, A. T. Cognitive and behavior therapy in chronic depression. *Behavior Therapy,* 1975, *6,* 398–404.

Rush, A. J., Kovacs, M., Beck, A. T., Weissenburger, J., & Hollon, S. D. Differential effects of cognitive therapy and pharmacotherapy on depressive symptoms. *Journal of Affective Disorders,* 1981, *3,* 221–229.

Rush, A. J., & Watkins, J. T. Group versus individual cognitive therapy: A pilot study. *Cognitive Therapy and Research,* 1981, *5,* 95–103.

Schmickley, V. G. *Effects of cognitive-behavior modification upon depressed outpatients.* Unpublished doctoral dissertation, Michigan State University, 1976.

Schmidt, M. M. *Amount of therapist contact and outcome in a multimodal depression treatment program.* Unpublished doctoral dissertation, University of New Mexico, 1980.

Shaffer, C. S., Shapiro, J., Sank, L. I., & Coghlan, D. J. Positive change in depression, anxiety, and assertion following individual and group cognitive behavior therapy intervention. *Cognitive Therapy and Research,* 1981, 5, 149–157

Shaw, B. F. Comparison of cognitive therapy and behavior therapy in the treatment of depression. *Journal of Consulting and Clinical Psychology,* 1977, *45,* 543–551.

Simons, A. D. *The process of change in cognitive therapy and pharmacotherapy of depression: Changes in mood and cognitions.* Unpublished doctoral dissertation, Washington University, 1982.

Spitzer, R. L., Endicott, J., & Robins, E. *Research Diagnostic Criteria (RDC) for a selected group of functional disorders (3rd ed.).* New York State Psychiatric Institute, Biometrics Research, 1978.

Taylor, F. G., & Marshall, W. L. Experimental analysis of a cognitive-behavioral therapy for depression. *Cognitive Therapy and Research,* 1977, *1,* 59–72.

Truax, C. F., & Mitchell, K. M. Research on certain therapist interpersonal skills in relation to process and outcome. In A. E. Bergin & S. L. Garfield (Eds.), *Handbook of psychotherapy and behavior change.* New York: Wiley, 1971.

Turner, J. A. Comparison of group progressive-relaxation training and cognitive-behavioral group therapy for chronic back pain. *Journal of Consulting and Clinical Psychology,* 1982, *50,* 757–765.

Wilson, P. H., Goldin, J. C., & Charbonneau-Powis, M. Comparative efficacy of behavioral and cognitive treatments of depression. *Cognitive Therapy and Research,* 1983, *7,* 111–124.

Woodward, R., & Jones, R. B. Cognitive restructuring treatment: A controlled trial with anxious patients. *Behavioral Research and Therapy,* 1980, *18,* 401–407.

Young, J. *Development of an instrument for rating cognitive therapy: The cognitive therapy scale.* Unpublished manuscript, Center for Cognitive Therapy, Philadelphia, 1980.

Zeiss, A. M., Lewinsohn, P. M., & Munoz, R. F. Nonspecific improvement effects in depression using interpersonal skills training, pleasant activity schedules, or cognitive training. *Journal of Consulting and Clinical Psychology,* 1979, *47,* 427–439.

7

Cognitive Therapy

PAUL R. LATIMER AND ANDREW A. SWEET

Psychology is said to have undergone a "cognitive revolution" during the past decade. The revolution is characterized by an emphasis on the private events or cognitive mechanisms and processes mediating behavior (Mahoney, 1974, 1977). Clinically it is reflected in the emergence of the "cognitive therapies," heralded in such works as Mahoney's *Cognition and Behavior Modification* (1974), Beck's *Cognitive Therapy and the Emotional Disorders* (1976), and Meichenbaum's *Cognitive-Behavior Modification* (1977). The cognitive therapy "revolutionaries" have championed their cause by claiming that behavior therapy is insufficiently attuned to the importance of cognitive processes in complex human behavior and that traditional learning theory is inadequate to explain therapeutic change.

That a vibrant new movement has formed is confirmed by all of the usual signs of professional special interest groups such as books, journals, organizations, and annual meetings, all bearing the title "cognitive." What remains debatable is whether this activity represents a "revolution." Is this a paradigm shift in the Kuhnian sense or a passing phase (Wilson, 1978)? In *The Structure of Scientific Revolutions,* Thomas Kuhn (1970) argues that scientific revolutions occur when an established paradigm is replaced in whole or in part by an incompatible new one. This occurs when there is a growing sense among some segment of the scientific community that an existing paradigm has ceased to function adequately. "Led by a new paradigm, scientists adopt new instruments and look in new places. Even more important, during revolutions scientists see new and different

Reprinted by permission of the publisher from Latimer, P. R., and Sweet, A. A., Cognitive versus behavioral procedures in cognitive-behavior therapy: A critical review of the evidence. *Journal of Behavior Therapy and Experimental Psychiatry, 15*(1), 9–22. Copyright © 1984, Pergamon Press, Ltd.

things when looking with familiar instruments in places they have looked before" (p. 111).

Any further consideration of this question requires some characterization of the behavioral and cognitive paradigms respectively. Just what do these terms subsume?

Behavior Therapy

What is frequently overlooked in these arguments is that there is no one learning theory. Wilson (1978) has outlined three major conceptual models which have been and continue to be influential in behavior therapy.

Applied Behavioral Analysis

This model is most closely identified with the radical behaviorism of Skinner (1953). Treatments based on the principles of operant conditioning focus primarily on overt behavior. Subjective or private events are regarded as epiphenomena which are determined by the external environment. While acknowledging the existence of subjective events, they are eschewed as subjects for scientific investigation for methodological reasons.

The Neobehavioristic Mediational S–R Model

This model derives primarily from the theories and experiments of Pavlov and his followers. Applied to clinical practices by Wolpe (1958), it is defined as the application of experimentally derived principles and paradigms of learning (and related principles) for the purpose of changing unadaptive behavior (Wolpe, 1973). It relies heavily on principles of classical conditioning and concerns itself primarily with anxiety-based disorders. Anxiety is hypothesized to be a classically conditioned autonomic response and to arise in response to conditioned stimuli. According to the two-factor theory of avoidance learning (Mowrer, 1947, 1960), escape/avoidance behavior is mediated by the occurrence of anxiety and reinforced by its reduction. More recently a three-systems view of anxiety acknowledges the fact that anxiety may be defined by behavior at three levels—verbal, physiological, and motoric (Lang, 1968; Rachman, 1978). Treatment methods such as systematic desensitization rely on both verbal and imaginal processes, whatever their mechanism of action.

Social-Learning Theory

This model attempts to be more comprehensive in scope by acknowledging the role of both classical and operant conditioning processes while emphasizing the importance of cognitive mediational processes. "The latter determine what environmental influences are attended to, how they are perceived, and whether they might affect future action" (Wilson, 1978, p. 11). Observational learning is used as an example of "cognitive" learning as opposed to operant or classical conditioning, and modeling is a treatment method derived from it.

Another feature of the social-learning theory is the cognitive concept of self-efficacy, according to which *all* behavior change procedures from psychotherapy to modeling work by changing expectations of self-efficacy. These expectations are supposed to provide the link between the classical, operant, and cognitive components of human learning.

Cognitive Therapy

There are several distinctive cognitive therapies. Three of the most influential are Ellis's (1962) Rational-Emotive Therapy (RET), Meichenbaum's (1977) Self-instructional Training (SIT), and Beck's (1976) Cognitive Therapy.

Rational Emotive Therapy

This approach is based on the assumption that the core of most neurotic problems is irrational beliefs. Twelve such beliefs identified by Ellis (1970) are shown in Table 7.1. Wilson (1978) has characterized the therapeutic method as consisting of the following steps:

a. Verbal persuasion aimed at convincing the client of the philosophical tenets of RET.
b. Identification of irrational thoughts through client self-monitoring and the therapist's feedback.
c. The therapist directly challenges irrational ideas and models rational reinterpretations of disturbing events.

TABLE 7.1
Common Irrational Beliefs

1. The idea that it is a dire necessity for an adult to be loved by everyone for everything he does.
2. The idea that certain acts are awful or wicked, and that people who perform such acts should be severely punished.
3. The idea that it is horrible when things are not the way one would like them to be.
4. The idea that human misery is externally caused and is forced on one by outside people and events.
5. The idea that if something is or may be dangerous or fearsome, one should be terribly upset about it.
6. The idea that it is easier to avoid than to face life difficulties and self-responsibilities.
7. The idea that one needs something other or stronger or greater than oneself on which to rely.
8. The idea that one should be thoroughly competent, intelligent, and achieving in all possible respects.
9. The idea that because something once strongly affected one's life, it should indefinitely affect it.
10. The idea that one must have certain and perfect control over things.
11. The idea that human happiness can be achieved by inertia and inaction.
12. The idea that one has virtually no control over one's emotions and that one cannot help feeling certain things.

d. Repeated cognitive rehearsal aimed at substituting rational self-statements for previously irrational interpretation.
e. Behavioral tasks ("shame exercises") designed to develop rational reactions where there were once irrational, distress-producing assumptions (p. 14).

Ellis (1979a) has emphasized that despite his designation as a cognitive therapist, he does not devote the bulk of his therapeutic effort to combating irrational beliefs.

Rational-emotive therapy (RET) is an exceptionally multifaceted or multimodal form of therapy that almost invariably includes a number of cognitive methods besides combating irrational beliefs—such as teaching clients coping statements, showing them how to focus on positive thoughts and feelings, teaching them methods of cognitive distraction (including Wolpe's reciprocal inhibition methods), employing rational-emotive imagery and other imagery techniques, using problem solving methods, giving relevant information, employing audiovisual aids, assigning cognitive homework, and consciously making use of

modeling, persuasion, philosophical analysis, semantic reeducation,
suggestion, auto suggestion, etc.

In addition, RET employs . . . a large number of emotive–evocative–
expressive methods (such as role playing, unconditional acceptance of
the client, self-disclosure, and shame-attacking exercises) and a sizable
number of behavioral methods (such as operant conditioning, in-vivo
desensitization, aversive penalties, and skill training. (pp. 98–99)

Self-instructional Training

Self-instructional training derives from RET but in addition was
influenced by the work of Luria (1961) concerning the developmental
sequence according to which children develop internal speech and
verbal–symbolic control over their behavior. It was hypothesized
that children's behavior was first regulated by the instructions of
others, then by overt self-instructions, and finally by covert self-
instructions. The translation of this process into therapy resulted in
SIT, which Wilson (1978) has characterized as follows:

> SIT involves the following steps:
> a. Training the client to identify and become aware of maladaptive
>   thoughts (self-statements).
> b. The therapist models appropriate behavior while verbalizing effec-
>   tive action strategies; these verbalizations include an appraisal of
>   task requirements, self-instructions that guide graded performance,
>   self-statements that stress personal adequacy and counteract worry
>   over failure, and covert self-reinforcement for successful perfor-
>   mance.
> c. The client then performs the target behavior first while verbalizing
>   aloud the appropriate self-instructions and then by covertly rehears-
>   ing them. Therapist feedback during this phase assists in ensuring
>   that constructive problem-solving self-talk replaced previously anxi-
>   ety-inducing cognitions associated with that behavior. (p. 15)

Beck's Cognitive Therapy

Beck's Cognitive Therapy is also based on the assumption that irrational, unadaptive thoughts are the primary problem in most neurotic disorders and are therefore the most appropriate primary target in
therapy. While there is evidence that stressful events such as illness
or loss of job frequently precede depressions, cognitive therapists
emphasize the role of the individual's interpretation of these events.

Depression results when cognitive distortion occurs such as equating the loss of a job with complete failure as a human being. Therapy consists of the following steps:

    a. Clients become aware of their thoughts.
    b. They learn to identify inaccurate or distorted thoughts.
    c. These inaccurate thoughts are replaced by accurate, more objective cognitions.
    d. Therapist feedback and reinforcement is a necessary part of this process. (p. 15)

Both behavioral and cognitive procedures are used to accomplish these objectives. The former include role-playing and the assignment of activity schedules and graded tasks which may include exposure to anxiety-producing circumstances. The latter include a variety of verbal techniques which are used to explore the logic behind specific cognitions and beliefs.

This combination of behavioral and cognitive techniques is common to all of the cognitive therapies and, as we shall see, is a severe impediment to testing the purported superiority of cognitive techniques. Beck, Rush, and Shaw (1979, p. 5) have explicitly stated that the behavioral techniques are generally more potent and therefore especially necessary toward the beginning of therapy and with the more severely depressed. The label "cognitive" therapy, therefore, has more to do with the underlying theory than with the therapy practiced. Beck et al. (1979) put it this way:

> The cognitive *therapy* of depression is based on the cognitive *theory* of depression. By working within the framework of the cognitive model, the therapist formulates his therapeutic approach according to the specific needs of a given patient at a particular time. Thus, the therapist may be conducting cognitive therapy even though he is utilizing predominantly behavioral or abreactive (emotional releasing) techniques. (p. 117; Beck's emphasis)

We shall return to this point later.

It is difficult to see these therapies as anything more than therapeutic innovations arising from a greater emphasis on one class of behaviors—cognitions.[1] The extent to which this is true and some of the historical reasons for this development are evident in the writings of Mahoney (1974). The argument that "cognitive therapy" is revolutionary is most defensible when cognitive therapy is con-

---

[1] Cognitions are inferred—usually from verbal behavior.

trasted with Skinnerian behavior modification practices. Indeed, Mahoney (1974) seems to develop his case for the "cognitive connection" almost entirely in reaction to radical behaviorism, à la Skinner. Wolpe (1958) was referred to only as "an occasional renegade exception." Mahoney devotes several chapters to the justification of invoking cognitive mediation, in spite of the fact that it was already common practice in the neobehavioristic and social-learning theory models of behavior therapy. Indeed, his first two chapters on cognitively based treatment procedures are devoted to such old standbys as systematic desensitization, thought stopping, covert control, covert sensitization, covert reinforcement, covert extinction, and covert modeling—hardly revolutionary.

To the extent that Mahoney's arguments establish the case for a paradigm shift based on the inclusion of cognitive mediation, the shift occurred earlier with the development of what Wilson (1978) called the neobehavioristic mediational S-R model. From this perspective, the more recent development of cognitive therapy is an elaboration or embellishment of an existing paradigm within the broader field of behavior therapy.

Beck et al.'s (1979) description of behavior therapy is also curiously outdated and misrepresentative, as illustrated by the following passage:

> Many of the techniques described in this chapter are also part of the repertoire of the behavior therapist. The impact of the therapeutic techniques derived from a strictly behavioral or conditioning model is limited because of the restriction to observable behavior and selective exclusion of information regarding the patient's attitudes, beliefs and thoughts—his cognitions. Hence, even though the behavior therapist induces the patient to become more active, his pessimism, self-disparagement and suicidal impulses may remain unchanged. For the behavior therapist, the modification of behavior is an end in itself; for the cognitive therapist it is a means to an end—namely, cognitive change.

To suggest that the behavior therapist seeks to increase the activity of depressed individuals as an end in itself rather than as a means of alleviating depressed affect is so far from the truth that it scarcely warrants serious consideration.

Likewise, Beck's list of "new" features of cognitive therapy do not distinguish it from neobehavioristic or social-learning theory–based behavior therapy, with the exception of its *greater emphasis* on the patient's internal experiences. The other features listed as being distinctive of cognitive therapy include:

1. An active therapist deliberately interacting with the patient.
2. A focus on "here-and-now" problems.
3. A collaborative relationship between therapist and patient.
4. An emphasis on empiricism (pp. 6–7).

Clearly, none of these features distinguishes cognitive and behavior therapy (Sweet, 1982; Wilson & Evans, 1977).

In criticizing behavior therapy for something it is not, that is, noncognitive, nonmediational, these critics become "malcontents," that is, critics who do not entirely understand what they are talking about (Wolpe, 1976).

All of the preceding discussion is based on the assumption that cognition is a subclass of behavior which is, nevertheless, governed according to the same principles as other behavior. This view is consistent with behavior therapy and with much of the writing of cognitive therapists. The latter sometimes come perilously close, however, to advocating the view that cognitive behavior has some degree of autonomy from the causal stream. This leads directly to the familiar arguments over free will versus determinism and, of course, is incompatible with the basic deterministic philosophy of behaviorism (for a more complete discussion, see Wolpe, 1978). This position would represent a paradigmatic shift from behavior therapy, and a retrogressive one at that (cf. Wolpe, 1978, p. 442). It is not, however, a fundamental or necessary assumption for the cognitive therapies described above nor, to the best of our knowledge, is this position explicitly taken by any of the major proponents of cognitive therapy.

Whether cognition is important or relevant is not the issue. The real issue is whether the therapies derived from cognitive theory are more effective or otherwise advantageous compared with behavior therapy. In this regard we will not consider the covert conditioning therapies since they arose within the field of behavior therapy and were based on existing learning theories. They have been extensively reviewed elsewhere (Heppner, 1978; Kazdin & Smith, 1979; Sohn & Lamal, 1982; Tryon, 1979). The remainder of this chapter will focus on the outcome evaluation of the cognitive therapies.

Outcome

The available cognitive therapy outcome literature will be evaluated subject to the following restrictions. Only studies which attempt to evaluate the efficacy of the procedures specific to cognitive therapy as defined above will be reviewed. To quote Ullmann (1981): "It is what we do that should be evaluated, not what we call ourselves or our efforts" (p. 21). Systematic desensitization is systematic desensitization whether conceptualized in cognitive or conditioning terms. Examples of studies excluded on this basis are Rush et al. (1977), Shaw (1977), and Comas-Diaz (1981). Each of these studies used Beck's cognitive therapy approach which, as described above, includes many traditional behavioral procedures. They did not include comparison groups employing *only* the *same* traditional behavioral procedures and thus do not provide evidence with which to evaluate procedures specific to cognitive therapy. The question that this paper will attempt to answer is whether the "cognitive revolution" has increased our therapeutic efficacy. A further restriction, which is implied by this question, is that only studies of clinical populations or of populations with clinically significant problems will be included. Although it is acknowledged that all studies are to a greater or lesser degree analogues of usual clinical treatment, some more nearly approximate it than others. Nor does this restriction imply a denigration of analogue research. Studies on nonclinical populations simply do not provide the most valid answer to the question of therapeutic efficacy in clinical practice. In addition to these restrictions, single-case studies are included only if they involve some experimental manipulation and group comparisons only if subject assignment to groups was random and if the study has been published in full (as opposed to an abstract or brief report).

A literature search included a review of the tables of contents of *Behavior Research and Therapy, Journal of Behavior Therapy and Experimental Psychiatry, Behavior Therapy, Cognitive Therapy and Research, and Journal of Consulting and Clinical Psychology*, from 1970 to 1983, and a systematic search of *Psychological Abstracts* covering the same period. Relevant articles were also culled from published reviews and articles on cognitive therapy and from the references of all studies included according to the above criteria. Eleven studies met these criteria and are summarized in alphabetical order in Table 7.2

As illustrated in Table 7.2, these studies involved a variety of clinical problems (simple phobias, agoraphobia, obsessive-compulsive disorder, tension headache, unassertive behavior, social anxiety, social skills deficits, depression), a variety of cognitive therapies, and group and individual sessions and were remarkably consistent in their results. These studies have approached the question we are asking in two ways. The first, and in our view the most defini-

TABLE 7.2
Summary of Cognitive Therapy Outcome Studies

Authors	Population and problem	Treatment groups	Dependent measures	Outcome
Biran, Augusto, & Wilson (1981)	Scriptophobia (subjects responded to ads in community newspaper)	1. In vivo exposure (IE) 2. Cognitive restructuring (CR) Multiple baseline across subjects: CR preceded IE in two subjects; one subject had only IE	Behavioral approach test (BAT) (a) anticipation BAT (b) performance BAT Subjective fear scale (0–10) Beck depression inventory Social avoidance and distress scale Rathus assertiveness scale Fear of negative evaluation Marital adjustment scale	1 > 2 behavioral approach test Subjective fear was lower posttreatment and 1 month follow-up but not at 9 month follow-up. Behavioral gains were maintained at 9 month follow-up. There were no significant changes on other self-report measures. In vivo exposure was clearly superior to cognitive restructuring. No conclusions can be drawn about the efficacy of cognitive restructuring
Biran & Wilson (1981)	Simple phobias (subjects responded to ads in community newspaper; only those with clinically significant fears were included)	1. Guided exposure 2. Cognitive restructuring	Behavioral approach test Subjective fear (a) anticipatory (b) performance Efficacy expectations Fear survey schedule Beck depression inventory	1 > 2 Approach behavior 9/11 of guided exposure group achieved maximal performance compared to one in the cognitive restructuring group 1 > 2 Self-efficacy expectations 1 > 2 Performance fear to familiar threat

(continued)

TABLE 7.2 *(continued)*

Authors	Population and problem	Treatment groups	Dependent measures	Outcome
			Social avoidance and distress scale Fear of negative evaluation Irrational beliefs test Heart rate and skin potential (with imaginal phobic scene)	Performance fear/initial level 1 > 2 Practicing phobic situations in real life 1 = 2 Self-report measures 1 > 2 Heart rate reduction Skin potential amplitude reduction Seven cognitive restructuring patients received guided exposure after one-month follow-up. Six of seven achieved maximal performance on behavioral tests 1 = 2 on credibility and expectation for improvement Guided exposure was clearly superior to cognitive restructuring No conclusions can be drawn about the efficacy of cognitive restructuring in the absence of an attention-placebo control group

Emmelkamp, Kuipers, & Eggeraat (1978)	Agoraphobic patients	1. Exposure in vivo 2. Cognitive restructuring	Measurement in vivo Phobic anxiety and avoidance scales (patient, assessor) Anxious mood scale (assessor) Fear survey schedule Internal–external control scale Self-rating depression scale (Zung) Adult self-expression scale	1 > 2 on all measures Exposure in vivo was significantly more effective than cognitive restructuring whether it was first or second treatment Cognitive restructuring led to only minimal improvement
Emmelkamp & Mersch (1982)	Agoraphobic patients	1. Exposure in vivo 2. Cognitive restructuring 3. Exposure in vivo plus self-instructional training	Measurement in vivo Phobic anxiety and avoidance scale (patient and assessor) Anxious mood scale—(assessor) Fear survey schedule Internal–external control scale Self-rating depression scale Adult self-expression scale (ASES)	Posttreatment 1 > 2 Total phobic anxiety as rated by patient. 1 > 2 Total phobic avoidance as rated by patient and assessor. 3 > 2 In vivo measurement, phobic anxiety as rated by patient and assessor and phobic avoidance as rated by patient Follow-up 1 = 2 = 3 All measures except ASES, where 2 > 1 Self-instructional training did not enhance in vivo exposure on any measure. 2 differed from 3 in that specific *(continued)*

TABLE 7.2 (continued)

Authors	Population and problem	Treatment groups	Dependent measures	Outcome
				irrational beliefs were not dealt with in 3 Specific effects of "cognitive" therapy were tested but not demonstrated
Emmelkamp, van der Helm, van Zanten, & Plochg (1980)	Obsessive-compulsive patients	1. Exposure *in vivo* 2. Exposure *in vivo* plus self-instructional training (both treatments included relaxation)	Anxiety and avoidance scales (patient, therapist, assessor) Anxious mood and depression (therapist and assessor) Leyton obsessional inventory Self-rating depression scale	1 = 2 Both groups improved significantly (statistically and clinically) Specific effects of "cognitive" therapy were tested but not demonstrated
Holroyd & Andrasik (1978)	Tension headache (subjects responded to ads and were selected for clinically significant headaches)	1. Cognitive self-control 2. Cognitive self-control plus relaxation training as a coping response 3. Headache discussion 4. Self-monitoring	Self-monitoring of headaches Psychosomatic checklist EMG activity level Expectancy ratings Miskimins self-goal other discrepancy scale	Post-treatment 1 = 2 = 3 > 4 headache frequency and intensity There were significant effects for 1, 2, and 3 1 = 2 = 3 = 4 on EMG Results the same at follow-up 1 = 2 = 3 on credibility ratings Specific effects of "cognitive" therapy were tested but not demonstrated

Study	Sample	Treatments	Measures	Results
Holroyd, Andrasik, Westbrook (1977)	Tension headaches (subjects responded to ads) Only subjects with clinically significant headaches were included	1. Stress coping training (cognitive) 2. Frontalis EMG biofeedback 3. Waiting-list control	Headache self-monitoring Psychosomatic checklist Frontalis EMG Trait anxiety Locus of control	Headaches $1 > 2 = 3$ at posttreatment and follow-up Psychosomatic Checklist $1 = 2 > 3$ at post treatment and follow-up Frontalis EMG $2 > 1 > 3$ at posttreatment; no relationship to headaches Stress coping training was administered by the two senior authors Biofeedback was administered by lab assistants The stress coping training was clearly superior to biofeedback A comparison of cognitive and behavioral stress coping training would be a better test of the cognitive theory

(continued)

TABLE 7.2 *(continued)*

Authors	Population and problem	Treatment groups	Dependent measures	Outcome
Jacobs & Cochran (1982)	Unassertive (subjects responded to ads and were selected to be unassertive to a clinically significant degree)	1. Behavior rehearsal 2. Behavior rehearsal plus lecture on rights 3. Behavior rehearsal plus lecture on rights plus cognitive restructuring 4. Waiting-list control	Rathus assertiveness scale Galassi assertion self-assessment table Self-monitoring of target unassertive situation	Post-treatment $1 = 2 = 3 = 4$ Rathus assertiveness scale $1 = 2 < 3 = 4$ Self-monitoring Six weeks follow-up Differences disappeared except for self-reported pre-behavior anxiety. Patients in 3 and 4 were more likely to attempt to act assertively in appropriate situations than those in 1 and 2 No waiting-list control group because six of nine dropped out. No assessment of generalization. Intervention involved only one situation/person Cognitive therapy added little to behavioral rehearsal No conclusions can be drawn about the efficacy of cognitive therapy in the absence of an attention-placebo group

Study	Subjects	Treatment	Measures	Results
Stravynski, Marks, & Yule (1982)	Socially dysfunctional neurotic outpatients. All were patients referred for treatment of social skills problems	1. Social skills training (SST) 2. Social skills training plus cognitive modification (SST + CM). Four patients in each group received individual treatment and seven received group treatment.	Self-monitoring of individual social targets and their associated subjective anxiety ratings; Social avoidance and distress inventory; Fear of negative evaluation inventory; Wakefield depression inventory; Irrational beliefs test; Structured and scaled interview to assess maladjustment (SSIAM); Blind assessor • SSIAM • Frequency of performance of social targets	1 = 2; Significant improvement occurred in both groups and was maintained; Specific effects of "cognitive" therapy were tested but not demonstrated
Wolfe & Fodor (1977)	Unassertive women (subjects responded to ads and were selected for clinically significant unassertiveness)	1. Modeling plus behavior rehearsal 2. Modeling plus behavior rehearsal plus rational therapy 3. Consciousness raising 4. Waiting-list control	Behavioral measure rated assertive responses to videotaped situations; Rathus assertiveness schedule (RAS); Social avoidance and distress scale (SAD); Fear of negative evaluation scale (FNE)	1 = 2 > 4 = 3; Assertiveness content scale 1 = 2 > 4, 3 > 4; 1 = 2 > 3; Assertiveness paralinguistic scale; There was generalization in 1 and 2; There were no treatment effects on the RAS, SAD, or FNE; Only group 2 led to less anxiety during behavioral measures; Specific effects of "cognitive" therapy were tested but not demonstrated

(continued)

TABLE 7.2 *(continued)*

Authors	Population and problem	Treatment groups	Dependent measures	Outcome
Zeiss, Lewinsohn, & Munoz (1979)	Depression (subjects responded to ad offering free therapy) Only subjects with clinically significant depression were included	1. Interpersonal skills training 2. Pleasant events scheduling 3. Cognitive therapy Patients in each group were randomly assigned to either immediate or delayed treatment	Interpersonal events schedule Coding of social skill in group interactions Group peer members ratings of social skills Pleasant events schedule Cognitive events schedule Personal beliefs inventory Subjective probability questionnaire Ratings of cognitive set Peer ratings of cognitive set MMPI, D Scale	$1 = 2 = 3$ No differential effects of treatments on specific dependent measures were demonstrated Patients receiving delayed treatment showed substantial improvement before treatment began Although all groups improved significantly, patients were, on average, still depressed at follow-up 44 patients completed treatment Cognitive therapy included elements of Beck, Ellis, Meichenbaum, and others No conclusions can be drawn about the efficacy of cognitive restructuring in the absence of an attention-placebo control group.

tive approach, is to compare a behavioral treatment of known efficacy to the same treatment *plus* the cognitive procedures to be evaluated. If the cognitive procedures address problems which are overlooked by the behavioral treatment and if the cognitive procedures are efficacious, then the combination treatment should yield superior results. For this design to address our question the added cognitive procedures must not include established behavioral methods simply relabeled as cognitive therapy. Five studies used this design and none demonstrated a clinically significant contribution for the cognitive procedures (Emmelkamp & Mersch, 1982; Emmelkamp, van der Helm, van Zanten, & Plochg, 1980; Jacobs & Cochran, 1982; Stravynski, Marks, & Yule, 1982; Wolfe & Fodor, 1977). The second approach used was to compare the cognitive therapy with other treatments. At best this design can demonstrate only the relative efficacy of the treatments compared. If there is an attention-placebo control group it can also demonstrate the efficacy of the cognitive therapy over and above the effects of expectancy. To answer the question addressed in this chapter, it is still essential that the cognitive therapy not include established behavioral methods. Among the seven[2] studies using this design, four have demonstrated the superiority of behavioral methods (Biran, Augusto, & Wilson, 1981; Biran & Wilson, 1981; Emmelkamp, Kuipers, & Eggeraat, 1978; Emmelkamp & Mersch, 1982), one the superiority of cognitive methods (Holroyd, Andrasik, & Westbrook, 1977), and two the equivalence of the cognitive and behavioral methods compared (Holroyd & Andrasik, 1978; Zeiss, Lewinsohn, & Munoz, 1979). The one study demonstrating the superiority of cognitive therapy (Holroyd et al., 1977) and one of the studies finding it equivalent to a behavioral treatment (Zeiss et al., 1979) did not have attention-placebo control groups or expectancy evaluations and thus no conclusions can be drawn about the absolute efficacy of the cognitive procedures. The other study which found equivalence compared cognitive self-control to cognitive self-control plus relaxation as a coping response and neither treatment was more effective than an equally credible headache discussion group (Holroyd & Andrasik, 1978).

In summary, the efficacy of cognitive therapy (excluding behavioral components) has not been demonstrated in clinical populations and what evidence there is suggests that the "cognitive" pro-

---

[2]Some studies used a design which includes both approaches described and are therefore found in both categories.

cedural component of the cognitive therapies is less potent than established behavioral methods such as exposure *in vivo*.

Those readers interested in a review of cognitive therapy including cognitive-behavioral treatments and analogue studies are referred to reviews by Rachman and Wilson (1980), Ledwidge (1978), and Phillips (1981).

Methodological Issues and Future Directions

For the most part the methodological issues relevant to the evaluation of cognitive therapy are not unique. These include issues of generalization, length of therapy, therapists' experience, therapists' bias, and expectancy controls.

Many of the existing studies of cognitive therapy are analogue studies, and these have not been reviewed in this paper. The chief shortcoming of analogue studies is the limitation they impose on generalizing the conclusions to clinical populations. The more closely the subject population approximates the clinical population in severity and character of the problem treated, the more valid it is to generalize from one to the other. Analogue studies involving undergraduate volunteers with severe test anxiety may be quite adequate to draw conclusions about the clinical treatment of test anxiety but are of less obvious relevance to the treatment of agoraphobics. Unfortunately, the problems treated in most analogue studies are less severe and of a different character from those usually encountered in clinical practice. Likewise, the more closely the therapy evaluated approximates clinical practice, the more valid the generalizations about that therapy in clinical practice. Many of the studies summarized in Table 7.2, for example, used extremely brief therapeutic interventions over short periods of time (see Table 7.3). Wolfe and Fodor (1977) used two two-hour group sessions one week apart in treating unassertive women. It is simply implausible that such a brief intervention, often by inexperienced therapists, will change lifelong irrational beliefs in the sense proposed by Ellis (1962).

The length of follow-up in the studies reviewed varies from zero to nine months (see Table 7.3). In view of the well-known difficulty in maintaining changes in behavior brought about by therapy of all types, across a wide variety of clinical problems, conclusions based on follow-up of less than six months are of questionable clinical significance. Only four of the studies summarized in Table 7.2 met this

TABLE 7.3
Methodological Features of Cognitive Therapy Studies

	Total duration		Therapists					
Authors	Number of Subjects	Therapy (hr)	Cognitive therapy (hr)	Graduate student	Experimenter	Follow-up (months)	Independent Assessment	Expectancy ratings
Biran, Augusto, & Wilson (1981)	3	15	7.5	Yes	?	9	No	No
Biran & Wilson (1981)	22	4	4	Yes	Yes	6	Yes	Yes
Emmelkamp, Kuipers, & Eggeraat (1978)	20	20[a]	10[a]	Yes	Yes[b]	1	Yes	No
Emmelkamp & Mersch (1982)	27	16[a]	16[a] or 11[a]	Yes	Yes[b]	1	Yes	No
Emmelkamp, van der Helm, van Zanten & Plochg (1980)	15	20	5	Yes	Yes[b]	6	Yes	No
Holroyd & Andrasik (1978)	39	8.75[a]	8.75[a] or 4.37[a]	?	Yes	1.5	No	Yes
Holroyd, Andrasik, & Westbroock (1977)	31	6	6	?	Yes	3.75	No	No
Jacobs & Cochran (1982)	42	16[a]	3[a]	Yes	?	1.5	No	No
Stravynski, Marks, & Yule (1982)	22	12	4	No	Yes	6	Yes	No
Wolfe & Fodor (1977)	64	4[a]	<4[a]	?	?	0	Yes	No
Zeiss, Lewinsohn, & Munoz (1979)	66	12	12	Yes	?	2	Yes	No

[a]Group therapy.
[b]Therapists supervised by experimenter.

199

criterion (see Table 7.3) and none of these demonstrated a significant contribution for cognitive therapy.

Studies are often conducted using graduate students or otherwise inexperienced therapists simply as a matter of expedience (see Table 7.3). Where comparisons are made between treatments and each treatment is equally susceptible to the effects of inexperience, the comparisons may yield valid conclusions of the relative efficacy of the treatments. Such studies may, however, underestimate the efficacy of all of the therapies, and this could result in a finding that the active treatment conditions were no more effective than an attention-placebo control group, as was found by Holroyd and Andrasik (1978).

Another common problem results when the experimenter is also the therapist or when the therapists are not blind to the hypothesis being tested. This may bias the way therapy is conducted and/or the therapists' ratings of patient progress. The use of independent assessors who are blind to the patient's treatment condition is one way of circumventing this latter problem.

As discussed above, unless there is evaluation of the patients' expectancy for improvement, the possibility exists that differences may be due to treatments of unequal credibility.

One problem to which these studies are particularly susceptible, and which surprisingly receives very little attention in the behavioral literature, is the possibility of a Type II or ß error, that is, concluding that there is no difference between treatments when, in fact, one exists. The small sample size employed in most of these studies and the probable poor compliance with therapeutic instructions make this a significant practical problem. The required sample size depends on the levels of α (Type I) error, ß (Type II) error, the size of a clinically significant difference between groups in the dependent measure, the standard deviation, and the kind of test statistic employed in the trial. Goldsmith (1979) has shown how a compliance rate of 50% can lead to a quadrupling of the sample size required to demonstrate a clinically significant effect. Fifty percent compliance is not uncommon in clinical outcome studies of various sorts (Dunbar, 1980).

The importance has already been emphasized of distinguishing "cognitive" therapy from therapies including innovative treatment procedures derived from cognitive theory *plus* behavioral methods of established efficacy. The objection may be raised that this distinction is academic and what really matters is that the therapy as actually practiced works. Cognitive therapists may object that the therapy they practice includes cognitive and behavioral methods and that they have never claimed that the cognitive procedures alone are sufficient (Beck et al., 1979; Ellis, 1979b). If these therapies are effective, however, only by virtue of their inclusion of existing behavioral methods, then nothing "revolutionary" has been added and perhaps nothing of value. The labeling of therapeutic practices is not without practical consequences. The vast majority of clinical psychotherapists are not familiar with the theoretical and practical intricacies discussed here; they equate cognitive therapy with the use of "cognitive" procedures whether Ellis, Beck, and Meichenbaum do or not. In the interests of effective therapy, it is important that the emphasis in labeling, teaching, and publications encourage the use of the most effective therapeutic strategies.

Future research could be improved by clearly defining the treatment procedures used in each treatment condition, by ensuring that therapists carry out the treatments defined, and by more frequent attention to component analysis designs. The cognitive therapies promoted by Ellis (1962) and Beck et al. (1979) are probably most in need of these improvements to future studies.

In this chapter we have deliberately chosen to focus on evaluating the clinical effects of those treatment procedures which have arisen as a result of the recent cognitive movement. We have eschewed evaluation of the cognitive theory underlying those procedures. It is worth stating, however, that there are many assumptions implicit in this approach to therapy which have not received empirical support and which have generally not been addressed in the studies reviewed here. Are cognitive distortions or irrational beliefs more common in neurotics than in normals? It is conceivable that cognitive distortions have more to do with treatment-seeking behavior than with neurotic behavior. Are they primary or secondary? Are they changed by effective therapy? Is cognitive therapy better at this than behavior therapy? Does changing these beliefs necessarily solve the clinical problem? Are the dependent measures used in these studies reliable and valid measures of these cognitive characteristics?

Conclusions

Cognitive therapy is an evolutionary rather than a revolutionary development in the field of behavior therapy. It is unique only in its greater emphasis on one class of behavior—cognitions. Several innovative therapeutic methods have been spawned as a result of this shift in emphasis, but these have not been demonstrated to be efficacious in the treatment of clinical populations. Cognitive therapy as actually practiced usually involves a variety of methods including behavioral procedures of established efficacy. Most of the claims made in support of cognitive therapy are based on studies employing these cognitive-behavioral methods. It remains to be demonstrated either that the new cognitive therapy procedures make a significant contribution to therapeutic outcome or that existing behavioral methods are rendered more effective when conceptualized in cognitive terms. The widespread adoption of cognitive treatment procedures is unwarranted on the basis of existing outcome data involving clinical populations.

References

Beck, A. T. (1976). *Cognitive therapy and the emotional disorders.* International Universities Press, New York.

Beck, A. T., Rush, A. J., Shaw, B. F. et al. (1979) *Cognitive therapy of depression.* Guilford Press, New York.

Biran, M., Augusto, F., & Wilson, G. T. (1981). In vivo exposure vs. cognitive restructuring in the treatment of scriptophobia. *Behav. Res. Ther.* 19, 525–532.

Biran, M., & Wilson, G. T. (1981). Treatment of phobic disorders using cognitive and exposure methods: A self-efficacy analysis. *J. Consult. Clin. Psychol.* 49, 886–899.

Comas-Diaz, L. (1981). Effects of cognitive and behavioral group treatment on the depressive symptomatology of Puerto Rican women. *J. Consult. Clin. Psychol.* 49, 627–632.

Dunbar, J. (1980). Adhering to medical advice: A review. *Int. J. Ment. Hlth* 9, 70–87.

Ellis, A. (1962). *Reason and emotion in psychotherapy.* Stuart, New York.

Ellis, A. (1970). *The essence of rational psychotherapy: A comprehensive approach to treatment.* Institute for Rational Living, New York.

Ellis, A. (1979a). On Joseph Wolpe's espousal of cognitive-behavior therapy. *Am. Psychol.* 34, 98–99.

Ellis, A. (1979b). A note on the treatment of agoraphobics with cognitive modification versus prolonged exposure in vivo. *Behav. Res. Ther.* 17, 162–164.

Emmelkamp, P. M. G., Kuipers, A. C. M. & Eggeraat, J. B. (1978). Cognitive modification versus prolonged exposure in vivo: A comparison with agoraphobics as subjects. *Behav. Res. Ther.* 16, 33–41.

Emmelkamp, P. M. G. & Mersch, P. P. (1982). Cognition and exposure in vivo in the treatment of agoraphobia: Short-term and delayed effects. *Cognit. Ther. Res.* 6, 77–88.

Emmelkamp, P. M. G., van der Helm, M., van Zanten B. L., & Plochg, I. (1980). Treatment of obsessive–compulsive patients: The contribution of self-instructional training to the effectiveness of exposure. *Behav. Res. Ther.* 18, 61–66.

Goldsmith, C. H. (1979). The effect of compliance distributions on therapeutic trials. In *Compliance in Health Care* (Edited by R. B. Haynes, D. W. Taylor & D. L. Sackett). Johns Hopkins University Press, Baltimore, Maryland.

Heppner, P. P. (1978). The clinical alteration of covert thoughts: A critical review. *Behav. Ther.* 9, 717–734.

Holroyd, K. A., & Andrasik F. (1978). Coping and the self-control of chronic tension headache. *J. Consult. Clin. Psychol.* 46, 1036–1045.

Holroyd, K. A., Andrasik, F. & Westbrook T. (1977). Cognitive control of tension headache. *Cognit. Ther. Res.* 1, 121–133.

Jacobs, M. K., & Cochran, S. D. (1982). The effects of cognitive restructuring on assertive behavior. *Cognit. Ther. Res.* 61, 63–76.

Kazdin, A. E., & Smith, G. A. (1979). Covert conditioning: A review and evaluation. *Adv. Behav. Res. Ther.* 2, 57–98.

Kuhn, T. A. (1970). *The structure of scientific revolutions* (2nd edn.). University of Chicago Press, Chicago, Ill.

Lang, P. J. (1968). Fear reduction and fear behavior: Problems in treating a construct. In *Research in Psychotherapy,* Vol. III, p. 90 (Edited by T. M. Shlein). American Psychological Association, Washington D.C.

Ledwidge, B. (1978). Cognitive behavior modification: A step in the wrong direction? *Psychol. Bull.* 85, 353–375.

Luria, A. (1961). *The role of speech in the regulation of normal and abnormal behavior.* Liveright, New York.

Mahoney, M. J. (1974). *Cognition and behavior modification.* Ballinger, Cambridge, Mass.

Meichenbaum, D. (1977). *Cognitive–behavior modification: An integrative approach.* Plenum, New York.

Mowrer, O. H. (1947). On the dual nature of learning: A reinterpretation of "conditioning" and "problem solving." *Harvard Educ. Rev.* 17, 102–148.

Mowrer, O. H. (1960). *Learning theory and the symbolic processes.* Wiley, New York.

Phillips, L. W. (1981). Roots and branches of behavioral and cognitive practice. *J. Behav. Ther. Exp. Psychiat.* 12, 5–17.

Rachman, S. J. (1978). *Fear and courage.* Freeman, San Francisco, California.

Rachman, S. J., & Wilson, G. T. (1980). *The effects of psychological therapy.* Pergamon Press, Oxford.

Rush, A. J., Beck, A. T., Kovacs, M., & Hollon, S. (1977). Comparative efficacy of cognitive therapy and pharmachotherapy in the treatment of depressed outpatients. *Cognit. Ther. Res.* 1, 17–37.

Shaw, B. F. (1977). Comparison of cognitive therapy and behavior therapy in the treatment of depression. *J. Consult. Clin. Psychol.* 45, 543–551.

Skinner, B. F. (1953). *Science and human behavior.* The Free Press, New York.

Sohn, D., & Lamal, P. A. (1982). Self-reinforcement: Its reinforcing capability and its clinical utility. *Psychol. Rec.* 32, 179–203.

Stravynski, A., Marks I., & Yule, W. (1982). Social skills problems in neurotic outpatients. Social skills training with and without cognitive modification. *Arch. Gen Psychiat.* 39, 1378–1385.

Sweet, A. A. (1982). The therapeutic relationship in behavior therapy. *Clinical Psychology Review,* in press.

Tryon, G. S. (1979). A review and critique of thought-stopping research. *J. Behav. Ther. Exp. Psychiat.* 10, 189–192.

Ullmann, L. P. (1981). Cognitions: Help or hindrance? *J. Behav. Ther. Exp. Psychiat.* 12, 19–23.

Wilson, G. T. (1978). Cognitive behavior therapy: Paradigm shift or passing phase? In *Cognitive behavior therapy: Research and application* (Edited by J. Foreyt and D. Rathjen). Plenum, New York.

Wilson, G. T., & Evans, I. M. (1977). The therapist–client relationship in behavior therapy. In *Effective psychotherapy: A handbook of research* (Edited by A. S. Gurman and A. M. Razin. Pergamon, New York.

Wolfe, J. L., & Fodor, I. G. (1977). Modifying assertive behavior in women: A comparison of three approaches. *Behav. Ther.* 8, 567–574.

Wolpe, J. (1958). *Psychotherapy by reciprocal inhibition.* Stanford University Press, Stanford, California.

Wolpe, J. (1973). *The practice of behavior therapy* (2nd Edn.). Pergamon Press, New York.

Wolpe, J. (1976). Behavior therapy and its malcontents—I. Denial of its bases and psychodynamic fusionism. *J. Behav. Ther. Exp. Psychiat.* 7, 1–5.

Wolpe, J. (1978). Cognition and causation in human behavior and its therapy. *Am. Psychol.* 33, 437–446.

Zeiss, A. M., Lewinsohn, P. M., & Munoz, R. F. (1979). Nonspecific improvement effects in depression using interpersonal skills training, pleasant activity schedules, or cognitive training. *J. Consult. Clin. Psychol.* 47, 427–439.

8

Paradoxical Intention in Behavior Therapy: A Review of the Experimental Literature

L. MICHAEL ASCHER AND ROBERT A. DiTOMASSO

One of the major aims of this book is to present to the reader a critical review of the research which tests the clinical efficacy of the most commonly employed behavioral techniques. The studies yielding the data which are considered in these reviews must meet the generally accepted criteria for valid experimental procedure. In comparison to the other techniques considered in this book, paradoxical intention, the focus of the present chapter, has a unique relationship with behavior therapy. Unlike other treatments such as desensitization, flooding, assertive training, and covert conditioning, the context within which paradoxical intention emerged was existential philosophy as opposed to learning theory. It is only recently, then, that behavior therapists, intrigued by reports of the success of paradoxical intention from other therapeutic orientations, have begun to incorporate this procedure into their repertoires. Since experimental validation of the clinical efficacy of therapeutic techniques employed by nonbehaviorally oriented therapists is generally not undertaken, a vast majority of the nonbehavioral literature supporting the utilization of paradoxical intention is composed of uncontrolled case studies.

More recently, however, the literature on paradoxical intention has begun to reflect the burgeoning interest of behavior therapists in this technique. This trend is evidenced by the appearance of well-

The authors wish to acknowledge the assistance of Ms. Ruth Greenberg in the preparation of this chapter.

controlled single-case experimental studies and between-subjects experiments designed to validate the successful clinical performance of the procedure. In this chapter we will present a critical review of those published studies which evaluate paradoxical intention and which adhere to accepted principles of experimental design. In view of the death of such reports, the reader may wonder about the timeliness of such a chapter. Some may even suggest that we have been premature in our contribution. However, our purpose is not merely to present a body of literature for critical review, but to suggest to behavior therapists the potential usefulness of a technique which has been successfully employed by clinicians of alternative orientations for more than three decades.

Paradoxical intention is a procedure developed by Victor Frankl (1955, first English reference) and employed within the context of logotherapy. The client is encouraged to intend, hope for, and court, the very thing that he or she is trying to avoid. Thus, the sleep onset insomniac is told to try to remain awake, the agoraphobic is instructed to leave the house and become as anxious as possible. The success of the technique is assumed to be due to the incompatibility of the paradoxical intention with the performance anxiety and the client's attempts to reduce this discomfort.

History

The historical roots of paradoxical intention in the field of behavior therapy can be traced to the initial experiments conducted by behavioral clinicians to study the technique. Although descriptions of paradoxical-like procedures (e.g., negative practice) have appeared in the behavioral literature for some years (e.g., Dunlap, 1928, 1932, 1946), the systematic application and experimental investigation of one of these techniques, paradoxical intention, did not occur until 1972. At that time, Solyom, Garza-Perez, Lediwidge, and Solyom (1972) conducted a pilot study to determine whether paradoxical intention could be useful in reducing the frequency of obsessions. Despite the failure to use adequate controls and some difficulty in assessing their data, this study was instrumental in demonstrating that paradoxical intention could serve as the focus of experimental scrutiny.

Ascher (1975) and Ascher and Efran (1978) presented the first controlled case studies utilizing paradoxical intention with sleep-onset insomnia. Their results indicated that paradoxical intention could be effective in reducing sleep-onset latency. This work was later corroborated by additional controlled case studies conducted by Relinger, Bornstein, and Mungus (1978) and by Relinger and Bornstein (1979).

Finally, Turner and Ascher (1979) conducted the first randomly assigned between-groups experiment which investigated the efficacy of paradoxical intention. Individuals complaining of clinically significant levels of sleep-onset insomnia were assigned to one of three treatment groups (paradoxical intention, progressive relaxation, stimulus control) or to one of two control groups (attention, waiting list). Analysis of the results failed to yield a significant difference among the three treatment groups, or between the two control groups, but did show a significant difference between the treatment groups on one hand and the control groups on the other. In a partial replication of this study, Ascher and Turner (1979) again randomly assigned sleep-onset insomniacs to a paradoxical intention treatment group, or to either an attention control group or a waiting-list control group. The results corroborated those of Turner and Ascher (1979) by indicating a significant difference between the paradoxical intention group and the two control groups. Later work has followed the model established by the aforementioned studies, but considerable investigation remains to be undertaken.

Cautions and Possible Contraindications

Although data permitting definitive statements regarding contraindications is lacking, the present section will be devoted to general hypotheses concerning selected issues.

Although therapist factors are important in the administration of any treatment procedure, certain techniques are probably more dependent upon therapist factors than others. For example, systematic desensitization has been employed, with excellent results, by a wide variety of clinicians exhibiting the full range of possible styles and characteristics. Because of the nature of the technique, it is not especially dependent upon the specific therapist (Wolpe, 1962) nor, for that matter, is even the presence of a therapist (at least in person) necessary for the effective use of this procedure (Lang, Melamed, & Hart, 1970). However, DeVoge and Beck (1978) have reviewed some evidence to suggest that therapist characteristics can interact with the desensitization technique and enhance its efficacy. The efficacy of this procedure, therefore, may to some extent be mediated by the characteristics of the therapist. As a further example of this notion, consider covert sensitization. Here the clinician must be skillful in presenting aversive scenes of sufficient detail to disgust the client without the therapist himself experiencing discomfort.

Paradoxical intention (and paradoxical interventions in general), we suspect, may be subsumed under the category of those techniques which are especially sensitive to therapist characteristics. One important aspect of the technique would appear to be the clinician's understanding of, and facility with, therapeutic paradox. It is perhaps best that the therapist view paradox as a pervasive phenomenon, rather than as a specific set of techniques to be applied in a relatively mechanical fashion. One of the dangers of the latter approach might be a tendency for the therapist to view paradoxical intention as a form of subterfuge (employed only for the client's benefit, of course). Under most circumstances, the therapist may somehow communicate this attitude to the client, who will either resist being "tricked" or having been "tricked," will feel foolish. In either case, damage to the therapeutic relationship will result.

Frankl (1955) suggests that the context of paradoxical intention is humor. While this possibly depends upon the clinician's theoretical position, an examination of the case reports of therapists espousing diverse orientations reveals the widespread, if not universal, use of a significant component of humor. To the extent that this humorous attitude on the part of the therapist facilitates the administration of the technique and enhances its probability of success, paradoxical intention is probably best employed by clinicians whose approach to therapy allows the use of humor. Naturally, since we are dealing with speculation rather than experimentally supported relationships, the above statement must not be interpreted to suggest that a clinician who is not comfortable or otherwise lacks the facility to operate therapeutically with humor should avoid paradoxical techniques; but rather that humor can aid the utilization of paradoxical intention in a variety of ways. On the other hand, such a clinician would probably be well-advised to avoid the use of humor in therapy, since the concomitant discomfort on the part of the therapist and the client would certainly not be helpful in achieving therapeutic goals.

In the case of client factors, the most obvious caution would seem to be directed toward the use of paradoxical intention with maladaptive approach behaviors such as pedophilia and other sexual offenses, as well as those behaviors which pose threats to health maintenance, for example, drug and alcohol abuse, smoking, or overeating. Most therapists would be well-advised to approach these problems utilizing well-supported treatments of choice noted for having good face validity and being devoid of paradox. On the other hand, some individual therapists who are comfortable with using paradox in therapy have successfully employed it to reduce these problem activities (e.g., Farrelly & Brandsma, 1974).

Paradoxical intention is possibly most successfully employed with clients who are generally compliant and who complain of anxiety-based behavior which seems to be out of their control (e.g., sexual dysfunction). On the other hand, this procedure would seem to be less useful with obviously resistive individuals who present with behavioral problems which appear to be emitted on a voluntary basis (e.g., aggressive behavior). Finally, paradoxical intention is probably best avoided in dealing with crisis situations or periods of instability, such as acute decompensation or situational grief (Rohrbaugh et al., 1977).

Description

Although the tenets of paradoxical intention have been in existence for some time, the specific label was first employed by Viktor Frankl in the context of logotherapy (1955). In his initial writing, as well as in the large body of subsequent work (e.g., 1975, 1978), Frankl details the role of paradoxical intention in logotherapy, suggests clinical problems with which it has been effective in his experience, and provides instructions for the utilization of the technique. Frankl has been primarily interested in using paradoxical intention to ameliorate the discomfort of agoraphobics, obsessives, and compulsives, though he has also addressed other difficulties, such as insomnia, hydrophobia, and erythrophobia. According to Frankl, anticipatory anxiety which the client experiences prior to entering a sensitive situation produces responses which are in opposition to the client's goal. For example, an individual who fears blushing in specific situations might become anxious and flushed prior to entering these situations. Frankl approaches his clients with instructions to increase the particular behavior that they wish to avoid. Thus, the agoraphobic who thinks that she will experience cardiac arrest if she leaves her home is encouraged to take a long walk and have numerous heart attacks.

Paradoxical intention is probably best administered with behaviors whose functioning can be influenced by the sympathetic nervous system. We use the term *influenced* to refer to processes which are directly affected by the sympathetic nervous system (e.g., blushing, perspiration) as well as those processes which are indirectly affected by this system through the mediation of anxiety (e.g., insomnia, travel restriction of agoraphobia). It is hypothesized that certain individuals become generally concerned about the performance of responses which are influenced by the sympathetic nervous system. Upon entering situations which are relevant to the operation of such responses, the individual attempts to take control of those aspects of sympathetic activity of which he or she is aware. Control takes the form of an attempt to reduce the anxiety which the individual experiences in anticipating the impending situation and the concomitant performance difficulties. The various coping strategies employed in an effort to maintain anxiety at a low level typically fail, resulting in an increasing spiral of discomfort which can, in some cases, end in a panic attack, as is often the case in agoraphobia (Ascher, 1980).

The goal of the paradoxical intention procedure is to move the client from the point at which he or she is seriously concerned about symptoms and is therefore resisting them, to a point at which he or she is more comfortable with the symptoms and is willing to "intend" them or bring them on. The central component of the paradoxical intention instructions requires the client to produce and enhance the symptoms which he or she is trying to resist. A number of ancillary aspects of the procedure are important in assisting the client to make the appropriate shift in attitude toward the symptoms which is necessary for him or her to carry out the paradoxical intention. For example, as was mentioned above, Frankl administers paradoxical intention in the context of humor (1955). It is his position that to the extent that the client can laugh at his or her symptoms, improvement has been demonstrated and the possibility of the client succeeding with paradoxical intention increases.

To support Frankl's contention of the efficacy of paradoxical intention, numerous uncontrolled case reports describing the success of the technique with a wide variety of disorders have continuously appeared in the literature over the course of more than two decades. Recently, a small number of papers have been published which present data from acceptably controlled studies. It is these data which will be the exclusive focus of this chapter. We have chosen to exclude the large body of case studies in an effort to increase the validity of any concessions which may be known. It is our purpose, then, in the research section of this chapter to critically examine the clinical research designed to evaluate the hypothesis that paradoxical intention is an effective technique for the treatment of behavior disorders.

Moreover, we will evaluate only those studies which are exclusively associated with paradoxical intention per se and thereby ignore studies of other similar paradoxical procedures, for instance, prescribing the symptom (Haley, 1963). This decision is based mainly on our desire that the orientations of the chapter and the book be congruent. Of the paradoxical procedures, paradoxical intention has been most closely associated with behavior therapy (e.g., Ascher, 1979; Frankl, 1975). Paradoxical intention can also be differentiated from other paradoxical techniques on the basis of the number of controlled experimental studies with which it has been associated.

Research

Agoraphobia

To date there are only two investigations of the use of paradoxical intention in the treatment of agoraphobics. In one study Ascher (1981) evaluated the effectiveness of paradoxical intention for the restriction of travel experienced by agoraphobics. Ten agoraphobics (nine females and one male) were randomly divided into two groups. In one group (A) subjects received gradual exposure *in vivo* for six sessions following a baseline period and subsequently were instructed to employ paradoxical intention. In the other group (B) subjects received paradoxical intention for six sessions immediately following a baseline period. Outcome was assessed by a behavioral approach test developed by the investigator. Two maximally difficult target locations were selected. The route from the client's home to the target was divided into 10 serial components. These components were generally based on geographical landmarks. Subjects were assigned a score of one point for the successful completion of each behavioral test component; thus their score could range from 0 to 20 on a single behavioral approach test. Clients were required to take this test once each week.

Analysis of pretest behavioral approach scores confirmed the comparability of the two groups. Intragroup statistical analysis in group A revealed that after six weeks of treatment with gradual exposure no change from baseline was evident. In contrast, after six weeks of paradoxical intention the subjects in group B moved significantly closer to their target. Moreover, a comparison of each treatment between groups revealed that subjects who received paradoxical intention were significantly more improved than subjects who received gradual exposure.

There is an important limitation in this study: the treatment was delivered by a single therapist (who was also the author). Therapist expectancy and personality are confounded with treatment and therefore limit generalizations in contrast to situations in which a blind therapist and therapists with different personalities are used. Second, in group A it is impossible to decipher the effects of paradoxical intention alone as multiple treatment interference jeopardizes the external validity of the design.

In a more recent study on the use of paradoxical intention with agoraphobics (Mavissakalian, Michelson, Greenwald, Kornblith, & Greenwald, 1983), 26 patients who met the *DSM III* criteria for agoraphobia were randomly assigned to either paradoxical intention or self-statement training conditions. Subjects were screened such that those included met the following criteria: (1) onset before age 40, (2) problem duration of at least one year, (3) absence of depression, (4) fear of leaving home or being in public places, and (5) a diagnosis of agoraphobia by *DSM III* criteria. All patients were instructed to gradually withdraw and stop all psychotropic medications two weeks prior to treatment. Despite this some continued to use tranquilizers. Thus, some subjects were taking medication while others were not. The sample comprised 22 females and 4 males with an average of 41.5 years and a mean problem duration of 10 years. About half of the subjects were unemployed and over 90% had received psychotherapy previously.

With regard to treatment each subject received twelve 90-minute sessions in a group of four or five subjects. There were three groups in each condition. Treatment was provided by a PhD clinical psychologist with experience in cognitive behavioral therapy. An MS research assistant who was present at all therapy sessions conducted three consecutive sessions for four groups, two in each condition, when the main therapist was absent. The therapists met to discuss and review treatment sessions.

The assessment battery for this investigation included clinical ratings of severity for the following variables: illness, phobia, anxiety, panic, and depression. Also, behavioral, self-report, and cognitive measures were gathered. All measures were obtained at pretest, midpoint, posttest, and one and six months follow-up. The behavioral measure consisted of a behavioral avoidance test. Cognitive assessments were obtained during the behavioral test by tape recordings which were then blind coded by three independent raters into four categories: self-defeating, coping, paradoxical, and neutral task-irrelevant conditions.

The findings indicated that there was a significant improvement on almost all measures with no differences between treatments. Analysis at midpoint, posttest, and follow-up holding pretest as a covariate revealed that paradoxical intention was significantly better on fear and anxiety measures. However, at one month the advantage was lost. Matched correlated *t* tests to evaluate within-group (pre–post) change revealed that paradoxical intention was significantly better on 10 variables, self-statement training on only 3. Paradoxical intention manifested improvements on measures not judged critical to agoraphobia.

From a methodological perspective there are several points to consider. First, the fact that over 90% of the subjects received prior treatment limits generalizability in contrast to a situation in which subjects received no prior therapy. Second, two of the patients dropped out of the study, but there is no mention about where the attrition occurred. Thus, subject mortality is an issue here. Third, during three consecutive sessions for four of the groups (two from each condition), the research assistant delivered treatment while the main therapist was absent. Third, univariate analyses were employed where multivariate analysis was indicated.

Functional Urinary Retention

There is only one quasi-experimental multiple-case investigation of paradoxical intention in the treatment of psychogenic urinary retention. In this study Ascher (1979) selected from a larger subject pool only those patients (*n* = 5) who were dissatisfied with the results of a conventional comprehensive behavioral treatment program for functional urinary retention. The research design was an ABC model. Subjects collected baseline measurements for two weeks (phase A), after which during an eight-week period (phase B) subjects received a behavioral package including systematic desensitization, covert positive reinforcement, thought stopping, a cognitive intervention, relaxation, imaginal exercises for homework, and *in vivo* assignments (e.g., increase fluid intake, enter bathroom when urinary urgency is experienced). In the final period (phase C) lasting from one to six weeks paradoxical intention was introduced whereby subjects were instructed to (1) enter a bathroom, (2) engage in all of the appropriate activities associated with urinating, and (3) not urinate (prohibition). Outcome was assessed by the subject's reports of discomfort ratings (0–100), which the author reported to be highly correlated with latency to urination.

The findings revealed a relatively rapid increase in comfort while urinating in public restrooms following the introduction of paradoxical intention. Moreover, within six weeks the subjects reported little or no anxiety when urinating in public restrooms and were satisfied with latency to urination. An informal follow-up at six months revealed that none of the subjects experienced an increase in anxiety while urinating in public restrooms. In addition, four of the five subjects remained completely satisfied with latency to urination. One individual experienced occasional difficulty, which was alleviated by the reintroduction of the paradoxical directive. The author concluded that paradoxical intention was effective with five cases which were resistant to a more comprehensive package.

This conclusion must be interpreted tentatively at best for a number of reasons. First, the paradoxical strategy was introduced after a multicomponent behavioral package and must be viewed in this context. In other words, multiple treatment interference or sequential confounding prevents one from concluding that similar change would have been observed had the paradoxical treatment been introduced initially. This limits generalizations to the situation in which paradoxical intention is presented alone without the prior behavioral package. Furthermore, one may reasonably make a case for a number of threats to internal validity such as history, maturation, testing, and regression artifacts. The reintroduction of a baseline phase would be needed to substantially increase the rigor of this design by ruling out the above-listed factors as sources of alternative hypotheses. In addition, the subjective nature of the dependent variable (SUDS) makes this measurement vulnerable to bias. Finally, replication by other therapists is indicated. In view of the above criticisms, then, the conclusions of this study can be viewed as a tentative demonstration in need of further replication.

Insomnia

The incorporation of paradoxical intention within a behavioral framework was initiated by Ascher (1975), who successfully treated insomniacs who had not responded well to systematic desensitization or to progressive muscle relaxation. Clients were instructed to remain awake as long as possible with a rationale that depended on their previous treatment. Unfortunately, however, the lack of data makes it difficult to ascertain the efficacy of the treatment in this study.

As a follow-up to Ascher (1975), Ascher and Efran (1978) conducted a multiple-case study of the ABC variety. Five sleep-onset insomniacs who were unusually resistant to a standard behavioral program were successfully treated with a course of paradoxical intention. Subjects collected baseline data for a two-week period and then received a 10-week conventional behavioral program comprising deep muscle relaxation, instructions designed to modify sleeping arrangements, systematic desensitization, and covert conditioning. After the traditional package failed to produce a desirable level of clinical improvement, paradoxical instructions were introduced and subjects were given the usual instruction to intentionally prolong their sleep-onset latency. For four of the subjects treatment was terminated at this point. However, for the remaining subject a return to baseline for three weeks was followed by a three-week course of paradoxical intention.

Thus, within this investigation we have four subjects studied in an ABC design and one subject clustered within an ABCAB design. An inspection of minutes to sleep onset latency revealed that while on the second week of baseline subjects took an average of about 50 minutes to fall asleep, the introduction of the conventional program reduced this variable to only 40 minutes on the average. However, following paradoxical intention the average sleep onset latency was about 10 minutes. For the remaining subject the reintroduction of baseline resulted in worsening, as evidence by an average of 30 minutes latency to sleep onset. Paradoxical intention resulted in a reduction again to about 7 minutes. A critical analysis of this study reveals that the ABC is only a weak test of treatment in that there is no return to baseline, which would rule out a number of internal validity threats. The ABCAB design is much better in this regard. Nonetheless, in both designs one cannot conclude that paradoxical intention alone accounted for the results, since the treatment was preceded by a multicomponent behavioral package.

Another study which suffers from some shortcomings was conducted by Relinger et al. (1978). In a follow-up to Ascher (1975), they treated a 31-year-old woman with chronic insomnia. The client suffered repeated awakenings and sleep onset difficulties of 20 years' duration. She was instructed to collect baseline recordings on eight self-report variables for three weeks and also during the treatment phase, which consisted of five daily 30-minute sessions. The paradoxical tactic involved having the client attempt to remain awake as long as possible in order that she could become aware of thoughts to be used in a quasi-desensitization placebo procedure. A counterdemand condition was also used in that the client was informed not to expect improvement until the end of treatment.

Time series analysis of the data revealed significant improvement on the following dimensions: sleep-onset latency, frequency of falling back to sleep with difficulty, degree of restfulness, and the patient's estimate of her personal functioning on the previous day. Finally, although the client's number of awakenings did not change during treatment, improvement on this variable was evident at follow-up. Despite the use of adequate control procedures to eliminate therapist attention and patient expectancies, as threats to internal validity, the weak nature of AB designs (Hersen & Barlow, 1976) allows only tentative conclusions to be drawn about the efficacy of the treatment. Moreover, it is important to recognize that counterdemand instructions conflict with the underlying rationale of paradoxical intention.

In another controlled multiple-case experimental design, Relinger and Bornstein (1979) studied the efficacy of paradoxical intention with chronic insomniacs who met several criteria. The authors employed a multiple baseline across subjects design. Outcome measures included daily sleep charts, the MMPI, and a questionnaire designed to assess subjective degree of improvement. To control for expectancy and attention, a counterdemand control was used. Moreover, treatment credibility and therapist characteristic ratings were gathered. Treatment consisted of five 30-minute daily sessions during which subjects were instructed to remain awake and record thoughts to be paired with neutral images in a quasi-desensitization paradigm. The data which were evaluated by statistics designed for single cases revealed that significant improvements occurred on the following variables: latency to sleep onset, number of awakenings, difficulty falling asleep, and degree of restfulness. These effects were maintained at 4-, 8-, and 12-week follow-up on estimates of subjective improvement on sleep-onset latency, subjective difficulty in falling asleep, and number of episodes of difficulty falling asleep.

Although the study was well executed, it did incorporate some difficulties. As mentioned previously, the use of a counterdemand is conceptually incompatible with that of paradoxical intention. In addition, the fact that the authors served as therapists permitted the possibility that they unintentionally biased the results. However, the use of a multiple baseline design, a good variety of dependent measures, and follow-up data yielded yet another reasonably good, multiple-case study supporting the efficacy of paradoxical intention.

In one of the most comprehensive and well-designed studies of paradoxical intention to date, Turner and Ascher (1979) compared this technique to two previously validated treatment strategies, progressive relaxation and stimulus control, as well as to a placebo condition and a no-treatment control group. Subjects who demonstrated clinically significant levels of primary insomnia were randomly assigned to one of the five experimental groups. The mean sleep-onset latency and mean problem duration were 62 minutes and 11 years, respectively. Outcome measures included the following: (1) latency to sleep onset, (2) number of awakenings with difficulty returning to sleep, (3) a restedness rating, (4) a rating of difficulty falling asleep, (5) number of hours of sleep, and (6) the number of nights per week on which medication was taken.

The findings demonstrated that the three treatments differed significantly from the control groups on all of the dependent measures except number of hours of sleep. Further, there were no significant differences among the three treatments, or between the two control conditions. These findings support the efficacy of paradoxical intention in the treatment of sleep-onset insomnia.

Particularly noteworthy from a methodological standpoint, Turner and Ascher (1979) employed a spouse-roommate reliability check, assessed the credibility of the treatments, and ruled out social acquiescence as an alternate hypothesis for the observed change. Moreover, the use of multivariate analysis for assessing outcome is striking in view of previous outcome research in behavior therapy. Thus, the statistical problem of probability pyramiding was effectively handled. One major flaw of this study was that all treatments were delivered by one of the authors. Consequently, therapist personality and expectancy cannot be ruled out as alternative hypotheses for change. The other difficulty was the strict reliance on subjective measures to assess therapeutic outcome.

In a replication study Ascher and Turner (1979) recruited insomniacs through newspaper ads. To be included in the study subjects had to meet one or more of the following criteria: (1) a one-hour sleep-onset latency on three or more occasions each week, (2) awakening subsequent to falling asleep on three or more occasions every week either with or without difficulty falling back to sleep, (3) feeling uncomfortable upon arising three or more times per week, and (4) experiencing primary as opposed to secondary insomnia. These criteria ensured the selection of a sample with clinically significant problems as evidenced by their mean sleep-onset latency of 65 minutes as well as the mean problem duration of 8 years. The sample included 10 males and 15 females with an average age of 39.

The authors collected four outcome measures based upon client self-ratings of the following: minutes to sleep-onset latency, number of night awakenings with difficulty returning to sleep, a restedness rating, and a rating of difficulty in falling asleep. Spouse-roommate checks were gathered to assess the reliability of information provided by the subjects. Finally, credibility ratings of the treatments as well as therapist ratings were obtained from the subjects.

Subjects were randomly assigned to three conditions: paradoxical intention, placebo, or wait-list control. In the paradoxical intention condition subjects were asked to remain awake as long as possible but not to engage in any activity incompatible with sleep. They were fully informed of the paradoxical rationale. Placebo subjects received a quasi-desensitization package which consisted of pairing 18 chronologically ordered bedtime activities with 6 neutral scenes plus homework practice. The no-treatment control subjects were not engaged in clinical activity during the study, although telephone contact was maintained approximately every 10 days.

A nonsignificant pretreatment MANOVA on the dependent variables ensured the comparability of the groups. A posttest Multivariate Analysis of Variance (MANOVA) revealed significant differences between groups. Post hoc analysis indicated that paradoxical intention differed from the controls on every variable except the restedness rating. The control groups did not differ from each other. Also, there was no difference in credibility across the conditions. Thus, this study provides support for the efficacy of paradoxical intention. Moreover, it does so using a clinical sample, reliability checks, and multivariate analysis of the data. Perhaps the two major shortcomings are reliance upon subject self-report and ambiguity regarding who delivered the treatment.

In a subsequent study Ascher and Turner (1980) evaluated the effectiveness of two methods of administering paradoxical intention. Again, subjects were recruited through newspaper ads and interviewed by an independent assessor to judge their appropriateness for the study. Subjects suffering from secondary insomnia were excluded. The final sample compared 40 subjects with a mean age of 37 years. The clinical nature of the sample was evidenced by the mean protracted sleep-onset latency of 70 minutes and a mean problem duration of 9 years. Subjects were randomly assigned to four conditions: paradoxical intention A (veridical explanation), paradoxical intention B (bogus explanation), placebo, and wait-list control. In condition A subjects were asked to remain awake and were informed of the relationship between performance anxiety and sleeping difficulties. In condition B subjects were asked to remain awake in order to become aware of anxiety-provoking thoughts. These thoughts were to be desensitized later. Placebo subjects received quasi-desensitization, the pairing of 18 hierarchical bedtime scenes with neutral images. Subsequent to treatment subjects completed a questionnaire designed to tap the credibility of the treatments and the quality of the therapeutic relationship. The following outcome measures were obtained: latency to sleep onset in minutes, number of awakenings with difficulty falling asleep, and number of hours of sleep.

The findings indicated that the type A procedure was significantly superior to the untreated control on every variable. Moreover, the type A treated subjects fared significantly better than the type B treated subjects and the placebo subjects on latency to sleep onset, restedness rating, and difficulty falling asleep. From a methodological standpoint these authors ruled out factors such as differential treatment credibility, therapist differences, and statistical probability pyramiding. However, one major concern relates to the identity of the therapist(s) in this study. Obviously, if the therapists were the authors, unintentional expectancy effects could be operating. Moreover, as pointed out by the authors, the type B subjects were told that desensitization would begin after the disturbing thoughts were collected. Consequently, these subjects were probably assuming that therapy had not yet begun, which may have diluted the potential effect of the type B procedure.

In the most recent study, Ott, Levine, and Ascher (1983) compared paradoxical intention, feedback from a sleep-monitoring unit, feedback plus paradoxical intention, and a no-treatment condition. Fifty-five subjects who had an average latency to sleep onset of 60 minutes were randomly assigned to groups. Random assignment as indicated by pretreatment analysis resulted in the groups being equivalent on age, problem duration, MMPI scores, and sex. Moreover, posttreatment analysis ruled out differences between the groups on adherence to instruction, correctness of the sleep log, and constancy of medication intake. Of special interest, these authors collected both subjective and objective measurements of sleep-onset latency. In addition, a counterdemand control was employed to counteract placebo effects. The findings of this investigation provide some support for the efficacy of paradoxical intention on both subjective and objective measures of sleep-onset latency. The major shortcoming of this study was the use of invariate analysis where a multivariate analysis was indicated. Thus, probability pyramiding is a statistical threat to validity. In addition, the senior author conducted all the sessions, introducing the possibility that his hypotheses might have biased the results. Also, the so-called objective measure of sleep onset was not completely objective in that it could be manipulated by the subject. Finally, the design does not seem suitable for the objectives as stated in the paper.

Encopresis and Chronic Constipation

Fecal incontinence, or encopresis, a lack of bowel control that results in the soiling of clothes, is usually associated with chronic constipation (Wright, 1973). It has recently been suggested that in those cases where traditional interventions have failed, a performance anxiety cycle may actually be operating to maintain and exacerbate this problem (Bornstein, Sturm, Retzlaff, Kirby, & Chong, 1981). In other words, the concern associated with defecation and appropriate toileting would increase anxiety, which in turn would further inhibit performance of the desired behavior.

In a recent single-case ABAB reversal design with one-year follow-up, Bornstein et al. (1981) treated a nine-year-old boy encopretic with paradoxical instruction. Although the child had been successfully toilet trained by age three, at age five he began to suffer infrequent bowel movements followed by soiling behavior for no apparent physical or psychological reason. Between the ages of five and nine the child had received a variety of interventions including laxatives, enemas, and hypnosis, all of which were to no avail. Soiling occurred on a daily basis while his bowel movements occurred once a week. Moreover, his encopresis was severely affecting his social interactions and peer relations. Behavioral analysis also revealed that the child had considerable anxiety associated with toileting and that the parents may have been inadvertently exacerbating the problem by forcing him to the bathroom whenever the duration of his constipation exceeded five days.

With the introduction of the ABAB design, the parents were asked to keep weekly records of soiling and bowel movements throughout the course of baseline and treatment. The paradoxical instruction was delivered in a form similar to the following prescription: (1) go to the bathroom every hour, (2) pull down your trousers, (3) sit on the toilet for five minutes, and (4) act as though you have to go but do not allow it to happen. The results were striking. During baseline I, the mean number of weekly soilings was approximately 7 with the mean number of appropriate bowel movements per week at .07. With the first introduction of paradoxical instruction soilings dropped to 0 and bowel movements increased to 4.3 per week. The reintroduction of baseline evidenced a reversal effect with a mean of 5 soilings and 5 bowel movements. Finally, paradoxical instruction was reinstituted with fading instructions in regard to visits to the bathroom. Soiling was completely eliminated and mean weekly bowel movements increased to 4.8. At one-year follow-up both changes were maintained.

The findings of this single-case study appear to support the efficacy and controlling effects of paradoxical instruction in the treatment of encopresis. Particularly noteworthy was the inclusion of a one-year follow-up. With regard to limitations, however, the investigators raise the important issue as to which among the components included in the treatment package actually accounted for change. Thus, paradoxical intention alone might not be validly credited with the total therapeutic gain.

Conclusion

The behavioral orientation to psychotherapy has as one of its requirements the empirical validation of those techniques subsumed under its label. Techniques which are initially of demonstrated effectiveness in the clinical setting, as reflected in uncontrolled case reports, must be experimentally validated through the collection of data yielded by appropriately controlled research. Behavior therapists, perhaps stimulated by the unsystematic reports of clinical success attributed to paradoxical intention, have recently begun to utilize this procedure in programs designed to modify behavioral complaints. It is characteristic that, as the result of this interest, a number of controlled case studies and experiments have appeared for the first time in the literature on paradoxical intention.

In the short time that such investigations have been conducted, the accumulation of data has not been sufficient to warrant valid conclusions regarding the efficacy of the technique. Further, although this small body of literature is composed of studies whose designs and data collection procedures generally compare favorably to the behavior therapy literature in general, there does exist one pervasive criticism. The possibility of experimenter bias is common to many of the studies. This is due to the fact that, in the relatively brief relationship which paradoxical intention has had with behavior therapy, a comparatively small number of investigators have been responsible for a majority of the reports. Notwithstanding this difficulty and some of the other shortcomings noted, the various studies taken as a whole do tentatively support the hypothesis that paradoxical intention, as a behavioral technique, is effective in modifying the specific complaints of clients suffering from primary insomnia and agoraphobia. The outcome data regarding the treatment of encopresis, although encouraging, are based on the results of one controlled single case. We therefore eagerly await direct and systematic replication in this area. Finally, at this time the available outcome data in the treatment of functional urinary retention are, relatively speaking, somewhat less convincing from a methodological standpoint and in our view remains undemonstrated. Our hope is that within the next few years more behavioral researchers will assume the task of further evaluating the efficacy of paradoxical intention in the context of methodologically sound single-case and between-group investigations. At this point paradoxical intention does indeed appear to be somewhat promising as a behavior therapy technique for certain problems.

References

Ascher, L. M. *Paradoxical intention as a component in the behavioral treatment of sleep onset insomnia: A case study.* Paper presented at the Association for the Advancement of Behavior Therapy, San Francisco, CA, December, 1975.

Ascher, L. M. Paradoxical intention in the treatment of urinary retention. *Behavior Research and Therapy*, 1979, *17*, 267–270.

Ascher, L. M. Paradoxical intention. In A. Goldstein & E. B. Foa (Eds.), *Handbook of behavioral interventions.* New York: Wiley, 1980.

Ascher, L. M. Employing paradoxical intention in the treatment of agoraphobia. *Behavior Research and Therapy*, 1981, *19*, 533–542.

Ascher, L. M., & Efran, J. S. The use of paradoxical intention in a behavioral program for sleep onset insomnia. *Journal of Consulting and Clinical Psychology*, 1978, *46*, 547–550.

Ascher, L. M., & Turner, R. M. Paradoxical intention and insomnia: An experimental investigation. *Behavior Research and Therapy*, 1979, *17*, 408–411.

Ascher, L. M., & Turner, R. M. A comparison of two methods for the administration of paradoxical intention. *Behavior Research and Therapy*, 1980, *18*, 121–126.

Bornstein, P. H., Sturm, C. A., Retzlaff, P. D., Kirby, K. L., & Chong, H. Paradoxical instruction in the treatment of encopresis and chronic constipation: An experimental analysis. *Journal of Behavior Therapy and Experimental Psychiatry*, 1981, *12*, 167–170.

DeVoge, J. T., & Beck, S. The therapist–client relationship in behavior therapy. In M. Hersen, R. M. Eisler, & P. M. Miller (Eds.), *Progress in behavior modification*. New York: Academic Press, 1978.

Dunlap, K. A revision of the fundamental law of habit formation. *Science*, 1928, *57*, 350–362.

Dunlap, K. *Habits, their making and unmaking*. New York: Liveright Publishing, 1932.

Dunlap, K. *Personal adjustment*. New York: McGraw-Hill, 1946.

Farrelly, F., & Brandsma, J. *Provocative therapy*, Fort Collins, CO: Shields, 1974.

Frankl, V. E. *The doctor and the soul: From psychotherapy to logotherapy*. New York: Knopf, 1955.

Frankl, V. E. Paradoxical intention and dereflection. *Psychotherapy: Theory, Research and Practice*, 1975, *12*, 226–237.

Frankl, V. E. The unheard cry for meaning. In *Psychotherapy and humanism*. New York: Simon & Schuster, 1978.

Haley, J. *Strategies of psychotherapy*. New York: Grune & Stratton, 1963.

Hersen, M., & Barlow, D. H. *Single case experimental designs: Strategies for studying behavior change*. New York: Pergamon Press, 1976.

Lang, P. J., Malamed, B. G., & Hart, J. A psychophysiological analysis of fear modification using all automated desensitization procedure. *Journal of Abnormal Psychology*, 1970, *76*, 220–234.

Mavissakalian, M., Michelson, L., Greenwald, D., Kornblith, S., & Greenwald, M. Cognitive-behavioral treatment of agoraphobia: Paradoxical intention vs self-statement training. *Behavior Research and Therapy*, 1983, *21*, 75–86.

Ott, B. D., Levine, B. A., & Ascher, L. M. Manipulating the explicit demand of paradoxical intention instructions. *Behavioral Psychotherapy*, 1983, *11*, 25–35.

Relinger, H., & Bornstein, P. H. Treatment of sleep onset insomnia by paradoxical instructions: A multiple baseline design. *Behavior Modification*, 1979, *3*, 203–222.

Relinger, H., Bornstein, P. H., & Mungas, D. M. Treatment of insomnia by paradoxical intention: A time series analysis. *Behavior Therapy*, 1978, *9*, 955–959.

Rohrbaugh, N., Tennen, H., Press, S., White, L., Raskin, P., & Pickering, M. *Paradoxical strategies in psychotherapy*. Paper presented at the American Psychological Association, San Francisco, CA, August, 1977.

Solyom, L., Garza-Perez, J., Ledwidge, B. L., & Solyom, C. Paradoxical intention in the treatment of obsessive thoughts: A pilot study. *Comprehensive Psychiatry,* 1972, *13,* 291–297.

Turner, R. M., & Ascher, L. M. Controlled comparison of progressive relaxation, stimulus control, and paradoxical intention therapies for insomnia. *Journal of Consulting and Clinical Psychology,* 1979, *47,* 500–508.

Wolpe, J. Isolation of a conditioned procedure as the crucial psychotherapeutic factor: A case study. *Journal of Nervous and Mental Disease,* 1962, *134,* 316–329.

Wright, L. Handling the encopretic child. *Professional Psychology,* 1973, *4,* 137–144.

9

The Token Economy

ALAN E. KAZDIN

Introduction

The token economy is an intervention based on the delivery of positive reinforcement for specific target behaviors. The reinforcers that are delivered consist of tokens (e.g., tickets, coins, stars, points) that can be exchanged for a variety of other rewards that vary with the particular clientele. The token economy has been used as a treatment or intervention technique with psychiatric patients, students (preschool through college age) in educational and special educational settings, delinquents, prisoners, alcohol and drug abusers, the mentally retarded, autistic children, geriatric patients, and others (see Kazdin, 1977). Also, many applications are conducted in community and other social settings and focus on energy conservation, littering, recycling of wastes, and job-related performance.

Evidence attesting to the effects of the token economy and the range of applications is too voluminous to review here. Rather than attempt a review, the present chapter examines characteristics of the token economy, conclusions that can be reached about its effects, contraindications and qualifications of treatment effects, and unresolved issues raised by the research. Substantive, assessment, and technological issues to which future research might be directed are also identified.

Completion of this paper was supported by a Research Scientist Development Award (MH00353) and a grant (MH35408) from the National Institute of Mental Health.

Historical Development

The token economy is based on extensions of basic research in operant conditioning, as elaborated by B. F. Skinner (1938). The intervention relies on the principle of positive reinforcement in which consequences are delivered contingent on behavior and increase the
frequency of that behavior. In a token economy, the consequences are
generalized conditioned reinforcers which refers to those events or
rewards that acquire their reinforcing value, because they can be
exchanged for, or are backed up by, a variety of other rewards.
Money, points, and tickets are common conditioned reinforcers used
in token economies and indeed in society at large.

Long before operant conditioning formally developed, generalized conditioned reinforcers had been used frequently to alter behavior in treatment, educational, and other settings (see Kazdin,
1978). Indeed, several historical applications closely resemble practices that would now be referred to as a token economy. One of the
more elaborate programs was developed in England by Joseph Lancaster (1778–1838), who was interested in providing education for
the poor in locations where resources for teachers or classrooms were
limited (Lancaster, 1805). In large classrooms ranging from 100 to
1,000 students, Lancaster implemented a "monitorial system"
whereby students in class served as assistants (or monitors) for their
peers. The monitors were responsible for such activities as teaching
small groups of students, asking questions, grading answers, and
noting misbehavior. Students received rewards for answering correctly on academic assignments and advancing through increasingly
difficult levels of work. Tickets were provided for mastery of lessons.
For especially excellent performance, students were given silver
medals to wear to convey their achievement. Prizes, pens, watches,
and other material rewards were also given to students or monitors
for their performance.

As another illustration, in the United States in the late 1880s,
also in educational settings, the "Excelsior School System" emerged
(Ulman & Klem, 1975). Students earned "merits" in various de-
nominations for such behaviors as punctuality, orderliness, and stu-
diousness. The merits could be exchanged for other rewards including special certificates of commendation from the teacher. An interesting component was involvement of the parents in the program
by providing them with feedback on their child's school performance
and encouraging them to ask their children about their earnings.

Precursors of contemporary token economies were evident in other settings. In Australia in the 1880s, Alexander Maconochie (1787–1860) developed the "mark system" in a prison for criminals with multiple convictions (Maconochie, 1847). The program was intended to overcome the inhumane methods of treating prisoners. A reward (mark) system was developed to promote positive behaviors that would facilitate subsequent adjustment of prisoners to society. Prison sentences were converted into a number of "marks" that needed to be earned. Marks were earned for work and appropriate conduct. They were exchangeable for essential items such as food and clothing; excess tokens could be saved to be exchanged for release.

These and other examples that might be cited convey the use of conditioned reinforcement antedating current applications of the token economy. The examples are especially interesting for two reasons. First, many of the programs closely resembled contemporary practices and utilized procedures (e.g., group contingencies, team competition, response cost) that only recently have been shown to enhance the efficacy of the token economy (see Kazdin, 1977). Second, some of the programs were applied widely. For example, in the late 1800s, Lancaster's system had spread rapidly in England and throughout the British Empire, Europe, Africa, Russia, Asia, South America, the United States, and Canada.

Despite the significance of the historical examples, contemporary token economies grew from direct extensions of laboratory research in operant conditioning (see Kazdin, 1978). Laboratory work, beginning in the 1930s, demonstrated the potency of reinforcement in altering behavior in a variety of infrahuman species. By the 1950s and 1960s, several laboratory extensions were underway to assess whether the methods of operant conditioning could be extended to human behavior (e.g., Ferster & DeMyer, 1961; Lindsley, 1956). Work initially focused on individual subjects who performed on laboratory tasks in experimental sessions. Extensions began to focus on clinical populations and the behaviors they performed in everyday life (e.g., Ayllon & Michaels, 1959).

The extension of token reinforcement to applied settings and to groups of subjects marks the emergence of contemporary token economies (e.g., Ayllon & Haughton, 1962). The program with the greatest impact was reported by Ayllon and Azrin (1965, 1968b), who devised a token economy to restructure a ward for psychiatric patients at Anna State Hospital in Illinois. Also, classroom applications emerged at the same time at Rainier School in Washington in which the effects of the token economy were demonstrated with mentally retarded students (e.g., Birnbrauer, Bijou, Wolf, & Kidder, 1965). These and several other programs provided the impetus for extension of the token economy to diverse clinical populations and settings.

Characteristics of the Token Economy

The Basic Token Program

Essentially, three ingredients are needed to begin a token program and include a token or medium of exchange, backup reinforcers and a set of rules that describe the interrelationships among behaviors and tokens and backup reinforcers. Tokens can consist of poker chips, cards, points, marks, stars, or any other medium that can be delivered and exchanged. Aside from the token, backup reinforcers are required. These reinforcers are purchased by the tokens. Backup events usually include consumables (e.g., food, chewing gum), high-probability behaviors (e.g., free time in class, watching television), money, clothes, cosmetics, and others. Backup reinforcers need not necessarily be elaborate or expensive. In many programs, persons can purchase free time to engage in activities on their own or are allowed to rent on a time-limited basis special equipment such as a radio or record player. The important feature of backup reinforcers is that persons are provided with a wide range of options. The initial and long-term value of the tokens depends upon the range of reinforcing events that back up the tokens. The selection of backup reinforcers for a given population is based upon identifying available privileges in the setting, observing behaviors and activities the clients perform when provided with free time, and soliciting client preferences for specific rewards.

The rules of the token economy require specifying several details about how and when tokens are earned, lost, and spent. It is useful to provide the rules in the clearest possible fashion. Indeed, clear instructions that specify the precise reinforcement contingencies can enhance the effects of reinforcement. To maximize clarity, some programs specify the contingencies in a written manual or post them conspicuously in the setting so that they can be referred to as needed.

An example of a recently reported token economy will help to illustrate the basic requirements. Token economies have been implemented in many hospitals that provide treatment for psychiatric patients. For example, Nelson and Cone (1979) used a token economy with 16 psychiatric patients on a locked ward. Both psychotic and mentally retarded patients were included in the sample. These patients were on a locked ward because of episodes of aggressive behavior and attempts to escape from the hospital. The program altered behavior in four general categories: general hygiene, personal management, work on the ward, and social skills. Within each category, several specific behaviors were identified. For example, social skills included behaviors such as verbally greeting staff, answering questions about the current hospital environment, and participating in group discussions. Behaviors that were included in each category were observed directly on the ward. Each behavior was associated with a value in terms of tokens (colored tickets) that would be delivered contingent upon its performance.

Patients were informed of the program in a general ward meeting in which the specific behaviors, tokens, backup events, and general rules were discussed. A "store" was made available in the setting which was opened at three different times during the day. Several commodities could be bought with token earnings including hot and cold beverages, fruit, biscuits, sweets, ice cream, cigarettes, records, wallets, and other items. To keep patients informed of the system, posters were placed on the ward that conspicuously indicated the target behaviors, token values, ward rules, and a schedule of activities.

The effects of the token reinforcement procedures were dramatic. Changes were evident for several behaviors within each general category mentioned earlier. In addition, ratings of the patients by the staff indicated improvements in several general areas such as social competence and interest, neatness, and decrements in patient irritability.

Options and Variations

Several procedures and technique options can be added to the basic program. The options and variations can be used for several reasons, such as increasing the effectiveness of the contingencies, making the program more acceptable to the clientele or staff, and making the procedures more convenient to implement. A few of the options that are commonly employed are noted briefly below.

The *type of contingencies* that are used provides several options in a token economy. Typically, reinforcement programs utilize contingencies based upon an individual client's performance. The client receives consequences for his or her own behavior. However, several other contingencies may be used in which the group is incorporated. One variation includes a group contingency in which performance of the *group as a whole* determines the consequences (tokens) that are administered to each individual. Another type of group contingency is *consequence sharing,* which often is used when a token program is designed for only one or a few persons. In such cases, the tokens earned by one person are delivered to that person as well as to his or her peers. The consequences are shared among persons even though these latter persons may not have worked for the tokens.

Several other variations of group contingencies and consequence sharing exist. The advantage of incorporating the group into the contingencies is that the group support, encouragement, and praise add important prompting and reinforcing consequences to the contingencies. For many populations and in many situations, peer-group contingencies may be more effective than those contingencies implemented by the staff. Group-based contingencies help take advantage of the important role of peers in altering behavior.

In addition to type of contingencies, token programs often vary in whether they use punishment. In particular, *response cost* has been used in many programs in the form of fines for engaging in undesirable behaviors. The convenience of response cost in part accounts for its extensive use. If tokens are provided for some behaviors, they can be withdrawn for others in the form of fines. Thus, a punishment contingency can be added to the program with little difficulty. Several studies have suggested that response cost is a valuable adjunct to a token program (see Kazdin, 1977).

Another option for a token economy is to utilize *peers* to administer the contingencies. In the usual program, of course, staff deliver tokens based upon their observations of the clients. However, peers may be used in this function as well. Occasionally, programs utilize *self-administered reinforcement* where persons provide their own consequences.

Group contingencies, consequence sharing, response cost, and peer- or self-administered contingencies represent major options for token economies. Variations of these procedures also exist, and so the basic token economy can be modified in several ways. Indeed, the large number of available options makes the token economy a highly flexible system. Perhaps it is this flexibility that partially accounts for its widespread application to diverse populations and settings.

Outcome Evidence

Types of Research

A major characteristic of operant conditioning research from which the token economy emerged has been investigation of one or a few subjects at one time in experimental designs in which subjects serve as their own controls. Frequency or rate of behavior is observed while the subject is exposed to different experimental and control conditions. Single-case designs rely on continuous assessment of performance for a period of several days or more in which the intervention is evaluated (see Hersen & Barlow, 1976; Kazdin, 1982). The designs can be extended to groups of subjects, the group (e.g., students in a classroom, patients on a ward) being treated as a single subject. Most investigations of the token economy have used single-case designs in which the token economy is alternately presented and withdrawn (ABAB design) or introduced to different clients at different points in time (multiple-baseline design).

Recently, between-group designs have been used with increased frequency, in part because of the type of experimental and clinical questions that have been asked of the token economy. Early research focused on the most basic outcome question, namely, does the token economy produce behavior change? Single-case designs, mentioned above, are quite well suited to this question by comparing performance of the same subjects across different phases. Changes in performance from baseline (no treatment) to intervention (token economy) phases usually can be readily detected, especially if the effects are replicated (repeated) at different points in time during the investigation. Between-group designs have become especially important to address many questions beyond the ability of the token economy to produce change.

First, with single-case designs, it is difficult to evaluate the magnitude of change produced by the token economy relative to no treatment or to an alternative intervention. In single-case designs, the token economy is often alternated with a no-treatment (baseline or return-to-baseline) phase. Yet pretreatment baselines may not remain constant over the course of an investigation and hence do not provide an estimate of the changes over time that might take place without treatment. Return-to-baseline phases also may not provide an estimate of what performance would be like because such phases follow the withdrawal of treatment. The level of performance after treatment is withdrawn may be very different from what it would be like if treatment had not been provided at all. Between-group designs have been useful in addressing the magnitude of change. Separate groups are used, one of which receives the token economy and the other which does not. The amount of change produced by the token economy over and above changes associated with the passage of time alone can be evaluated. Of course, when the investigator is interested in evaluating the magnitude of change over the course of a long-term follow-up, between-group designs are essential. Comparisons of the token economy and no treatment or routine treatment control groups have demonstrated marked effects of the token economy (e.g., Herman, deMontes, Dominguez, Montes, & Hopkins, 1973; McAllister, Stachowiak, Baer, & Conderman, 1969).

A second reason for the increased use of between-group designs has been the interest in comparative research where separate interventions are contrasted. It may not be feasible to present the separate interventions to the same subjects because the procedures provide conflicting rationales or techniques. Even if two or more treatments could be applied, their juxtaposition in different phases of a within-subject design might be problematic. When two or more treatments are given to the same subjects, the possibility of multiple-treatment interference exists, that is, the effects of one treatment may be influenced by other, preceding treatment(s) the subjects received. Comparison of alternative treatments in between-group designs permits evaluation of each treatment without the influence of the other(s). Major comparative studies, utilizing between-group designs, have contrasted the token economy with such alternative procedures as milieu therapy and routine hospital care for psychiatric patients (Paul & Lentz, 1977), diverse educational programs for disadvantaged children in classroom settings (Bushell, 1978), and detention and probation for delinquent youths (Jones, Weinrott, & Howard, 1981; Kirigin, Wolf, Braukmann, Fixsen, & Phillips, 1979).

Often, the investigator is interested in constructing a new treatment by combining alternative techniques. Such research evaluates the effects of a procedure such as the token economy alone and when combined with some other treatment. Evaluation of different combinations of treatment usually requires between-group comparisons to avoid the problem of multiple-treatment interference. Several studies have evaluated the token economy alone and in combination with other active treatments. For example, investigations with psychiatric patients have compared the token economy alone and in combination with milieu treatment (e.g., Greenberg, Scott, Pisa, & Friesen, 1975) and antipsychotic medication (e.g., McCreadie, Main, & Dunlop, 1978).

A third use of between-group designs has been to evaluate large-scale applications of the token economy. Large-scale investigations utilize several settings and locations. Also, alternative treatments commonly are compared in the design. Given the magnitude of the project (e.g., several schools, cities, hospitals), continuous assessment on a daily basis over time may not be feasible because the requisite resources (e.g., number of observers, daily travel) are prohibitive. Assessment at a few points in time (e.g., pretreatment, posttreatment, and follow-up), commonly used in between-group designs, may present a more feasible alternative. Relatively few large-scale applications of the token economy exist, but they convey the utility and need for between-group designs (e.g., Bushell, 1978; Jones et al., Note 1; Rollins, McCandless, Thompson, & Brassell, 1974).

Finally, between-group research is essential for examining the separate and combined effects of different variations of a token economy. The investigator may be interested in studying two or more variables simultaneously (e.g., feedback and token reinforcement). Two levels of each variable (feedback vs. no feedback; contingent vs. noncontingent token reinforcement) may be combined. It is extremely cumbersome to investigate the different conditions and their interaction in a single-case design, leaving aside the problems of sequence and multiple-treatment interference effects. However, factorial designs permit evaluation of the separate and combined effects of different variables by providing different levels and combinations of variables to different groups (e.g., Kazdin, 1973).

In general, evaluation of treatment techniques such as the token economy can raise a variety of outcome questions. These questions entail whether the token economy is more effective than no treatment, what components encompassed by the technique are essential, what parameters can be varied to enhance outcome, whether entirely new procedures can be combined with the token economy to make it more effective, and whether the token economy is more effective in achieving a particular end than alternative treatments. With increased demonstrations of the effectiveness of the basic procedure, research attention has shifted to the broader range of questions and to the increased use of between-group designs.

Efficacy of the Token Economy

The token economy has been evaluated in hundreds of outcome studies which, of course, are beyond review here (see Kazdin, 1977). As noted earlier, applications have encompassed a large variety of populations. Even within particular populations the diversity of applications is broad. For example, among psychiatric populations, token economies have been applied to acute, chronic, organic brain syndrome, psychosomatic and neurotic patients, and children, adolescents, and adults. The token economy has also been extended in several demonstration projects applied outside of the traditional realm of treatment, education, and rehabilitation to the community and social problems (e.g., consumption of home energy or car fuel). Indeed, there probably is no other psychosocial intervention that has been applied as broadly to diverse populations and settings and at the same time has generated as much empirical research as the token economy.

The outcome evidence has indicated that the token economy is extremely effective in producing change in specific target behaviors while the program is in effect. Also, the changes in specific behaviors often are reflected in much broader changes as well. For example, reinforcement of specific adaptive behaviors on the ward among psychiatric patients often is associated with other changes such as improvements in symptomatic behaviors, mood, social interaction, and subsequent community adjustment (e.g., Gripp & Magaro, 1971; Grzesiak & Locke, 1975; Nelson & Cone, 1979; Paul & Lentz, 1977).

The outcome studies attesting to the efficacy of the token economy are not without exceptions. Occasionally, studies report little or no effect with the procedures. More commonly, in an effective program, not all persons invariably improve. In several studies, clients can be identified who fail to respond to the contingencies, a point discussed later in more detail.

The evidence attesting to the efficacy of the token economy consists largely of short-term evaluations while the program is in effect. During the course of an investigation, the program often is temporarily suspended, as part of a single-case design, and is associated with decreases in the target behaviors to a level at or near baseline performance. The changes associated with suspension of the program during an investigation previews what is likely to happen long after the client leaves the setting and the program is completely terminated. Relatively few reports exist that evaluate the long-term effects of the token economy.

The results from different studies with extended follow-up show that gains produced by token economies are not inevitably lost. For example, Paul and Lentz (1977) compared social learning, milieu therapy, and routine hospital care for the treatment of chronic psychiatric patients. The social learning program was based primarily on a token economy in which patients received incentives for a variety of adaptive behaviors on the ward such as attending activities and engaging in self-care or social interaction. Although patients in both social learning and milieu programs improved, the social learning program was consistently more effective on measures in the hospital and regarding discharge of patients and their status in the community from 1.5 up to 5 years after termination of the program.

In school settings, follow-up data have also indicated that intervention effects are at least partially maintained. For example, the most extensive application of the token economy has been the Behavior Analysis Follow Through program for disadvantaged elementary school children (Bushell, 1978). The program has been implemented in kindergarten through third grades and has included over 7,000 children in approximately 300 classrooms and 15 cities throughout the United States. The program utilizes a token economy to reinforce academic performance. Changes in academic achievement evident while the program was in effect were still evident two years after the program had been terminated and the children had entered ordinary classrooms (Bushell, 1978). Similarly, in a junior high school program for adolescents with serious behavior problem, token economies led to reductions in expulsions, suspensions, and grade failure. At follow-up three to four years later, gains were still evident (Heaton & Safer, 1982; Safer, Heaton, & Parker, 1981). Adolescents who participated in the program showed higher rates of entrance into high school and of school attendance, better classroom conduct, and lower rates of withdrawal from school relative to control subjects. However, by the end of senior high school, token economy and control groups showed comparable rates of school enrollment and high school graduation.

With delinquent youths, follow-up results have been obtained for the teaching-family model (based on Achievement Place) (Wolf et al., 1976). The model has been extended to approximately 150 different group homes throughout the United States and a few foreign countries (Jones et al., Note 1). Evaluations of large-scale extensions of the model have shown that measures of offenses and reinstitutionalization from one to three years after the program are no different for youths who complete the program and those who participate in more traditional programs (Jones et al., Note 1; Kirigin, Braukmann, Atwater, & Wolf, 1982). In contrast, an extensive evaluation of the Achievement Place home where the procedures have been especially well developed and monitored has shown that youths who participate in the program have much lower rates (approximately one half) of reinstitutionalization and a much higher rate of school attendance in the community than youths in a more traditional detention setting (Kirigin et al., 1979). However, in the follow-up period, contact with the police and the courts was no different between groups.[1]

In general, the above programs show that the effects of participation in a token economy may still be evident up to a few years after the program has been terminated. Yet important qualifiers need to be highlighted to place the follow-up data in perspective. First, in many instances a token economy is only one component of the program. For example, in school programs the token economy has been associated with smaller classroom size, individualized instruction, parent involvement in classroom procedures, home-based reinforcement, and other procedures that may contribute to maintenance and transfer in their own right (e.g., Bushell, 1978; Safer et al., 1981). Similarly, in the Achievement Place program, the token economy is only part of a much more comprehensive program including client self-government, a skills training curriculum, a relationship with the teaching parents, and procedures to reintegrate youths into the community (Kirigin et al., 1982). Thus, follow-up results cannot be attributed specifically to the token reinforcement contingencies. However, the primary applied concern is whether after participation in a token economy, the gains in behavior are necessarily lost; several programs indicate that they are not.

Second, in many cases, follow-up data show that gains are sustained in some areas of performance but lost in others. For example, in the junior high school program of Safer et al. (1981), some measures reflected maintenance of intervention effects (school attendance) and others did not (graduation from high school). The same was true for the comparison of Achievement Place and other facilities where follow-up gains for delinquents were different on some measures but not on others (Jones et al., 1981; Kirigin et al., 1979, 1982).

Finally, with long-term follow-up, intervening experiences (e.g., hospital aftercare) can obfuscate the effects of the original program. Intervening and current environmental contingencies may exert

---

[1]The absence of differences on police and court contacts is difficult to interpret. Non-Achievement Place youths were more likely to be reinstitutionalized at follow-up and consequently were less available for police and court contacts.

more immediate impact on performance than a program completed a few years earlier. Thus, several investigators have cautioned that token programs may have immediate impact but perhaps should not be expected to alter future performance unless the environments to which persons return promote continuation of the gains (Bushell, 1978; Kirigin et al., 1982; Paul & Lentz, 1977).

In general, the token economy has an extensive literature attesting to its efficacy with diverse populations. At present, there is no clear evidence suggesting that the token economy is less effective with one population rather than another. Similarly, there is no clear evidence that would suggest that some disorders or target behaviors respond more readily to token economies than others. The token economy refers to a type of program that can alter behavior. Its success as a treatment modality depends in large measure on the extent to which the clinical disorder can be translated into specific behaviors.

Whether the effects of a token economy are maintained after clients leave the program is not clear. Evidence suggests that the gains are at least partially maintained. However, programs demonstrating long-term maintenance usually have exposed clients to the contingencies for an extended period (e.g., several months). It is not clear whether changes would be sustained after participation in a program in effect for a relatively brief period.

Several procedures have been suggested to increase the likelihood that behaviors are maintained and extend to new settings (see Kazdin, 1980b; Stokes & Baer, 1977). The proposed strategies include removing the token economy gradually so that behaviors are maintained with less direct reinforcement; reinforcing behaviors under a variety of situations so that the behaviors are not restricted to a limited range of cues; substituting naturally occurring reinforcers such as praise and activities in place of tokens; altering the schedule and delay of reinforcement to prolong extinction; and utilizing peers and clients themselves as reinforcing agents to sustain long-term performance across a variety of situations. The effects of these procedures on long-term follow-up remain to be evaluated.

Contraindications

Few contraindications or deleterious side-effects have been noted in token economies. Problems that emerge in selected programs usually appear to result from how the particular token economy is designed and implemented and hence may be controverted with changes in the contingencies. One issue that has occasionally emerged is client resistance, which refers to expressions of anger, complaints, and rule breaking in response to the token economy. Although only a few reports indicate client resistance, adverse client reactions are important to mention for different reasons. First, a token economy restructures much of the reward system in most settings. Consequently, the potential for coercion is great. Conceivably, basic amenities previously provided noncontingently might be withheld until they are earned. Second, legal issues raised by token economies in institutional settings have received increased attention in the United States (Martin, 1975). In specifying patient rights and basic conditions of institutional care, the courts have influenced the types of events that can be used as reinforcers (see Kazdin, 1977).

Within legal guidelines, it is still possible to design programs that clients find aversive. For example, Biklen (1976) reported a token economy in a psychiatric hospital that led to patient anger at the system and rejection of the tokens. Objections were based in part on the contingent delivery of many rewards that were given freely before the program. Also, many of the reinforced activities seemed puerile (e.g., games, crafts, childlike parties). Similarly, Zeldow (1976) noted adverse reactions of psychiatric patients to a system that seemed to consist of inflexible rules that staff rigidly imposed and the lack of patient recourse for complaints about the system.

Consideration of client reactions to token economies is critical because in institutional settings, residents usually have the legal right to withdraw from the program. Because the courts have been involved increasingly in the rights of involuntarily confined persons, programs have changed. The onus has fallen on investigators to identify and provide reinforcers that are ordinarily unavailable in the setting rather than to use basic amenities to which persons are entitled by right (Wexler, 1973). With creative selection of incentives, client resistance is less likely to result because existing reinforcers from the setting are not lost. Indeed, because of the diverse rewards that are added to the setting, there is an incentive for participants to remain willingly in the program. Also, in some programs, clients are explicitly given the option of leaving the program without penalty (e.g., Ayllon, Milan, Roberts, & McKee, 1979). Other procedures can be utilized to overcome client resistance and to help protect client rights. For example, providing opportunities for clients to have input into the system such as selecting rewards or negotiating the contingencies may augment positive reactions to the program (see Karraker, 1977; Kazdin, 1980a). In short, several options are available to overcome client resistance.

Client resistance is less likely to be a problem than is the finding that a small number of persons fail to respond to the program. The failure to respond can be evident in different ways including little or no change in performance once the program has been implemented, change in only some behaviors but not others, or only transient changes. Rarely is actual deterioration in performance found. In one example with psychiatric patients, implementation of a response cost contingency to punish failure of patients to attend a ward meeting actually decreased attendance (Boren & Colman, 1970). However, the clients generally responded to other contingencies in the program and increased their attendance to the ward meeting when the response cost contingency was lifted. Thus, decreases in the target behavior were specific to the particular contingency.

Considerably more evidence is available indicating that some clients may show little or no change during a program (see Kazdin, 1983). When clients fail to respond, or respond minimally, the results are often difficult to evaluate. In some programs, clients are included because they have already proven to be refractory to other treatments. For example, Hofmeister, Scheckenbach, and Clayton (1979) utilized a token economy for chronic schizophrenic patients, many of whom have already failed to respond to a milieu program and evidenced a decline in social and adaptive behaviors. After a year of follow-up, 80% of the patients continued to remain in the community (i.e., no recidivism). Although it is tempting to refer to the other 20% as "failures" in some way, the initial selection of patients makes the percentages difficult to evaluate. Similarly, in a token economy for criminal offenders, Moran, Kass, and Munz (1977) reported that 35% of the sample were "failures" (i.e., recidivists and parole or probation violators). This too is difficult to evaluate because the population was viewed as a high-risk group for future crime; the effects of the token program in altering the rate of recidivism that would otherwise have been evident are not known.

Research has not revealed client characteristics that consistently predispose one not to respond to a token economy. In token economies for psychiatric patients, most investigators have reported that the degree of patient withdrawal, social isolation, and length of hospitalization are negatively correlated with improvement (e.g., Ayllon & Azrin, 1968a; Butler, 1979; Fullerton, Cayner, & McLaughlin-Reidel, 1978). On the other hand, other authors have reported that length of hospitalization is not related to responsiveness to the contingencies (Allen & Magaro, 1971) and may even be positively correlated with success in the program (Birky, Chambliss, & Wasden, 1971). In the same vein, age has been positively associated with improvements for adult psychiatric patients in some programs (Last, Ginor, Lowental, & Klein, 1978) but not in others (Allen & Magaro, 1971; Fullerton et al., 1978; Mishara, 1978). Unfortunately, the actual range of patient ages has not been provided among the alternative studies to clarify one possible basis for the discrepancy. At this point, across several adult populations including geriatric patients (Mishara, 1978), age does not seem to be a significant correlate of responsiveness to the program.

Other variables for psychiatric patients have been investigated. For example, in one token economy, IQ was positively related to responsiveness. Patients with IQs over 80 performed better than those with IQs under 80 (Fullerton et al., 1978). Also, success in a token economy has been associated with staff-rated attractiveness (Choban, Cavior, & Bennett, 1974). Patients judged as more attractive tended to earn more tokens and showed a higher discharge rate than those judged as less attractive.

In general, data indicate many inconsistencies in the type of persons who respond or fail to respond to token economies. The difficulty has been the heterogeneity of populations investigated and the methods of investigation. Typically, one or two client variables are examined in isolation. An improved approach might be to examine several variables and the manner in which they combine to predict responsiveness to treatment. For example, using multiple regression techniques, Mishara (1978) identified a constellation of variables including the degree of psychotic disorganization, total years of hospitalization, self-care habits, and physical condition that predicted responsiveness to a token program for geriatric psychiatric patients. Regression analyses can provide a more useful tool for predicting responsiveness than isolated correlations with one or two variables.

A more productive approach to the lack of responsiveness among clients has been to explore program variations that can enhance performance. Performance often can be improved in nonresponsive clients by varying the parameters of reinforcement, altering economic variables (e.g., savings, costs of back-up reinforcers) of the system, using peer and group contingencies, and combining the token economy with alternative procedures. In many investigations, changes in only one of these areas has had marked effects on responsiveness and the conclusions that would be reached about a particular program or client. The fact that many variables can overcome initial unresponsiveness to the program does not mean that token economies do not "fail." However, the lack of responsiveness often can be readily controverted with changes in the contingencies. Treatment options need to be explored during a program, if preliminary data suggest lack of responsiveness or insufficient change.

In general, few contraindications are evident in applications of the token economy. Because programs are often implemented in institutional settings with involuntary clients (e.g., psychiatric patients, prison inmates), the potential exists for coercion. The program conceivably can rely on aversive contingencies and deprive persons of basic amenities to which they are entitled by right. In recent years, involvement of the courts, the use of institutional review committees, professional guidelines for treatment, and direct involvement of clients in the design and implementation of the contingencies operate to combat the potential coerciveness of the system.

Future Directions

Over the last several years, investigations of the token economy and dimensions that contribute to its efficacy have proliferated. Several issues have emerged that may shift the research focus in future years.

Current Issues

Treatment Integrity. Several procedures often are included in effective token economies to monitor the program and to ensure its correct implementation. These procedures, rarely subject to research, may be critical to the successful implementation of token economies and their effective extension across settings and populations (Kazdin, 1982b).

To convey the point, consider the token economy reported by Paul and Lentz (1977) which produced marked changes in chronic psychiatric patients. Several features of the program probably contributed to its success. First, training of staff to implement the treatments was extensive. Clinical staff received academic training that consisted of carefully planned instruction in the different procedures, using a detailed treatment manual as a guide. Training included opportunities for role-playing, modeling, rehearsal, and feedback. The academic training was followed with on-the-job training and supervised practice.

Second, monitoring of treatment was extensive to ensure that the programs were administered as planned. Supervisory staff monitored data on staff–patient interaction daily and provided positive feedback to staff for flawless performance or corrective feedback for departures from the desired procedures. Professional observers monitored staff and patients over the entire course of the program, which provided a further check on execution of the program.

Third, the program included several personnel in roles that depart from the usual staffing of inpatient programs. Among the positions were interns who helped implement and evaluate the program, persons to monitor staff–patient interactions, professional observers, and PhD level staff to supervise the research. Separate research and clinical staff and PhD level research supervisors to monitor the day-to-day program may have added a special feature to ensure proper implementation of the treatments.

Finally, the treatment was described in manual form. Constant updating of procedures was handled through memoranda to clarify implementation of practices, to answer questions, and so on. Both the subtle day-to-day details and the resources to have knowledgeable personnel to address such questions are very special program features that may have helped ensure that treatment was conducted as intended.

Characteristics such as those mentioned above may have had major bearing on the clinical impact of treatment and the generality of results to other clinical settings. The reslts, viewed superficially, suggest that a token economy can produce dramatic inhospital and extrahospital changes and return chronic patients to the community. However, the Paul and Lentz program was implemented with multiple procedures to evaluate and monitor the execution of treatment. Programs without these latter procedures may produce less marked changes in client performance.

One of the major problems of treatment and program evaluation is ensuring the *integrity of treatment,* that is, that treatment is carried out as intended (Scheirer, 1981; Sechrest, West, Phillips, Redner, & Yeaton, 1979). Monitoring the integrity of treatment is essential to ensure that the program is being conducted correctly. Different reports have indicated that token economies deteriorate when supervision over execution of the program is withdrawn or is not in place from the beginning (Rollins et al., 1974; Scheirer, 1981; Thompson, Brassell, Persons, Tucker, & Rollins, 1974). For example, Bassett and Blanchard (1977) reported a token economy in a prison setting for male adult offenders. When the director took a leave of absence and provided supervision only on a consulting basis, the program deteriorated rapidly. Staff withheld tokens for appropriate behaviors, increased the use of fines, and became inconsistent in the magnitude of fines that were invoked. The eventual return of the program director and careful monitoring of the contingencies returned the program to its original state.

In general, the potent effects of token economies may result in part from procedures included to ensure treatment integrity. Perhaps a minimal condition to monitor treatment execution is continuous data collection on client or staff behavior. In many institutional settings, continuous data collection is often difficult to implement unless special consultants with outside resources are available (see Scheirer, 1981). With little or no feedback about direct execution of the program or its effects on client behavior, the integrity of treatment and the efficacy of the program are likely to be sacrificed.

Administrative and Organizational Issues. Token economies are frequently implemented in institutional settings such as schools, psychiatric facilities, and institutions for the mentally retarded. Programs must work within the confines of organizational structures, administrative heirarchies, and external regulatory procedures. Organizational and administrative issues frequently dictate the extent to which implementing an effective token economy is feasible (see Scheirer, 1981). Constraints in permissible practices within the institution, lack of authority or power to follow through on program decisions, limited resources, and a variety of other sociopolitical issues may interfere with beginning the program and maintaining the integrity of treatment once the program is initiated. Although organizational obstacles have long been recognized in applied research (e.g., Tharp & Wetzel, 1969), their significance in delimiting the effects of token economies has been fully appreciated only relatively recently (Ayllon et al., 1979; Bushell, 1978; Liberman, 1979; Reppucci & Saunders, 1974; Scheirer, 1981).

Professionals who are responsible for designing, implementing, and evaluating token economies may not initially recognize organizational and administrative issues as central to the program until they affect more familiar variables that are known to influence program effectiveness. For example, limited resources within an institution may be translated into a small budget for backup reinforcers, insufficient staff to reward clients as frequently as might be required, and absence of personnel to assess behavior of clients or staff. In one instance, a limited budget resulted in the absence of backup reinforcers in the store when psychiatric patients were to spend their tokens (Scheirer, 1981).

Administrative and institutional obstacles often become obvious when beginning staff training. For example, the administration of direct reinforcement to staff has been an important ingredient in many staff training programs. Yet potent reinforcers (e.g., money, vacations, shift preferences, work breaks) usually are unavailable for contingent application. Thus, staff training programs often rely on inservice training, workshops, and feedback which by themselves may be less effective training procedures than when used in conjunction with potent reinforcers. Even if incentives (e.g., certificates, recognition in an institutional newsletter) are provided, staff behavior is not always easily assessed to ensure that incentives are applied contingently.

Whether the program variations known to be effective can be implemented or implemented routinely in applied settings is a major question facing the field at the present time. Questions about administrative and organizational issues have become more prominent over the last decade because they have direct implications for the disseminability of the token economy.

Dissemination of the Token Economy. A major research and clinical issue related to the integrity of treatment and administrative and organizational obstacles highlighted above is whether the token economy can be extended effectively on a large scale. Most token economies are part of demonstration projects for which external resources (e.g., federal, state, or local funding) provide services (e.g., money to hire extra staff or observers) to help implement or monitor the program. Also, most programs are usually conducted on a relatively small scale (e.g., individual classrooms or wards) where many of the administrative and organizational obstacles and threats to treatment integrity are more readily managed. A major issue in need of additional research is whether the programs can be disseminated widely without loss of the marked effectiveness often evident in demonstration projects.

The Behavior Analysis Follow Through program, mentioned earlier, is an example of a large-scale application of the token economy (Bushell, 1978). The program was part of a specially funded, nationwide, research project and was monitored centrally and locally. Teacher and student performance were regularly evaluated. The favorable results suggest that the token economy can be extended on a large scale if the mechanisms for close monitoring and supervision are in place as well. However, it is important to note that treatment integrity and program effectiveness varied considerably across different sites. Thus, additional work may be needed to reduce variability of implementation and effectiveness across sites.

If token economies are to be extended effectively, additional research will be needed to show that programs can produce marked changes without the extensive outside assistance that characterizes most programs reported to date. A few attempts have been reported in which programs depend minimally on extraneous resources. For example, token programs in the schools developed by Rollins et al. (1974) depended on extensive training and supervision by outside consultants. To make the programs less dependent on outside resources, principals were trained in behavioral techniques so that they could return to their schools, train teachers, and monitor the programs (Rollins & Thompson, 1978). Extrainstitutional resources continued to be used to monitor program effectiveness. Yet the attempt to develop programs that can function autonomously is an important step.

Recommendations for Research

The token economy is an area where several questions remain to be addressed. Based on current progress, three general areas can be identified to which future research should be directed. These include substantive, assessment, and technological issues and are highlighted below.

Substantive Issues. The bulk of the research has investigated extensions of the token economy to new populations and settings, procedural variations, and their relative effectiveness, the contribution of specific components (e.g., response cost) to outcome, and the comparison of the token economy with other procedures. Although this work is likely to continue, the most salient area for future research pertains to the long-term effectiveness of the token economy.

Several procedures to enhance maintenance and generalization of behavior have been advanced, as noted earlier. Systematic research has not begun to examine their impact. Indeed long-term follow-up data beyond a few months after program termination are rarely collected. Thus, a two-fold approach to the questions of maintenance is warranted.

First, data need to be gathered to assess whether treatment

effects are maintained at all once the client leaves the setting where the token economy was conducted. This research would determine whether the token economy accomplishes anything more than short-term changes. Programs with favorable long-term follow-up results (e.g., Bushell, 1978; Paul & Lentz, 1977) usually have been implemented for long periods. Yet most programs reported in the literature are in effect for relatively brief periods and may be less likely to produce sustained effects. Second, alternative maintenance and generalization strategies need to be tested and compared. Many procedures have been outlined; they remain to be evaluated empirically.

Both of the above areas of research address important substantive questions about the token economy. The research requires investigation of the token economy over a period of years. A few studies of long-term effects of the token economy at this point are likely to be much more valuable for further progress than more studies of short-term effects.

Assessment Issues. Most programs assess multiple target behaviors to reflect intervention effects. Occasionally more general characteristics are assessed as well such as adjustment or social functioning of psychiatric patients or grades and achievement test performance of students. Yet another level of assessment needs to be pursued in future research. Additional attention needs to be directed to outcome measures that are regarded as highly socially relevant. Examples of the measures include recidivism, arrest records, and contact with the courts for delinquents or prisoners; days out of the hospital, discharge, and readmission rates for psychiatric patients; graduation and continuation in the educational system among disadvantaged students. These measures have been used in token economies, but the uses are exceptions rather than the rule.

The use of socially relevant criteria is essential. Marked changes in target behaviors in the treatment setting may not be reflected on other measures. The excellent research that has emerged from the Achievement Place program provides an illustration of the problem as well as a model for outcome assessment. Evaluations of the token economy and the larger teaching-family model of which it is a part have repeatedly shown the effects of the overall intervention and procedural variations on specific target behaviors within the setting. Additional studies have shown that the token economy is superior to alternative residential procedures for delinquent youths, as reflected in such measures as school attendance and reinstitutionalization

(Kirigin et al., 1979). A more recent investigation compared multiple group homes devised on the teaching-family model with other residential homes that did not rely on this model (Kirigin et al., 1982). While the different programs were in effect, children who participated in the teaching-family homes showed greater reductions in the number of offenses, derived from police and court records. However, one year after completion of the program, differences in the number of offenses or reinstitutionalization from the different programs were no longer evident (see also Jones et al., Note 1). Research on the teaching-family program presents a model for assessment by its inclusion of socially relevant criteria. However, the results also provide an implicit caveat to those whose programs are evaluated solely by changes in specific target behaviors and only while the program is in effect.

Ultimately, the contribution of the token economy to social problems is likely to be evaluated by its direct impact on socially relevant measures of the sort mentioned above. Legislators, policymakers, and others in critical decision-making positions are likely to demand evidence that participation in a token program has impact on the client's future social functioning in recognizable ways. Research needs to address the concern directly by including measures that assess the social impact of treatment.

Socially relevant measures often are based on archival records which present their own methodological problems (Kazdin, 1979). For example, measures of recidivism, discharge, and readmission do not necessarily reflect the behaviors that might be of interest. Former psychiatric patients who have no further significant contact with mental health system may still be suffering greatly in terms of their adjustment. Also, reduced contact with the courts or police among ex-prisoners does not necessarily reflect reduced crime or positive social functioning (e.g., employment). Despite interpretive difficulties, such measures provide critical information regarding the ultimate contribution of a particular intervention and need to be incorporated in future research.

Technological Issues. Even though much more research is needed to learn about the token economy and its effects, sufficient information exists to recommend its use as an alternative to many routine interventions in institutional and educational settings. However, dissemination of the token economy will require consideration and investigation of several program evaluation issues. To begin with, mere demonstration of the efficacy of the token economy will not ensure that it is widely adopted. Research may need to investigate how to promote program adoption.

Characteristics of the programs themselves are likely to contribute to their adoption. Fawcett, Mathews, and Fletcher (1980) have drawn on dissemination work in other fields (e.g., extension of technology to underdeveloped countries) to identify important characteristics that enhance program adoption. They suggest that interventions are more likely to be adopted if they are (1) effective, (2) relatively inexpensive, (3) decentralized and controlled by local participants, (4) flexible enough to permit local input, (5) sustainable with local rather than outside resources, (6) relatively simple and comprehensible, and (7) compatible with existing values, goals, and perceived needs of the setting.

Some of the above conditions have begun to be addressed in relation to token economies. For example, the expense (cost) of token economies has been examined in different ways. Operating costs, cost-effectiveness, and cost–benefit analyses have shown that major benefits accrue from adopting token economies in relation to existing alternatives such as routine psychiatric care or detention centers for juvenile offenders (e.g., Foreyt, Rockwood, Davis, Desvousges, & Hollingsworth, 1975; Kirigin et al., 1979; Paul & Lentz, 1977). Certainly the favorable results pertaining to cost analyses may help to promote adoption of the token economy.

The impact of other program characteristics may warrant investigation. One avenue of research is to examine the acceptability of the token economy to administrators, staff, and clients (cf., Kazdin, 1980a; Kazdin, French, & Sherick, 1981). The token economy is a highly flexible procedure and allows many program options based on the type of contingencies, range of backup reinforcers, roles of staff, clients, and peers, and so on. Alternative program variations may influence the acceptability of the program and its potential adoption.

Once a program is adopted, other issues become important. In particular, procedures must be included to provide feedback to staff regarding program efficacy. Although assessment procedures that permit close monitoring of the program have been well developed and frequently illustrated in research, strategies that are consistent with and feasible within existing resources of most institutional settings need to be developed. The assessment procedures need to be feasible and acceptable to staff as well as provide essential information for decision making. The development of intervention and assessment procedures that can be used routinely and that can still achieve potent effects of treatment represents an important area for future research.

Summary and Conclusions

The token economy has been extensively investigated with multiple populations in a variety of treatment and institutional settings. Program effects often are dramatic, as demonstrated by marked changes in specific target behaviors while the program is in effect. Occasionally, some persons fail to respond to the contingencies. Yet evidence suggests that variations of the contingencies often improve program effectiveness in general as well as for persons who were initially unresponsive.

Perhaps the most salient issue regarding the efficacy of the token economy is the long-term effects of treatment. The long-term effects no doubt are likely to vary as a function of the clients, setting, type of program, duration of the program, settings to which the clients will be returned or in which they will continue after the program has been terminated, and so on. The long-term effects of treatment and procedures to promote durable changes have not been systematically evaluated. Promising follow-up results are available in a few programs to suggest that the gains may be maintained after treatment. But the programs in which such gains are evident often differ in important ways (e.g., duration of the intervention) from the usual programs that have been reported.

Even with the limitations of current evidence, the token economy has been shown to provide a more effective and cost-efficient intervention relative to routine practices in many institutional settings. Increased efforts may be needed to encourage adoption of the program and to develop program variations that meet the needs of applied settings. Many of the programs to date have been based on demonstration projects and depend heavily on outside resources. Programs need to be designed that can achieve the dramatic effects often reported in well-controlled investigations but that rely primarily, if not exclusively, on the existing resources within institutional and educational settings.

References

Allen, D. J., & Magaro, P. A. Measures of change in token-economy programs. *Behaviour Research and Therapy*, 1971, *9*, 311–318.

Ayllon, T., & Azrin, N. H. The measurement and reinforcement of behavior of psychotics. *Journal of the Experimental Analysis of Behavior*, 1965, *8*, 356–382.

Ayllon, T., & Azrin, N. H. Reinforcer sampling: A technique for increasing the behavior of mental patients. *Journal of Applied Behavior Analysis,* 1968, *1,* 13–20. (a)

Ayllon, T., & Azrin, N. H. *The token economy: A motivational system for therapy and rehabilitation.* New York: Appleton-Century-Crofts, 1968. (b)

Ayllon, T., & Haughton, E. Control of the behavior of schizophrenic patients by food. *Journal of the Experimental Analysis of Behavior,* 1962, *5,* 343–352.

Ayllon, T., & Michael, J. The psychiatric nurse as a behavioral engineer. *Journal of the Experimental Analysis of Behavior,* 1959, *2,* 323–334.

Ayllon, T., Milan, M. A., Roberts, M. D., & McKee, J. M. *Correctional Rehabilitation & Management: A Psychological Approach.* New York: Wiley, 1979.

Bassett, J. E., & Blanchard, E. B. The effect of the absence of close supervision on the use of response cost in a prison token economy. *Journal of Applied Behavior Analysis,* 1977, *10,* 375–379.

Biklen, D. P. Behavior modification in a state mental hospital: A participant-observer's critique. *American Journal of Orthopsychiatry,* 1976, *46,* 53–61.

Birky, H. J., Chambliss, J. E., & Wasden, R. A comparison of residents discharged from a token economy and two traditional psychiatric programs. *Behavior Therapy,* 1971, *2,* 46–51.

Birnbrauer, J. S., Bijou, S. W., Wolf, M. M., & Kidder, J. D. Programmed instructions in the classroom. In L. P. Ullmann & L. Krasner (Eds.), *Case studies in behavior modification.* New York: Holt, Rinehart, & Winston, 1965.

Boren, J. J., & Colman, A. D. Some experiments on reinforcement principles within a psychiatric ward for delinquent soldiers. *Journal of Applied Behavior Analysis,* 1970, *3,* 29–37.

Bushell, D., Jr. An engineering approach to the elementary classroom: The Behavior Analysis Follow Through project. In A. C. Catania & T. A. Brigham (Eds.), *Handbook of applied behavior analysis: Social and instructional processes.* New York: Irvington, 1978.

Butler, R. J. An analysis of individual treatment on a token economy for chronic schizophrenic patients. *British Journal of Medical Psychology,* 1979, *52,* 235–242.

Choban, M. C., Cavior, N., & Bennett, P. *Effects of physical attractiveness of patients on outcome in a token economy.* Paper presented at 82nd Annual Convention of the American Psychological Association, New Orleans, August 1974.

Fawcett, S. B., Mathews, R. M., & Fletcher, R. K. Some promising dimensions for behavioral community technology. *Journal of Applied Behavior Analysis,* 1980, *13,* 505–518.

Ferster, C. B., & DeMyer, M. K. The development of performances in autistic children in an automatically controlled environment. *Journal of Chronic Diseases,* 1961, *13,* 312–345.

Foreyt, J. P., Rockwood, C. E., Davis, J. C., Desvousges, W. H., & Hollingsworth, R. Benefit-cost analysis of a token economy program. *Professional Psychology,* 1975, *6,* 26–33.

Fullerton, D. T., Cayner, J. J., & McLaughlin-Reidel, T. Results of a token economy. *Archives of General Psychiatry,* 1978, *35,* 1451–1453.

Greenberg, D. J., Scott, S. B., Pisa, A., & Friesen, D. D. Beyond the token economy: A comparison of two contingency programs. *Journal of Consulting and Clinical Psychology,* 1975, *43,* 498–503.

Gripp, R. F., & Magaro, P. A. A token economy program evaluation with untreated control ward comparisons. *Behaviour Research and Therapy,* 1971, *9,* 137–149.

Grzesiak, R. C., & Locke, B. J. Cognitive and behavioral correlates to overt behavior change with a token economy. *Journal of Consulting and Clinical Psychology,* 1975, *43,* 272.

Heaton, R. C., & Safer, D. J. Secondary school outcome following a junior high school behavioral program. *Behavior Therapy,* 1982, *13,* 226–231.

Herman, J. A., de Montes, A. I., Dominguez, B., Montes, F., & Hopkins, B. L. Effects of bonuses for punctuality on the tardiness of industrial workers. *Journal of Applied Behavior Analysis,* 1973, *6,* 563–570.

Hersen, M., & Barlow, D. H. *Single case experimental designs: Strategies for studying behavior change.* New York: Pergamon, 1976.

Hofmeister, J. F., Scheckenbach, A. F., & Clayton, S. H. A behavioral program for the treatment of chronic patients. *American Journal of Psychiatry,* 1979, *136,* 396–400.

Jones, R. R., Weinrott, M. R., & Howard, J. R. *The national evaluation of the teaching-family model.* Final report to the National Institute of Mental Health, Center for Studies in Crime and Delinquency, June 1981.

Karraker, R Self versus teacher selected reinforcers in a token economy. *Exceptional Children,* 1977, *43,* 454–455.

Kazdin, A. E. Role of instructions and reinforcement in behavior changes in token reinforcement programs. *Journal of Educational Phychology,* 1973, *64,* 63–71.

Kazdin, A. E. *The token economy: A review and evaluation.* New York: Plenum, 1977.

Kazdin, A. E. *History of behavior modification: Experimental foundations of contemporary research.* Baltimore: University Park Press, 1978.

Kazdin, A. E. Unobtrusive measures in behavioral assessment. *Journal of Applied Behavior Analysis,* 1979, *12,* 713–724.

Kazdin, A. E. Acceptability of alternative treatments for deviant child behavior. *Journal of Applied Behavior Analysis,* 1980, *13,* 259–273. (a)

Kazdin, A. E. *Behavior modification in applied settings* (2nd ed.). Homewood: IL: Dorsey, 1980. (b)

Kazdin, A. E. *Single-case research designs: Methods for clinical and applied settings.* New York: Oxford University Press, 1982. (a)

Kazdin, A. E. The token economy: A decade later. *Journal of Applied Behavior Analysis,* 1982, *15,* 431–445. (b)

Kazdin, A. E. Failure of persons to respond to the token economy. In E. B. Foa and M. G. Emmelkamp (Eds.), *Failures in behavior therapy.* (pp. 335–354) New York: Wiley, 1983.

Kazdin, A. E., French, N. H., & Sherick, R. B. Acceptability of alternative treatments for children: Evaluations by inpatient children, parents, and staff. *Journal of Consulting and Clinical Psychology,* 1981, *49,* 900–907.

Kirigin, K. A., Braukmann, C. J., Atwater, J. D., & Wolf, M. M. An evaluation of teaching-family (Achievement Place) group homes for juvenile offenders. *Journal of Applied Behavior Analysis,* 1982, *15,* 1–16.

Kirigin, K. A., Wolf, M. M., Braukmann, C. J., Fixsen, D. L., & Phillips, E. L. Achievement Place: A preliminary outcome evaluation. In J. S. Stumphauzer (Ed.), *Progress in behavior therapy with delinquents.* Springfield, IL, Charles C. Thomas, 1979.

Lancaster, J. *Improvements in education, as it respects the industrious classes of the community* (3rd ed.). London: Darton and Harvey, 1805.

Last, R., Ginor, M., Lowental, U., & Klein, H. A token economy in the framework of a hospital therapeutic community—Practice and psychosocial implications. *Mental Health Society,* 1978, *5,* 200–214.

Liberman, R. P. Social and political challenges to the development of behavioral programs in organizations. In P. Sjoden, S. Bates, & W. S. Dockens, III (Eds.), *Trends in behavior therapy.* New York: Academic Press, 1979.

Lindsley, O. R. Operant conditioning methods applied to research in chronic schizophrenia. *Psychiatric Research Reports,* 1956, *5,* 118–139.

Maconochie, A. *Norfolk Island.* Hobart, Australia: Sullivan's Cove, Publisher, 1973. (Original publication date 1847.)

Martin, R. *Legal challenges to behavior modification: Trends in schools, corrections and mental health.* Champaign, IL: Research Press, 1975.

McAllister, L. W., Stachowiak, J. G., Baer, D. M., & Conderman, L. The application of operant conditioning techniques in a secondary school classroom. *Journal of Applied Behavior Analysis,* 1969, *2,* 277–285.

McCreadie, R. G., Main, C. J., & Dunlop, R. A. Token economy, pimozide and chronic schizophrenia. *British Journal of Psychiatry,* 1978, *133,* 179–181.

Mishara, B. L. Geriatric patients who improve in token economy and general milieu treatment programs: A multivariate analysis. *Journal of Consulting and Clinical Psychology,* 1978, *46,* 1340–1348.

Moran, E. L., Kass, W. A., & Munz, D. C. In-program evaluation of a community correctional agency of high-risk offenders. *Corrective and Social Psychiatry,* 1977, *23,* 48–52.

Nelson, G. L., & Cone, J. D. Multiple-baseline analysis of a token economy for psychiatric inpatients. *Journal of Applied Behavior Analysis*, 1979, *12*, 255–271.

Paul, G. L., & Lentz, R. J. *Psychosocial treatment of chronic mental patients: Milieu versus social-learning programs*. Cambridge, MA: Harvard University Press, 1977.

Reppucci, N. D., & Saunders, J. T. Social psychology of behavior modification: Problems of implementation in natural settings. *American Psychology*, 1974, *29*, 649–660.

Rollins, H. A., McCandless, B. R., Thompson, M., & Brassell, W. R. Project Success Environment: An extended application of contingency management in inner-city schools. *Journal of Educational Psychology*, 1974, *66*, 167–178.

Rollins, H. A., & Thompson, M. Implementation and operation of a contingency management program by the elementary school principal. *American Educational Research Journal*, 1978, *15*, 325–330.

Safer, D. J., Heaton, R. C., & Parker, F. C. A behavioral program for disruptive junior high school students: Results and follow-up. *Journal of Abnormal Child Psychology*, 1981, *4*, 483–494.

Scheirer, M. A. *Program implementation: The organizational context*. Beverly Hills, CA: Sage, 1981.

Sechrest, L., West, S. G., Phillips, M. A., Redner, R., & Yeaton, W. Some neglected problems in evaluation research: Strength and integrity of treatments. In L. Sechrest, S. G. West, M. A. Phillips, R. Redner, & W. Yeaton (Eds.), *Evaluation studies: Review annual* (Vol. 4). Beverly Hills: Sage, 1979.

Skinner, B. F. *The behavior of organisms*. New York: Appleton-Century-Crofts, 1938.

Stokes, T. F., & Baer, D. M. An implicit technology of generalization. *Journal of Applied Behavior Analysis*, 1977, *10*, 349–367.

Tharp, R. G., & Wetzel, R. J. *Behavior modification in the natural environment*. New York: Academic Press, 1969.

Thompson, M., Brassell, W. R., Persons, S., Tucker, R., & Rollins, H. Contingency management in the schools: How often and how well does it work? *American Educational Research Journal*, 1974, *11*, 19–28.

Ulman, J. D., & Klem, J. L. Communication. *Journal of Applied Behavior Analysis*, 1975, *8*, 210.

Wexler, D. B. Token and taboo: Behavior modification, token economies, and the law. *California Law Review*, 1973, *61*, 81–109.

Wolf, M. M., Phillips, E. L., Fixsen, D. G., Braukmann, C. J., Kirigin, K. A. Willner, A. G., & Schumaker, J. B. Achievement Place: The teaching-family model. *Child Care Quarterly*, 1976, *5*, 92–103.

Zeldow, P. B. Some antitherapeutic effects of the token economy: A case in point. *Psychiatry*, 1976, *39*, 318–324.

10
Punishment

JOHNNY L. MATSON

Introduction

Punishment has been a fundamental and highly studied area in the basic and applied literature for some time (Matson & DiLorenzo, 1984). Many of the early successes with recalcitrant behaviors have included the effective treatment of behaviors that were considered intractable, and these singular accomplishments led to the acceptance, at least to some degree, of the new field of behavior therapy. For example, the work of Lovaas with seemingly untreatable behaviors of autistic children, Risley's (1968) classic study in which contingent electric shock was used to curb the climbing of a mentally retarded child, and the overcorrection studies of Foxx and Azrin (1972, 1973) are some of the most quoted studies in the field of clinical psychology and behavior therapy. Despite these early successes, however, there have been a number of highly restrictive mandates from within the fields of mental health and mental retardation and from legislative bodies that have curtailed the initial enthusiasm of some investigators and clinicians toward the use of at least some types of punishment.

What led to this rather quick and broad-based change even given the fact that contingent shock is one of the most highly documented of the behavioral approaches (see Wyatt v. Stickney, 1974)? Certainly the legal emphasis on least restrictive treatments and least restrictive environments has played a part (Martin, 1975). Similarly, there have been a number of more positively oriented methods to decelerate behavior. The procedures of DRO and social skills training are two such examples (Matson & Stephens, 1978; Repp & Deitz, 1978).

However, it is likely that these procedures are effective with only some problem behaviors. It has been aptly pointed out that the potential applicability of various punishment conditions is great. It is this author's contention that many problems confronted in the real world do not respond in the same manner that we would have hoped based on theory. Similarly, there is empirical evidence that punishment may frequently be more effective than reinforcement (Spence & Segner, 1967).

A second possible explanation of this situation is that a gap may be forming between legal mandates and available practical strategies for the solution of major clinical problems. Similarly, the legal system has been notorious in its selective attention to some types of empirical data and its general lack of interest in other information (e.g., data which supports the effectiveness of punishment procedures) (Bersoff & Prasse, 1978). It is not suggested by the author that punishment procedures should be applied in all situations or without careful supervision. However, as Repp and Deitz (1978) forcefully argue, it may also be inappropriate to ignore a potentially effective treatment strategy, particularly for life-threatening problems such as self-injury or infantile rumination when other effective treatments are not available. This problem, it is argued, could be construed as a violation of patient rights. However, at present there is a movement toward a total ban of such methods. A move of this sort would be in this author's opinion highly unfortunate and would be antiscientific, since much of the current empirical evidence on treatment procedures would be ignored. The seriousness of this problem is greatly enhanced when one considers that the agency proposing this ban is composed of factions within the American Psychological Association. Division 25 (Applied Behavior Analysis) is fighting this ban (Lutzker, 1982), but the ramifications of such a state of affairs is ominous and suggests that many professionals are not completely conversant in the potential benefits of such methods under controlled and properly supervised conditions. Despite the reservations noted above, however, punishment as a theraputic treatment is in widespread use. For example, in a recent survey it was reported that 98% of the parent and teachers interviewed used punishment (Sears, Maccoby, & Levin, 1957). Similarly, as noted in more detail later in this chapter, the development of effective punishment techniques in behavior therapy is still widespread.

The climate toward punishment has an important bearing on any review of punishment procedures and new developments, we as researchers and practitioners must be concerned that continued and ever-increasing negative press and litigation may result in a slowing in the development of punishment-based training techniques in future years. However, it will be shown that at least relative to research on punishment this trend has not appeared yet. In the following section a brief review of some developments and trends in behavior therapy will be made.

History

The historical use of punishment procedures is as old as man himself. The Greeks and Romans used various forms of penalties such as fines, scorn from a large body of individual's peers and penalties as severe as death for behaviors and deeds considered to fall outside the purview of socially acceptable behavior. These forms of punishments were given in a rather haphazard fashion, though, and the scientific use of punishment as a theraputic method is relatively new.

The trend toward using punishment methods for the treatment of emotionally disturbed and other handicapped persons followed closely, based on the history of mankind and on the development of psychiatry and psychology. In terms of scientific disciplines these are relatively new professions. Psychiatry, for example, is the newest of the disciplines within medicine and has been formally recognized for only the last 150 years (Mora, 1978). Prior to this time those with mental illness were considered to fall under the general ruberic of philosophy. The development of psychology as a science is even newer, having emerged only within the last 100 years (Boring, 1963). The work of Wundt in Germany and James in the United States was the basis for the first promulgation of the scientific study of mental disorders. These trends and the development of clinical psychology as a discipline soon after provided for an interface between scientific method and the application of such principles in applied settings. This trend was further spurred by learning-based theory through laboratory research and later applied work of behavior therapists.

Azrin and Holz's (1966) now classic paper which synthesized the research that had appeared on the operant conditioning of animals using punishment procedures was an important work that still influences the applied field. Of particular importance was the recognition that the systematic application of aversive stimuli using operant conditioning methods was exceedingly powerful compared to methods that had come before. Soon after the appearance of this paper, there was an explosion of scientific literature with respect to the volume of studies using these operantly oriented punishment methods with humans.

Also based on this review of Azrin and Holz (1966) is a list of principles for the application of punishment procedures that are still of great value in applied research. Among the recommendations were that (1) escape from the punishing stimulus should be possible; (2) the punishing stimulus should be intense; (3) the punishing stimulus should be presented after every occurrence of the target behavior; (4) the punishing stimulus should be administered immediately after the response to be punished; (5) the punishment should be introduced at the maximum intensity; (6) the punishment should be brief; (7) the punishing stimulus should not be differentially associated with reinforcement; (8) the degree of motivation to emit the punished response should be reduced; (9) an alternative response that can be reinforced should be available; and (10) if punishing stimuli could not be given, then a reduction of reinforcement should be used as a means of punishment.

Beginning in the 1960s and 1970s a rather large amount of empirical data was amassed pointing to the effectiveness of punishment techniques for a wide range of problem areas. Among the populations and behaviors treated were life-threatening rumination of children (Sajwaj, Libet & Agras, 1974), aggressive behaviors of mentally retarded adults (Matson, Ollendick, & DiLorenzo, 1980), and various inappropriate behaviors of chronic schizophrenic adults (Matson, 1980; Matson & Stephens, 1978), mentally retarded and autistic children (Lovaas & Simmons, 1969; Risley, 1968), alcoholics (Baker & Cannon, 1979), persons with weight problems (Harmatz & Lapuc, 1968), as well as inappropriate vocalizations of children (McLaughlin & Malaby, 1972), persons with tics (Azrin, Nunn, & Frantz, 1980), and clothes stripping of mentally retarded persons (Foxx, 1976) to name a few. These data exemplify what has been an exponential growth in behaviorally based punishment procedures in recent years. Hamilton (1982) among others has argued that punishment methods should not be abandoned without effective alternatives. The necessity for continued growth and development will be covered next.

The Need for Punishment Procedures

Despite the inherent positive nature of various differential reinforcement procedures to curb inappropriate behaviors, as noted earlier, there is little research to support the efficacy of these methods rela-

tive to the numerous studies demonstrating the viability of punishment procedures. Further, the problems for which DRO (differential
reinforcement of other behavior), DRI (differential reinforcement of
incompatible behavior), and related methods have proven useful
typically involve less severe problems than many of those mentioned
here, and the research is erratic, tending to be grouped around a few
select problems. Why is this the case? First, the lack of studies may
say something about the effectiveness of these differential reinforcement procedures when used alone for deceleration of very extreme
recalcitrant behaviors. Also, at least from this author's experience, it
is often difficult to find reinforcers powerful enough to use that do not
greatly restrict the patient's freedom and at the same time do not
result in a highly aversive situation. After all, for a behavior to be
reinforcing a deprivation state must exist and for many patients
access to food or freedom to move around the hospital may be among
the only reinforcing behaviors sufficiently powerful to compete with
the problem behavior. Third, reinforcement is often impractical. For
example, when a patient is attacking another patient or a staff
member, ignoring the problem is not sufficient. Some type of active
intervention in the form of a punishment procedure such as contingent restraint, time-out, or overcorrection is necessary. Also, in the
case of some patient groups such as chronic schizophrenics, reinforcers are hard to come by. (Chronic here refers to person with many
years of inpatient hospitalization.) Most state psychiatric hospitals
have many of these persons who may have had numerous ECT
treatments, lobotomies, and little contact with the public in many
months or years. With such persons, combinations of various punishment procedures and/or tranquilizing drugs may be necessary to
control the behavior displayed in some of these agitated states (see
Matson, 1980; Matson & Stephens, 1977). For example, the author
has had firsthand experience with patients who during extreme
agitation while restrained to a bed nonetheless markedly disrupted
the ward with violent and very loud screaming in conjunction with
the possibility of physical injury to themselves through contusions on
arms or legs that can be caused by *extreme* thrashing about. Further,
in some cases agitation is so great that several punishment procedures in combination may be necessary based on various possible
situations that may require intervention (see Matson & DiLorenzo,
1984). In this instance the patient was required to perform an overcorrection procedure contingent on picking trash up from the floor
and throwing it in people's faces. However, while being overcorrected
this mentally retarded, chronic schizophrenic female would often

resist overcorrection to such a degree that the procedure could not be continued. Under these conditions she was placed in time-out until agitation subsided and then the overcorrection procedure was begun again.

These are not the typical mild forms of disruption for which reinforcement alone is sufficient. The problems are nonetheless of a type that cannot be simply ignored, nor can solutions be left to direct-care staff, who may try any one of a number of homemade remedies. Additionally, these conditions are very prevalent in the most severe chronic patients (those who have been hospitalized continuously for many years). For these and other reasons the use of punishment procedures in a selective and caring fashion is considered necessary given the "state of the art" relative to intervention strategies.

Contraindications

Perhaps more than any other treatment technique of the behavior therapist, punishment must be viewed carefully with respect to possible contraindications. This situation is of course due to the negative aspects of the method. At least five categories which should be reviewed exist and will be discussed here. These include side-effects, resistence to the use of these procedures, consideration of alternative procedures, cost, and proficiency of staff in treatment implementation. The contraindications discussed are not in order of degree of importance. This order must be established based on the problem treated, the type and severity of the behavior, and related issues to a particular individual patient.

Side-Effects

An area which has received some attention in the empirical literature and a great deal of discussion among clinicians is the side-effects of the punishment procedures (in this case defined as any effect resulting from treatment other than those specific to the target behavior(s)). It is often inferred, and unfortunately so, that these procedures are in fact always negative responses. Of course, many negative behaviors do occur and these include hyperactivity, incessent talking, masturbation, and self-injurious behavior. (A side-effect is defined here as any behavior that occurs other than those responses that are specifically designated to receive the punishing stimulus.)

On the other hand, a number of studies have reported the occurrence of positive behaviors. For example, Lovaas and others (Doleys, Wells, Hobbs, Roberts, & Cartelli, 1976; Foxx & Azrin, 1972; Lovaas & Simmons, 1969) have reported behaviors such as increased positive affect and decreased negative affect, not directly associated with the treated behavior, that changed in positive directions when punishment procedures were implemented. Similarly, in a recent review Hamilton (1982) discussed a number of positive side-effects of punishment as they related to the use of contingent electric shock with mentally retarded persons. Positive side-effects to be noted include sociability, happiness, play activity, accessibility for teachers, table manners, affection, attentiveness, alertness, and spontaneous communication. These data are consistent with previous reviews and suggest that if these behaviors are to be found with contingent electric shock they are also likely to be present with less aversive methods or at least punishers perceived by the public to be less aversive such as overcorrection and time-out. The existing data are primarily antecdotal, and more systematic research on side-effects is needed. However, based on existing research it would seem that punishment does not necessarily produce only negative side-effects despite this general assumption among many researchers and clinicians.

Resistence to Procedures

A second factor in the use of any treatment procedure, but perhaps with punishment more so than other methods, is resistence to its use. This situation is likely to be evinced in several ways, not the least of which is an inaccurate application of the methods. Obviously for this reason and the potential harm to the patient that may arise from misapplications, punishment should be monitored very carefully. A second potential problem is that many of these methods may result in a good deal of work and effort for the staff member, who may be resistant to the use of the procedures for that reason. A good example is overcorrection, in which the staff member is often called upon to manually guide the patient in the performance of the response associated with the punishment. A final reason frequently given for resisting these methods is based on moral and legal grounds. In other words, the procedures are seen as unduly painful for use. Compromise on these issues is of course necessary if the treatment program is to be implemented and still prove successful.

Consideration of Alternative Procedures

For at least some problem behaviors there are alternatives to punishment, and these options should be considered before punishment procedures are used, where practical. The difficulty arises when punishment procedures are well supported by empirical data and behavior decelerators such as DRO are not and when the behavior is likely to result in permanent harm to self or others in a short period of time. A self-injurious behavior such as head banging might be one example of this problem.

Cost

Another important consideration in the application of treatment procedures is cost, particularly when there are two treatments that are of fairly equal probability to result in the type of effect that is desired. Similarly, if two punishment procedures are likely to have equal or near equal cost and effects, and one method is viewed as much more aversive than another, then the less aversive method is to be preferred.

Proficiency of Staff in Treatment

Ease of administration is the final variable that the behavior therapist should strongly consider in the selection of a particular treatment procedure or in the selection of one treatment procedure over another. This consideration may also be important in maintaining staff morale and the degree of accuracy with which a particular treatment is administered.

General Considerations in Evaluating Punishment

The issue of interpreting treatment effectiveness is at best difficult and at worst nearly impossible. This conclusion is of course neither new nor specific to punishment or even behavior therapy for that matter (Gottman & Markman, 1978). Even with the advent of new procedures such as meta-analysis to make statistical rather than more subjective evaluations of treatment effectiveness (e.g., Glass, McGaw, & Smith, 1981), conclusive and objective decisions as to efficacy of various procedures remains elusive. Also of importance is what constitutes effectiveness. Subjectivity becomes less critical in a review such as the one described here since the theoretical orientation of the researchers and the similarities of treatment makes comparisons at least somewhat easier. For example, unlike dynamic versus behavior therapy approaches, there is some consensus as to what are appropriate and what are inappropriate goals for therapy. In the case of the dynamically oriented therapist emphasis is more likely to be on treatment goals such as group cohesion, self-actualization, self-awareness, openness, free flow of feelings, self-exploration, and related variables (Yalom, 1975). The behavior therapist, on the other hand, is more likely to concentrate on functional, overt, operationally defined behaviors that are directly manipulated by the treatment. These vast differences in desired outcome invariably affect the choice of dependent variables in behavior therapy and psychotherapy research as even the most cursory review of the literature will show.

Given these caveats to treatment comparisons, there are a number of variables that when used should assist in the evaluation of well versus poorly conducted research. These points are reviewed at length by Matson and DiLorenzo (1984). Some of the factors deemed most important for adequately evaluating treatment effectiveness are briefly noted.) The first of these is the rapidity with which the effects of treatment occur. (This variable is most likely to be detected with the single-case research designs; Hersen & Barlow, 1976.) Second, there are a number of assessment methods for evaluating the behaviors being studied. This second point is considered of particular importance since the research to date shows that a number of punishment procedures are effective for a variety of problem behaviors. The effects of treatment have typically been very narrow, however, and suggest that more breadth of measurement would now be a priority in establishing the side-effects of punishment procedures both positive and negative. (See the preceding section for a discussion of side-effects.) Among the types of assessments suggested as a means of augmenting direct observations of target behaviors are checklists rated by patients and informed others, social validation criteria (Kazdin & Matson, 1981), and reports of peers (Asher, Oden, & Gottman, 1976; La Greca, 1981). All these methods have been used in treatment outcome research but rarely have they been used together in punishment research.

A third consideration is to be sufficiently precise when interpreting results of a particular treatment procedure. For example, overcorrection is a rather generic term that refers to a number of treatment procedures. The method typically used for stereotypic hand or arm movements involve having the patient raise the hand over the head, straight out from the body, and down to the sides while keeping the arms in a straight line with the hands. Each of these positions would be held for a period of a minute or two; then the patient would be asked to assume another position (e.g., see Foxx & Azrin, 1972, for further details of this overcorrection procedure). A second overcorrection procedure is oral hygiene training (see Foxx & Martin, 1975). In this case the person is treated for mouthing unsanitary/inedible objects by brushing the patient's teeth or gums with Listerine, usually for two or three minutes contingent on an episode of the inappropriate behavior.

Evaluating Treatment Effects

The difference in treatments may be quite difficult to evaluate in many cases. There are, however, a number of different procedures that should be considered in comparative treatment studies. One such method is to ask the opinion of ward staff or other professionals. However, rarely are decisions made based on a systematic evaluation of the behavior to be treated relative to severity of the behavior as perceived by the patients or their families as a means of social validation (see Kazdin & Matson, 1981). (Thus, social skills training with children as one example may in fact vary widely from social norms.) Behavioral studies across cultures can be even more problematic on this dimension (see Ardila, 1978). Additionally, what impact will changing one behavior have on other behaviors or other individuals? These and many other questions need to be addressed, particularly with punishment procedures. (If it can be established that a different behavior should be modified or the same behavior should be modified in a different way, then this may obviate the use of the punishment.)

Another problem concerns when to terminate treatment, or when the therapist may be able to switch to a less aversive procedure, to maintain a target response at a particular strength or frequency. Solutions that incorporate a social validation criterion or other methods for systematically determining clinical significance are suggested (Kazdin & Matson, 1980).

Another issue of concern is the type of research methodology used to evaluate treatment outcome. Group studies would seem to be the most efficacious method for treatment comparisons, since within-subject problems such as order effects are not present. If this method is not feasible, then the researchers should consider single-case methodologies such as the reversal, simultaneous treatment designs (see Kazdin, 1982), or the random stimulus design (see Matson & Ollendick, 1981).

A third comparitive approach used by the author and many other researchers (e.g., Chassan, 1979) involves the description of antecdotal treatment attempts or using treatments as baseline. This type of treatment comparison can generally be considered invalid. First of all, these preliminary evaluations may not be compared with the degree of systematization evident with effective treatments. This situation is readily apparent as with the study by Foxx and Azrin (1973). (This paper is used only as an example of what has generally been a common procedure in the evaluation of differential effectiveness in treatment procedures.) They compared various punishments used with two mentally retarded children. With one subject reinforcement for nonmouthing, noncontingent reinforcement and physical punishment via slaps produced a stepwise decrease in behavior, followed by overcorrection, which proved to be the most effective of these methods. The second child was given physical punishment via slaps, noncontingent reinforcement, reinforcement for nonmouthing, a distasteful solution, and finally overcorrection. Stepwise decrements in the treatments effectiveness were also noted. The problem, as mentioned before, is how to interpret order effects in punishment research of this sort. At the very best, it is difficult and at the worst impossible.

These are only some of the issues that need to be addressed more frequently, if adequate evaluations of punishment methods are to result. Obviously, these procedures have not been followed in many instances with much of the punishment research that has appeared. This state of affairs seems reasonable in the development of punishment research since these studies constitute an evolution to other and more difficult topics of study. However, much of the punishment research published to date focused more on the variety of demonstrations of treatment effectiveness. Some of the outcome data obtained to date will be reviewed in the following section.

Comparative Treatment Studies

While comparisons of various treatments by effectiveness are relatively rare, some research on this issue has appeared. One proposed approach to this type of assessment is described by Ollendick, Shapiro, and Barrett (1981). They compared positive practice overcorrection to a traditional correction procedure used by teachers to no treatment. Neither the traditional method nor no treatment proved to be as effective as overcorrection and positive reinforcement for treating of spelling deficits of the children who were hospitalized at Western Psychiatric Institute and Clinic in the University of Pittsburgh School of Medicine. An antecdotal problem that the author would like to note in using this design is that it may prove difficult or even impossible for the clinician-researcher to discern an inability of the patient to discriminate between the treatment conditions since they are usually presented during the same day and sequence effects can result in treatment comparisons of this type. Therefore, while single-subject approaches are highly endorsed, they do have many limitations in evaluating differential effectiveness of two or more treatments. Group research may be the design of choice in this latter situation.

Of the treatment studies recently conducted with punishment, very few have been comparative. Research methods from the treatment studies conducted will be briefly reviewed with some general statements about treatment outcome and what all this may mean. The first procedure to be discussed will be covert sensitization.

Covert sensitization is a procedure that has received a good deal of attention in recent years (see asterisked articles in the references section) and has proven to be a successful means of controlling aberrant behavior. The basic premise of the technique is that images of aversive events should be paired with undesired behavior in an attempt to decrease the targeted problem.

A recent study exemplifies the potential of covert sensitization. In this instance the two treatments compared were covert sensitization and contingent electric shock. Patients were 20 homosexuals who wished to change their sexual preference (McConaghy, Armstrong, & Blaszcyzynski, 1981). Equal numbers of subjects received each of the two treatments. In one instance, electric shock was administered to the fingertips while the patient was viewing slides of homosexual behavior. Covert sensitization, on the other hand, involved having the patient engage in the practice of visualizing three or four scenes in which they engaged in homosexual activity while pairing them with scenes of vomiting and other highly aversive situations. Both treatments were similar in effectiveness. Such a finding may not be as negative as would appear at the outset since the results leave the clinician with at least two treatment options for this problem behavior. Furthermore, one cannot assume that each method will be effective in all instances. Therefore, having an alternative treatment is important. Furthermore, since recent trends relative to legal actions may limit or restrict the use of certain treatment methods, the results are of even greater importance. For these and other reasons comparative research should be encouraged based on current findings.

A second treatment approach to be briefly discussed is overcorrection. This method consists of restitution (reinstating an environment to one vastly superior to the original one) and positive practice (practicing new, alternative behaviors). The procedure is a mix of many treatments including work and effort and time-out, and it is generally viewed to be most effective when applied in a topgraphically specific manner. It has been one of the most favored of the punishment approaches based on recent studies, and it has been applied to a vast array of problems, primarily with institutionalized persons. The problems typically selected for treatment have been those which are exceedingly resistant to change such as aggression (Matson & Stephens, 1977; Matson, Stephens, & Horne, 1978; Webster & Azrin, 1973). Disruptive behaviors of a more general nature that have also been treated include thumbsucking (Freeman, Moss, Somerset, & Ritvo, 1977), scavering (Foxx & Martin, 1975), reluctance to engage in self-help behaviors (Foxx, 1976), and self-injury (Kelly & Drabman, 1977). Unfortunately, comparative studies that involve group research between overcorrection and other methods is basically nonexistent. The only comparative group study found compared restitutional and positive practice overcorrection (Matson, Horne, Ollendick, & Ollendick, 1979). In this instance both methods were highly effective.

A number of single-case studies have been carried out with overcorrection, but the problems inherent with this method are to be found in abundance. For example, only a few of the studies use the more preferred comparison procedures in single-case methodology such as the simultaneous treatment design. Generally what is shown with these comparisons is that overcorrection is more effective with a wide range of problems than just about any other form of reinforcement or punishment. However, these data must, as noted earlier, be interpreted with considerable caution.

A third procedure to be briefly reviewed is response cost. This approach is primarily a penalty system typically used in conjunction with token economies. Extensive reviews of this procedure and the problems for which it has proven effective are presented elsewhere (Kazdin, 1973). The comparative research using group designs is impressive, with response cost compared to other treatment procedures, and may be due in part to the fact that problems receiving attention with this method have been more frequent than what has been the case with many other treatments (e.g., overcorrection). Additionally, since response cost has typically been used with token economy programs, the likelihood of establishing treatment situations with large groups of subjects is made more feasible. A few representative studies conducted in the 1970s will now be highlighted.

In one of these treatment studies, Kazdin (1973) evaluated 48 mentally retarded patients in a sheltered workshop. A response cost procedure of withdrawing tokens when speech dysfluencies occurred was compared to aversive stimulus in the form of loud noise. A third treatment used in this research consisted of information feedback via turning on a light that the patient could see whenever a speech dysfluency was noted. The response cost procedure proved to be highly effective while the other two methods produced little effect.

A second demonstration of response cost's effectiveness was reported by Humphrey, Karoly, and Kirschenbaum (1978). In their study 18 children with reading deficits were evaluated. Children were treated with one of two methods. The first of these, self-reward, consisted of moving tokens from one cup to another contingent on accurate reading performance thereby signifying that a reinforcer had been earned. The second treatment method involved removing tokens from the cup as a penalty when inappropriate behavior was exhibited (making a reading error). Both methods resulted in positive change; however, the self reinforcement method was the more effective.

Another comparative study using response cost that had some substantial methodological weaknesses was reported by Thompson, Kodluboy, and Heston (1980). They treated a 22-year-old mildly mentally retarded woman with Prader-Willi syndrome for her obesity. One treatment method consisted of losing tokens and being socially isolated for gaining weight while the other treatment method involved pairing a shock with preferred high-calorie foods. The point loss and isolation procedure was noted by the authors to be the most effective method of the two described.

Other comparative studies have been made, with response cost generally proving to be the most successful. Some of the other problems effectively treated with response cost include disruptive behavior, anxiety and depression (Reisinger, 1972), and errors in learning (McLaughlin & Malaby, 1972).

Time-out is one of the most widely used of the punishment techniques and has also been subject to comparison with other treatment methods. In one of the more recently reported studies, time-out was compared to command training (having parents issue specific instructions followed by a five-second interval in which the parent did not physically interfer or verbally interrupt the child) alone and in combination.

In this instance the problem behavior to be treated was mouthing of objects by mentally retarded children. Treatment consisted of a number of components, but the most time consuming of the procedures was brushing the child's teeth with a solution of Listerine and water for several minutes. As the reader can readily detect, these methods are vastly different from each other with the latter method involving the use of an aversive stimulus while the former more nearly fits the work and effort concepts central to most of the overcorrection procedures. Thus, saying that overcorrection works or that it works better with some types of problems than others can be misleading in many instances. Considerable precision in making definitive statements about treatment effectiveness with punishment procedures is therefore advised, particularly with overcorrection, time-out, and other methods which have many variations.

A fourth variable that is important in evaluating treatment outcome with punishment procedures is effects of long-term follow-up. In other words, are treatment effects maintained? Very few studies of this nature have been made in the punishment literature. The study by Matson et al. (1979) on overcorrection is one such example. In their case a one-year follow-up of a number of experimental studies was conducted, and effects were maintained in only a few of these persons for one year without treatment. Obviously, this variable should be of critical importance in establishing differential effectiveness of treatments.

Another variable which has plagued research on punishment is whether the treatment is both reliable and valid. In general, behavior therapists should feel confident at least compared to other researchers in psychotherapy. However, while we have done rather systematic and careful analysis of these data, one must wonder why the selection of target behaviors among those using behavior therapy methods has been so haphazard. These variables need closer attention in future research.

Research Trends with Punishment

To provide a representative example of trends in the use of punishment procedures in behavior therapy, four journals that publish such research on a routine basis were reviewed. Journals consulted were *Behavior Therapy,* the *Journal of Behavior Therapy and Experimental Psychiatry, Behavior Modification,* and *Behaviour Research and Therapy* between 1977 and 1982. From these journals 466, 387, 147, and 379 articles were reviewed, respectively. Instrumentation papers and brief reports were not counted. Review papers were included in the count but were not among those studies evaluated as empirical papers and used to determine trends in empirical research. Of the total number of 1,379 studies, 110 or 8% were empirical demonstrations of punishment based on the author's judgment. It is not meant to imply that this number is comprehensive or entirely scientific since studies appear in other journals. Similarly, some procedures might be viewed as borderline. Some studies categorized as interruption procedures, or measures to break an inappropriate response chain, in some cases could be viewed as punishment while in other instances they may not and some methods might be wrongly categorized within this gray area. (For a list of punishment procedures used in the studies mentioned above, see Table 10.1.)

The number of studies on punishment was plotted for each year: 20 (1977), 18 (1978), 20 (1979), 16 (1980), 17 (1981), and 19 (1982), respectively. These data are graphically presented in Figure 10.1. A number of breakdowns of this general set of data were also performed. Figure 10.2 presents one of these breakdowns and is by treatment procedure. In this instance four groups or categories of treatments were delineated. These were time-out and facial screening which appeared in 15 studies, overcorrection and habit reversal were noted in 36 studies, and 25 examples of cognitively oriented aversive training methods were reviewed. Among the methods grouped under this heading were flooding, thought stopping, covert sensitization, and implosive therapy. Time-out and overcorrection methods have been popular for some time. This rather large number

TABLE 10.1
List of Punishment Procedures Employed in Studies Reviewed

Thought stopping	Negative practice
Response prevention	Overcorrection
Behavioral interruption	Flooding
Contingent exercise	Facial screening
Time-out	Response cost
Contingent work	Covert sensitization
Implosive therapy	Scolding
Habit reversal	Rubbing a rubber tube on the neck
Water squirts	Physical restraint
Restraint	Lemon juice therapy
Contingent shock	Snapping wrist with rubber band
Aromatic ammonia	Taste aversion
Social disapproval	Aversive smell
Aversive noise	

The different punishment procedures used in the empirical studies reviewed from 1977 to 1982 from *Behavior Therapy, Journal of Behavior Therapy and Experimental Psychiatry, Behavior Modification,* and *Behaviour Research and Therapy.*

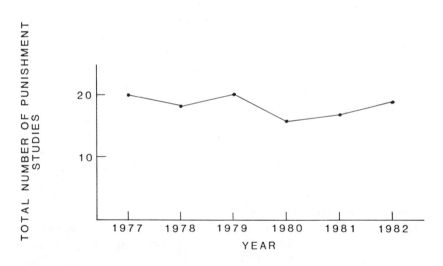

FIGURE 10.1 Total number of empirically based punishment studies in *Behavior Therapy, Journal of Behavior Therapy and Experimental Psychiatry, Behavior Modification,* and *Behaviour Research and Therapy* from 1977 to 1982, by year. (Asterisked articles in the reference section were those used to compile the tables. As a result the bulk of these studies will not be cited directly in the text.)

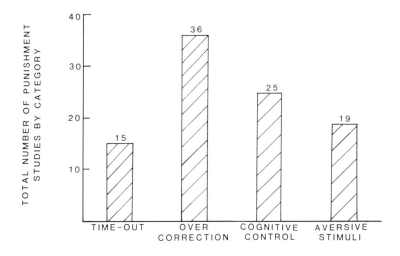

TIME-OUT: TIME-OUT AND FACIAL SCREENING

OVERCORRECTION: OVERCORRECTION AND HABIT REVERSAL

COGNITIVE CONTROL: FLOODING, THOUGHT STOPPING, COVERT SENSITIZATION, IMPLOSIVE THERAPY

AVERSIVE STIMULI : CONTINGENT SHOCK, DISTASTEFUL NOISES AND SUBSTANCES, SOCIAL DISAPPROVAL

FIGURE 10.2 Total number of empirically based punishment studies in *Behavior Therapy, Journal of Behavior Therapy and Experimental Psychiatry, Behavior Modification,* and *Behaviour Research and Therapy* by major categories of punishment. These categories include time-out, overcorrection, covert procedures, and aversive stimuli. (*The number of procedures noted is not a reflection of the total number of studies since some procedures were miscellaneous. These procedures were not included in the tally. Also, some studies used two or more punishment procedures.)

of studies under cognitive control (second of the four groupings) attests to the popularity and effectiveness of cognitive behavior therapy approaches. The fourth of these groupings is categorized as aversive stimuli and consisted of contingent shock, distasteful noises and substances, and social disapproval.

A third breakdown was made on type of problem treated and is represented in Figure 10.3. Once again a grouping procedure was used. In this case one grouping was psychiatric disorders, by far the

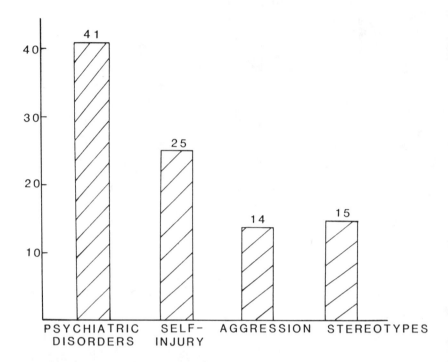

FIGURE 10.3 Total number of empirically based punishment studies in *Behavior Therapy, Journal of Behavior Therapy and Experimental Psychiatry, Behavior Modification,* and *Behaviour Research and Therapy* by problem behaviors. Behaviors are grouped in general areas and include: Psychiatric disorders: depression, obsessive-compulsive behavior, combat fears, public speaking fears, shoplifting, food refusal, fire fetish, pedophilia, alcoholism, hallucinations, homosexuality, exhibitionism, transvestism. Self-injury: chronic rumination, biting, bruxism, thumb-sucking, nail-biting, hair pulling, eye gouging, chronic hicupping, persistent vomiting. Aggression: hitting, tantruming, noncompliance, classroom disruptions. Stereotypes: fondling privates, handshaking, tics.

most frequently occurring problem area. Of the 41 studies which described treatments in this area, the problems noted included depression, obsessive-compulsive behavior, combat fears, public speaking fears, shoplifting, food refusal, fire fetishes, pedophilia, alcoholism, hallucinations, homosexuality, exhibitionism, and transvestism. The second area treated with considerable regularity was self-injurious behavior. Twenty-five studies were found in which this problem was treated including the problems of chronic rumination,

biting, bruxism, thumb-sucking, nail-biting, hair pulling, eye gouging, chronic hiccupping, and persistent vomiting. The third problem
area was aggression, with hitting, tantrums, noncompliance, and
classroom disruptions characterizing this problem area. Finally,
stereotypic behaviors such as fondling privates, handshaking, and
tics were noted as those frequently treated. These data should not be
particularly surprising, since the general areas for study are typical
of past research on punishment procedures in behavior therapy. One
particularly interesting result, from this reviewer's point of view,
was the rather small number of studies on aggression compared to
self-injury and self-stimulation. As it turned out self-injury was
much more frequently treated than aggression, and aggression and
self-stimulation were studied almost equally. These data are particularly surprizing given the recent controversy about whether punishment procedures should be used at all in the treatment of self-
stimulatory behavior. Thus, some contradiction between actual research and practice compared to conceptual-philosophical discourse
seems apparent.

A final comparison based on the studies reviewed involves patient characteristics. This analysis was quite general and consisted of
males ($n = 78$) versus females ($n = 69$), adults ($n = 59$) versus
children ($n = 54$), and developmentally disabled persons ($n = 40$)
such as those with decrements in intelligence, vision, and hearing
problems, versus nonhandicapped ($n = 70$). The total for these de-
mographics typically go over the total number of empirically based
punishment studies due to overlap in variables. The only exception
was that no studies had both developmentally disabled and normal
subjects. Another interesting characteristic was that cognitive control procedures never employed developmentally disabled patients.
Hopefully this problem will be rectified in the future since a number
of self-control studies have demonstrated the effectiveness of cognitive behavior therapy methods with the developmentally disabled.

These data provide some interesting and revealing aspects of
punishment research in the area of behavior therapy. First, the trend
in using these treatment methods continues despite controversy
about their use. One change that may have resulted from objections
to punishment procedures, however, is the shift in the type of punishment methods. Overcorrection and cognitively based punishment
methods are now frequently employed whereas they were infrequently used prior to 1975. (Overcorrection first appeared in print as a
punishment procedure in 1972.) This trend shows flexibility and a
willingness to adapt on the part of behavior therapists.

Nearly equal numbers of males to females and children to adults were evident in the published literature, although the behaviors treated and the therapy methods used varied considerably. In the case of adults, covert sensitization, thought stopping, flooding, and related cognitively based procedures were frequently used to curb sexual disorders, obsessions, and related psychiatric problems of an obviously adult nature. Children, on the other hand, most frequently received treatment for self-injurious and other stereotyped acts as well as aggression. In a majority of cases operantly based procedures such as overcorrection, time-out, or aversive stimuli such as water-squirts or lemon juice therapy were the treatments of choice. These findings provide some rather clear trends that are likely to continue in the next few years.

Unique Applications of Punishment

As noted in the preceding section, the number of punishment studies appearing in behavior therapy have remained relatively stable in the past six years. Despite this, some rather unique and highly innovative applications of punishment have occurred. In this section some of these innovative studies will be briefly reviewed. The intent is not to give an exhaustive discussion of all studies but, rather, a flavor of new developments in the area.

The first procedure to be discussed is habit reversal, which seems to be very similar, at least from this author's view, to positive practice overcorrection, and it is so classified for the present discussion. A fairly large number of studies have been conducted with this method and nailbiting and tics have often been treated. A typical example of habit reversal is presented by Azrin, Nunn, and Frantz (1980), who emphasize teaching the patient to identify the situational, social, and postural precursors of nailbiting and practice these so that self-awareness and thus self-control of habit reversal can be instituted. Contingent on each nailbiting episode, the patient was to engage in a grasping response for three minutes. Additionally, positive nail care to reduce frayed nails and cuticles was taught using a nail file and hand lotion. These behaviors were to be performed based on each biting episode. Many patients of both sexes and both adults and children have been treated with this highly effective method.

Another interesting approach is described by Singh (1979). He treated a 15-month-old boy for holding his breath resulting in his becoming unconscious. This behavior was evinced when in aversive situations, such as getting a shot or being interrupted during play or sleep. Treatment was carried out in the children's ward of a public hospital by crushing a vial of aromatic ammonia, which was then held four inches from his nose based on a breath-holding incident. The procedure was paired with verbal reprimands. Holding and cuddling of the child were used if he did not hold his breath for three-minute intervals during treatment sessions. Positive effects of the study were rapidly apparent.

Hayashida (1982) is another author who demonstrated a unique punishment treatment in behavior therapy. The patient in this instance was an 18-year-old coed with "pervasive and repetitive compulsive checking," a frequent response among obsessive-compulsive individuals, triggered by many common events of daily life. In this instance, she would repeatedly look to ascertain whether particular items or objects remained in previously designated spots such as continually checking to see whether doors, windows, and so forth had been closed. The effective treatment in this instance consisted of *in vivo* exposure and punishment. The latter method consisted of response prevention, whereby the patient was taken to settings in which she frequently engaged in checking behaviors, without allowing her to perform these responses. Unfortunately, the methods used to enforce response prevention were not well detailed. It may be assumed that verbal reprimands were an integral aspect of this procedure, however.

Another method related to response prevention aimed primarily at breaking a response chain is described by Belcher, Conetta, Cole, Iannotti, and McGovern (1982). They refered to the method as behavioral interruption. Their method, which is likened to overcorrection in that it consisted of mild, physically oriented intervention, is made up of a verbal reprimand followed by pulling a severely mentally retarded, blind 19-year-old male's chair away from his work table. He was then required to stand, make one 360° revolution with minimal physical prompting, and then resume his seat. The targeted problem, severe tantruming (stripping nude, throwing chairs, screaming and crying, scratching others, and so on) was rapidly decreased (within two weeks) after the initiation of treatment.

Another interesting and highly innovative application of punishment has been described by Gauthier and Pellerin (1982). They used covert desensitization and thought stopping to treat the compulsive shoplifting of a 30-year-old woman. Apparently the behavior was at a very high rate since the patient admitted that she acted on these urges almost every time she went to a store. To further exacerbate her problem, she had four previous convictions and had recently been charged for a fifth. Initially, the patient was asked to use thought stopping whenever she began to consider engaging in thoughts related to shoplifting. This procedure was used for one week with no positive effects. Next, the patient was instructed to apply covert sensitization which consisted of having her imagine different aversive consequences of stealing when the urge arose and at least 10 times a day, even if sufficient instances when the urge to shoplift were not evident. Of the methods employed, only covert sensitization proved effective.

Severe chronic hiccupping which resulted in gastrointestinal bleeding in an epileptic mentally retarded male patient is a novel problem recently treated effectively with punishment. This patient received a behavior therapy program that consisted of verbal reprimands plus moving a rubber tube up and down the patient's throat contingent on every occurrence of hiccupping until gagging occurred. While the procedure was a rather radical one, from this author's point of view, mild bleeding may be an unfortunate choice of terms given the other symptoms evinced by the patient during hiccupping attacks. These responses included high rates of coughing, vomiting, spitting up food, saliva, and blood, iron deficiency anemia, and severe forms of food rejection.

These studies highlight some rather unique applications of punishment. It should be cautioned, however, that the problem should be quite severe before such methods are employed. Furthermore, reinforcement and other milder forms of punishment should be tried first if there is time and staff available and some likelihood based on past research that such methods may work.

Future Directions

Based on what has occurred in the field of behavior therapy to this point, it is likely that punishment procedures will remain an important part of the behavior therapist's therapeutic approach. There are some data that would seem to support this position. First, there is a long tradition (relative to the brief time that behavior therapy has been a treatment approach) confirming the importance of various punishment procedures as useful means of treating problem behaviors. When learning-based procedures were first introduced to the

fields of psychiatry and clinical psychology, only the most recalcitrant problems were open to investigation, since mild anxiety-based
problems were considered the purview of the pyschodynamically
based psychotherapists. Thus, problems such as self-injurious behavior, toileting problems, self-help skills, and aggression of mentally retarded and chronic schizophrenic patients received attention by
the behavior therapist to the exclusion of other problem areas. A
major aspect of the successful treatment regimes employed were
behavior therapy programs that had as a principle component
punishment. While the scope of the problems treated has expanded,
these areas continue to be prominent.

One trap that the behavior therapist, as well as the fields of
psychiatry and clinical psychology, has fallen prey to in this writer's
opinion is that the mentally retarded and other developmentally
disabled patients have not been a target for treatment with cognitively based methods and with traditional psychiatric problems. Thus,
for example, no mentally retarded patients have received treatment
for sexual dysfunctions, phobias, or anxiety-based disorders using
cognitively oriented treatments. The prevalence of psychiatric problems has been shown to be much higher in the developmentally
disabled than in patients without such handicaps, and this problem
area is one of many that are in urgent need of attention from the
behavior therapist.

Punishment procedures in general have come under considerable attack not only from outside but from within clinical psychology
and psychiatry. Such attacks are a challenge that should be and have
been addressed by behavior therapists. Thus, while the use of punishment does not seem to have greatly decreased, if one can infer anything from research reports in behavioral journals, there has been a
major shift in the techniques and to a lesser extent the problems
receiving treatment. This trend is likely to continue. One reason for
such a conclusion is that the courts have generally determined that
behavior therapy is a less intrusive alternative than drugs, and
reinforcement procedures alone do not seem to be the total answer to
the treatment of many of the problems punishment methods have
traditionally been employed to check, at least to this point. The data
on studies published in the field would seem to support such a conclusion.

Three methods of punishment that have received considerable
attention within the last six years are cognitive methods, overcorrection, and aversive substances such as lemon juice therapy and water
squirts. Far and away the most researched of these techniques is

overcorrection, but this state of affairs may be attributed at least to some degree to the prolific and excellent research of Dr. Nathan Azrin and his associates. Overcorrection would have a similar trend in studies conducted as the other two methods had these studies not been included. The major contributions of Azrin's research group are to be complemented. Rather, a trend line not including the Azrin et al. studies is pointed out merely to demonstrate that overcorrection is probably having an impact more nearly equal to cognitive procedures and aversive substances than what is reflected in the data on number of treatment studies by procedure presented here.

It can be concluded from this review that punishment procedures continue to be viable and a growing number of options in treatment strategies are apparent. As noted above, however, the types of punishment procedures and the areas which are emphasized may be changing to some degree. As such, the tradition of punishment methods as one of the major treatment tools of the behavior therapist, particularly with very recalcitrant patients and problems, is likely to continue.

References

*Altman, K., Haavik, S., & Cook, J. W. Punishment of self-injurious behavior in natural settings using contingent aromatic ammonia. *Behaviour Research and Therapy*, 1978, *16*, 85–96.

*Andrasik, F., Turner, S. M., & Ollendick, T. H. Self-report and physiologic responding *in vivo* flooding. *Behaviour Research and Therapy*, 1980, *18*, 593–594.

Ardila, R. Behavior modification in Latin America. In M. Hersen, R. M. Eisler, & P. M. Miller (Eds.), *Progress in behavior modification*. New York: Academic Press, 1978.

*Arrick, M. C., Voss, J., & Rimm, D. C. The relative efficacy of thought-stopping and covert assertion. *Behaviour Research and Therapy*, 1981, *19*, 17–24.

Asher, S., Oden, S., & Gottman, J. Children's friendships in school settings. In L. Katz (Ed.), *Current topics in early childhood education* (Vol. 1). Hillsdale, NJ: Lawrence Erlbaum Associates, 1976.

Azrin, N. H., & Holz, W. C. Punishment. In W. K. Honig (Ed.), *Operant behavior: Areas of research and application*. New York: Appleton-Century-Croft, 1966.

*Asterisked articles were used to compile the table and figures in this chapter.

*Azrin, N. H., Nunn, R. G., & Frantz, S. E. Habit reversal vs. negative practice treatment of nervous tics. *Behavior Therapy*, 1980, *11*, 169–178.

*Azrin, N. H., Nunn, R. G., & Frantz, S. E. Treatment of hairpulling (Trichotillomania): A comparative study of habit reversal and negative practice training. *Journal of Behavior Therapy and Experimental Psychiatry*, 1980, *11*, 13–20.

*Azrin, N. H., Nunn, R. G., & Frantz-Renshaw, S. Habit reversal treatment of thumbsucking. *Behaviour Research and Therapy*, 1980, *18*, 395–400.

*Azrin, N. H., Nunn, R. G., & Frantz-Renshaw, S. E. Habit reversal vs. negative practice treatment of self-destructive oral habits (biting, chewing or licking of the lips, cheeks, tongue or palate). *Journal of Behavior Therapy and Experimental Psychiatry*, 1982, *13*, 49–54.

*Baker, T. B., & Cannon, D. S. Taste aversion therapy with alcoholics: Techniques and evidence of a conditioned response. *Behavior Research and Therapy*, 1979, *17*, 229–242.

*Ball, T. S., Campbell, R., & Barkemeyer, R. Air splints applied to control self-injurious finger sucking in profoundly retarded individuals. *Journal of Behavior Therapy and Experimental Psychiatry*, 1980, *11*, 267–271.

*Barmann, B. C., & Murray, W. J. Suppression of inappropriate sexual behaviors by facial screening. *Behavior Therapy*, 1981, *12*, 730–735.

*Barmann, B. C., & Vitali, D. L. Facial screening to eliminate trichotillomania in developmentally disabled persons. *Behavior Therapy*, 1982, *13*, 735–742.

*Barrett, R. P., & Shapiro, E. S. Treatment of stereotyped hair-pulling with overcorrection: A case study with long term follow-up. *Journal of Behavior Therapy and Experimental Psychiatry*, 1980, *11* 317–320.

*Belcher, T. L., Conetta, C., Cole, C., Iannotti, E., & McGovern, M. Eliminating a severely retarded blind adolescent's tantrums using mild behavioral interruption: A case study. *Journal of Behavior Therapy and Experimental Psychiatry*, 1982, *13*, 257–260.

*Berecz, J. M. Maintenance of nonsmoking behavior through self-administered wrist-band aversive therapy. *Behavior Therapy*, 1979, *10*, 669–675.

Bersoff, D. N., & Prasse, D. Applied psychology and judicial decision making: Corporal punishment as a case in point. *Professional Psychology*, 1978, *9*, 400–411.

*Black, J. L., & Keane, T. M. Implosive therapy in the treatment of combat related fears in a World War II veteran. *Journal of Behavior Therapy and Experimental Psychiatry*, 1982, *13*, 163–165.

*Boland, F. J., Mellor, C. S., & Revusky, S. Chemical aversion treatment of alcoholism: Lithium as the aversive agent. *Behaviour Research and Therapy*, 1978, *16*, 401–410.

*Bollard, J., Nettlebeck, T., & Roxbee, L. Dry-bed training for childhood bedwetting: A comparison of group with individually administered parent instruction. *Behaviour Research and Therapy*, 1982, *20*, 209–218.

Boring, E. *History, psychology and science: Selected papers.* New York: Wiley, 1963.

*Bornstein, P. H., Hamilton, S. B., & Quevillon, R. P. Behavior modification by long-distance: Demonstration of functional control over disruptive behavior in a rural classroom setting. *Behavior Modification*, 1977, *1*, 369–380.

*Boudreau, L., Landry-Martin, T., & Killorn, L. H. Multiple behavior therapy techniques applied to a case of forcible sexual assault. *Journal of Behavior Therapy and Experimental Psychiatry*, 1978, *9*, 335–337.

*Carstens, C. Application of a work penalty threat in the treatment of a case of juvenile fire setting. *Journal of Behavior Therapy and Experimental Psychiatry*, 1982, *13*, 159–161.

*Castro, L., & Rachlin, H. Self-reward, self-monitoring and self-punishment as feedback in weight control. *Behavior Therapy*, 1980, *11*, 38–48.

*Chanbless, D. L., Foa, E. B., Groves, G. A., & Goldstein, A. J. Flooding with brevital in the treatment of agoraphobia: Countereffective? *Behaviour Research and Therapy*, 1979, *17*, 243–251.

*Chaplin, E. W., & Levine, B. A. The effects of total exposure duration and interrupted versus continuous exposure in flooding therapy. *Behavior Therapy*, 1981, *12*, 360–368.

*Chassan, J. B. *Research design in clinical psychology and psychiatry.* New York: Wiley, 1979.

*Cimenero, A. R., & Davidson, R. S. Free-operant avoidance of alcohol: An analogue study of alcohol aversion. *Journal of Behavior Therapy and Experimental Psychiatry*, 1977, *8*, 371–376.

*Cincirpini, P. M., Epstein, L. H., & Kotanchik, N. L. Behavioral intervention for self-stimulatory, attending and seizure behavior in a cerebral palsied child. *Journal of Behavior Therapy and Experimental Psychiatry*, 1980, *11*, 313–316.

*Cipani, E. Modifying food spillage behavior in an institutionalized retarded client. *Journal of Behavior Therapy and Experimental Psychiatry*, 1981, *12*, 261–265.

*Clements, J., & Dewey, M. The effects of overcorrection: A case study. *Behaviour Research and Therapy*, 1979, *17*, 515–518.

*Coleman, R. S., Whitman, T. L., & Johnson, M. R. Suppression of self-stimulatory behavior of a profoundly retarded boy across staff settings: An assessment of situational generalization. *Behavior Therapy*, 1979, *10*, 266–280.

*Conley, O. S., & Wolery, M. R. Treatment by overcorrection of self-injurious eye gouging in preschool blind children. *Journal of Behavior Therapy and Experimental Psychiatry*, 1980, *11*, 121–125.

*Cook, J. W., Altman, C. K., Shaw, J., & Blaylock, M. Use of contingent lemon juice to eliminate public masturbation by a severely retarded boy. *Behaviour Research and Therapy,* 1978, *16,* 131–133.

*Crowley, C. P., & Armstrong, P. M. Positive practice overcorrection and behavior rehearsal in the treatment of three cases of encopresis. *Journal of Behavior Therapy and Experimental Psychiatry,* 1977, *8,* 441–416.

*Czyzewski, M. J., Barrera, R. D., & Sulzer-Azaroff, B. An abbreviated overcorrection program to reduce self-stimulatory behaviors. *Journal of Behavior Therapy and Experimental Psychiatry,* 1982, *13,* 55–62.

*Daniel, W. H. Management of chronic rumination with a contingent exercise procedure employing topographically dissimilar behavior. *Journal of Behavior Therapy and Experimental Psychiatry,* 1982, *13,* 149–152.

*Delparto, D. J., Aleh, E., Bambusch, J., & Barclay, L. A. Treatment of fingernail biting by habit reversal. *Journal of Behavior Therapy and Experimental Psychiatry,* 1977, *8,* 319.

*Doleys, D. M., Ciminero, A. R., Wallach, E. S., & Davidson, R. S. Responding by alcoholics during aversive conditioning: Implications for treatment. *Behavior Modification,* 1977, *1,* 205–220.

Doleys, D. M., Wells, K. C., Hobbs, S. A., Roberts, M. W., & Cartelli, L. M. The effects of social punishment on noncompliance: A comparison with time-out and positive practice. *Journal of Applied Behavior Analysis,* 1976, *9,* 471–482.

*Drabman, R. S., Cruz, G. C., Ross, J., & Lynd, S. Suppression of chronic drooling in mentally retarded children and adolescents: Effectiveness of a behavioral treatment package. *Behavior Therapy,* 1979, *10,* 46–56.

*Fairbank, J. A., & Keane, T. M. Flooding for combat-related stress disorders: Assessment of anxiety reduction across traumatic memories. *Behavior Therapy,* 1982, *13,* 499–510.

*Fischer, J., & Nehs, R. Use of a commonly available chore to reduce a boy's rate of swearing. *Journal of Behavior Therapy and Experimental Psychiatry,* 1978, *9,* 81–83.

*Fleming, A., & Nolley, D. A comparison of techniques for the elimination of self-injurious behavior in a mildly retarded woman. *Journal of Behavior Therapy and Experimental Psychiatry,* 1981, *12,* 81–85.

*Foa, E. B., & Chambless, D. C. Habituation of subjective anxiety during flooding in imagery. *Behaviour Research and Therapy,* 1978, *16,* 391–399.

*Fonagy, P., & Slade, P. Punishment vs negative reinforcement in the aversive conditioning of auditory hallucinations. *Behaviour Research and Therapy,* 1982, *20,* 483–492.

Foxx, R. M. Increasing a mildly retarded woman's attendance at self-help classes by overcorrection and instruction. *Behavior Therapy,* 1976, *7,* 390–396.

Foxx, R. M., & Azrin, N. H. The elimination of autistic self-stimulatory behavior by overcorrection. *Journal of Applied Behavior Analysis,* 1973, *6,* 1–14.

Foxx, R. M., & Azrin, N. H. Restitution: A method of eliminating aggressive-disruptive behaviors of retarded and brain damaged patients. *Behaviour Research and Therapy,* 1972, *10,* 15–27.

*Foxx, R. M., & Martin, E. D. Treatment of scavenging behavior (coprophagy and pica) by overcorrection. *Behaviour Research and Therapy,* 1975, *13,* 153–162.

*Freeman, B. J., Moss, D., Somerset, T., & Ritvo, E. R. Thumbsucking in an autistic child overcome by overcorrection. *Journal of Behavior Therapy and Experimental Psychiatry,* 1977, *8,* 211–212.

*Gauthier, J., & Pellerin, D. Management of compulsive shoplifting through covert sensitization. *Journal of Behavior Therapy and Experimental Psychiatry,* 1982, *13,* 73–75.

Glass, G. V., McGaw, B., & Smith, M. L. *Meta Analysis & Social Research.* Beverly Hills, CA.: Sage Publications, 1981.

Gottman, J. M., & Markman, H. J. Experimental designs in psychotherapy research. In S. L. Garfield & A. E. Bergin (Eds.), *Handbook of psychotherapy and behavior change.* New York: Wiley, 1978.

*Gray, J. J. Positive reinforcement and punishment in the treatment of childhood trichotillomania. *Journal of Behavior Therapy and Experimental Psychiatry,* 1979, *10,* 125–129.

*Gross, A. M., Berler, E. S., & Drabman, R. S. Reduction of aggressive behavior in a retarded boy using a water squirt. *Journal of Behavior Therapy and Experimental Psychiatry,* 1982, *13,* 95–98.

Hamilton, D. I. The side effects of electric shock employed with mentally retarded persons. *Australian and New Zealand Journal of Developmental Disabilities,* 1982, *8,* 133–140.

Harmatz, M. G., & Lapuc, P. Behavior modification of overeating in a psychiatric population. *Journal of Consulting and Clinical Psychology,* 1968, *32,* 583–587.

*Hayashida, M. Successful response prevention of rituals producing increase then decrease of untreated rituals. *Journal of Behavior Therapy and Experimental Psychiatry,* 1982, *13,* 225–228.

*Hayes, S. C., Brownell, K. D., & Barlow, D. H. The use of self-administered covert sensitization in the treatment of exhibitionism and sadism. *Behavior Therapy,* 1978, *9,* 283–289.

Hersen, M., & Barlow, D. *Single case research designs.* New York: Pergamon Press, 1976.

*Hobbs, S. A., Forehand, R., & Murray, R. G. Effects of various durations of timeout on the noncompliance behavior of children. *Behavior Therapy,* 1978, *9,* 652–656.

Humphrey, L. L., Karoly, P., & Kirschenbaum, D. S. Self-management in the classroom. Self-imposed response cost versus self-reward. *Behavior Therapy,* 1978, *9,* 592–601.

*Ingersoll, B., & Curry, F. Rapid treatment of persistent vomiting in a 14-year old female by shaping and time-out. *Journal of Behavior Therapy and Experimental Psychiatry,* 1977, *8,* 305–307.

*Jenkins, J. O., & Peterson, G. R. Self-monitoring and self-administered aversion in the treatment of Bruxism. *Journal of Behavior Therapy and Experimental Psychiatry,* 1978, *9,* 387–388.

*Johnson, M. R., Whitman, T. L., & Barloon-Noble, R. A home-based program for a preschool behaviorally disturbed child with parents as therapists. *Journal of Behavior Therapy and Experimental Psychiatry,* 1978, *9,* 65–70.

*Josiassen, R. C., Fantuzzo, J., & Rosen, A. C. Treatment of pedophilia using multistage aversion therapy and social skills training. *Journal of Behavior Therapy and Experimental Psychiatry,* 1980, *11,* 55–61.

Kaufman, K. F., & O'Leary, K. D. Reward, cost, and self-evaluation procedures for disruptive adolescents in a psychiatric hospital school. *Journal of Applied Behavior Analysis,* 1972, *5,* 293–309.

Kazdin, A. E. The effect of response cost and aversive stimulation in suppressing punished and nonpunished speed dysfluencies. *Behavior Therapy,* 1973, *4,* 73–82

Kazdin, A. E. *Single-case research designs: Methods for clinical and applied settings.* New York: Oxford, 1982.

Kazdin, A. E., & Matson, J. L. Social validation with the mentally retarded. *Applied Research in Mental Retardation,* 1981, *2,* 39–54.

Kelly, J. A., & Drabman, R. S. Generalizing response supression of self-injurious behavior through an overcorrection punishment procedure: A case study. *Behavior Therapy,* 1977, *8,* 468–472.

*Kenny, F. T., Moubray, R. M., & Lalaini, S. Faradic disruption of obsessive ideation in the treatment of obsessive neurosis: A controlled study. *Behavior Therapy,* 1978, *9,* 209–221.

*Labouceur, R. Habit reversal treatment: Learning an incompatible response or increasing the subject's awareness? *Behaviour Research and Therapy,* 1979, *17,* 313–316.

La Greca, A. M. Peer acceptance: The correspondence between children's sociometric scores and teachers' rating of peer interactions. *Journal of Abnormal Child Psychology,* 1981, *9,* 167–178.

*Lande, S. D. A combination of orgasmic reconditioning and covert sensitization in the treatment of a fire fetish. *Journal of Behavior Therapy and Experimental Psychiatry,* 1980, *11,* 291–296.

*Lassen, M. K., & Fluet, N. R. Elimination of nocturnal thumbsucking by glove wearing. *Journal of Behavior Therapy and Experimental Psychiatry,* 1978, *9,* 85.

*Laws, D. R., Meyer, J., & Holmen, M. L. Reduction of sadistic sexual arousal by olfactory aversion: A case study. *Behaviour Research and Therapy,* 1978, *16,* 281–284.

*Leger, L. A. An outcome measure for thought-stopping examined in three case studies. *Journal of Behavior Therapy and Experimental Psychiatry*, 1979, *10*, 115–120.

*Lewis, M., Shilton, P., & Fugua, R. W. Parental control of nocturnal thumb-sucking. *Journal of Behavior Therapy and Experimental Psychiatry*, 1981, *12*, 87–90.

*Lombardo, T. W., & Turner, S. M. Thought-stopping in the control of obsessive ruminations. *Behavior Modification*, 1979, *3*, 267–272.

Lovaas, O. I., & Simmons, J. Q. Manipulation of self-destruction in three retarded children. *Journal of Applied Behavior Analysis*, 1969, *2*, 143–157.

*Luiselli, J. K., & Greenidge, A. Behavioral treatment of high-rate aggression in a rubella child. *Journal of Behavior Therapy and Experimental Psychiatry*, 1982, *13*, 152–157.

*Luiselli, J. K., Helfen, C. S., Pemberton, B. W., & Reisman, J. The elimination of a child's in-class masturbation by overcorrection and reinforcement. *Journal of Behavior Therapy and Experimental Psychiatry*, 1977, *8*, 201–204.

*Luiselli, J. K., Suskin, L., & McPhee, D. F. Continuous and intermittent application of overcorrection in a self-injurious autistic child: Alternating treatments design analysis. *Journal of Behavior Therapy and Experimental Psychiatry*, 1981, *12*, 355–358.

Lutzker, J. A frank word about division membership from John Lutzker. *Division 25 Recorder*, 1982, *17*, 7.

*Mansdorf, I. J. Reinforcer isolation: An alternative to subject isolation in time-out from positive reinforcement. *Journal of Behavior Therapy and Experimental Psychiatry*, 1977, *8*, 391–393.

*Marholin, D., & Townsend, N. M. An experimental analysis of side effects and response maintenance of a modified overcorrection procedure. *Behavior Therapy*, 1978, *9*, 383–390.

*Marshall, W. L., Parker, L., & Hayes, B. J. Treating public speaking problems: A study using flooding and the elements of skills training. *Behavior Modification*, 1982, *6*, 147–170.

*Martin, G. L. Thought-stopping and stimulus control to decrease persistent disturbing thoughts. *Journal of Behavior Therapy and Experimental Psychiatry*, 1982, *13*, 215–220.

Martin, J. E., Weller, S., & Matson, J. L. Eliminating object transferring of a profoundly retarded female by overcorrection. *Psychological Reports*, 1977, *8*, 327–328.

Martin, R. *Legal challenges to behavior modification*. Champaign, IL: Research Press, 1975.

*Matson, J. L. Social reinforcement by the spouse in weight control: A case study. *Journal of Behavior Therapy and Experimental Psychiatry*, 1977, *8*, 327–328.

Matson, J. L. Behavior modification procedures for training chronically institutionalized schizophrenics. In M. Hersen, R. M. Eisler, & P. M.

Miller, *Progress in behavior modification*. New York: Academic Press, 1980.

Matson, J. L., & DiLorenzo, T. M. *Punishment and behavior modification: New perspectives and alternatives.* New York: Springer Publishing, 1984.

*Matson, J. L., Esveldt-Dawson, K., & O'Donnell, D. Overcorrection, modeling, and reinforcement procedures for reinstating speech in a mute boy. *Child Behavior Therapy*, 1980, *1*, 363–371.

*Matson, J. L., & Horne, A. M. A comparison of modeling, desensitization, flooding, study skills, and control groups for reducing test anxiety. *Behavior Therapy*, 1977, *8*, 1–8.

Matson, J. L., Horne, A. M., Ollendick, R. G., & Ollendick, T. H. Overcorrection: A further evaluation of restitution and positive practice. *Journal of Behavior Therapy and Experimental Psychiatry*, 1979, *10*, 295–298.

Matson, J. L., & Ollendick, T. H. The random stimulus design. *Child Behavior Therapy*, 1981, *5*, 491–502.

Matson, J. L., Ollendick, T. H., & DiLorenzo, T. M. Time-out and the characteristics of mentally retarded institutionalized adults who do or do not receive it. *Mental Retardation*, 1980, *18*, 181–184.

*Matson, J. L., Ollendick, T. H., & Martin, H. E. Overcorrection revisited: A long-term follow-up. *Journal of Behavior Therapy and Experimental Psychiatry*, 1979, *10*, 11–13.

*Matson, J. L., & Stephens, R. M. Overcorrection of aggressive behavior in a chronic mental patient. *Behavior Modification*, 1977, *1*, 559–564.

Matson, J. L., & Stephens, R. M. Increasing appropriate behavior of explosive chronic psychiatric patients with a social-skills training package. *Behavior Modification*, 1978, *2*, 61–76.

*Matson, J. L., & Stephens, R. M. Overcorrection treatment of stereotyped behaviors. *Behavior Modification*, 1981, *5*, 491–502.

*Matson, J. L., Stephens, R. M., & Horne, A. M. Overcorrection and extinction-reinforcement as rapid methods of eliminating the disruptive behaviors of relatively normal children. *Behavioral Engineering*, 1978, *1*, 89–94.

*McConaghy, N., Armstrong, M. S., & Blaszczynski, A. Control comparison of aversive therapy and covert sensitization in compulsive homosexuality. *Behaviour Research and Therapy*, 1981, *19*, 425–434.

McLaughlin, T., & Malaby, J. Reducing and measuring inappropriate verbalizations in a token classroom. *Journal of Applied Behavior Analysis*, 1972, *5*, 329–333.

*Miller, A. J., & Karatochwill, T. R. Reduction of frequent stomachache complaints by time-out. *Behavior Therapy*, 1979, *10*, 211–218.

Mora, G. Historical and theoretical trends in psychiatry. In A. M. Freedman, H. I. Kaplan, & B. J. Sadock (Eds.), *Comprehensive textbook of psychiatry* (Vol. 1). Baltimore: Williams & Wilkins, 1978.

*Murray, R. G., & Hobbs, S. A. The use of a self-imposed timeout procedure in the modification of excessive alcohol consumption. *Journal of Behavior Therapy and Experimental Psychiatry*, 1977, *8*, 377–380.

*Nettlebeck, T., & Bollard, J. A comparison of dry-bed training and standard urine-alarm conditioning treatment of childhood bedwetting. *Behaviour Research and Therapy*, 1981, *19*, 215–226.

*O'Brien, J. S. A modified thought stopping procedure for the treatment of agoraphobia. *Journal of Behavior Therapy and Experimental Psychiatry*, 1979, *10*, 121–124.

*Ollendick, T. H. Self-monitoring and self-administered overcorrection: The modification of nervous tics in children. *Behavior Modification*, 1981, *5*, 75–84.

*Ollendick, T. H., Shapiro, E. S., & Barrett, R. P. Reducing stereotypic behaviors: An analysis of treatment procedures utilizing an alternating treatment design. *Behavior Therapy*, 1981, *12*, 570–577.

*Paquin, M. J. The treatment of a nail-biting compulsion by covert sensitization in a poorly motivated client. *Journal of Behavior Therapy and Experimental Psychiatry*, 1977, *8*, 181–183.

*Rabavilas, A. D., Boulougouris, J. C., Perissaki, C., & Stefanis, C. Premorbid personality traits and responsiveness to flooding in obsessive-compulsive patients. *Behaviour Research and Therapy*, 1976, *17*, 575–580.

Repp, A. C., & Deitz, D. E. D. On the selective use of punishment-suggested guidelines for administrators. *Mental Retardation*, 1978, *16*, 250–254.

Risley, T. R. The effects and side effects of punishing the autistic behaviors of a deviant child. *Journal of Applied Behavior Analysis*, 1968, *1*, 21–34.

*Roberts, M. W., Hatzenbuehler, C., & Bean, A. W. Effects of differential attention and timeout on child noncompliance. *Behavior Therapy*, 1981, *12*, 93–99.

*Rollings, J. P., Baumeister, A. A., & Baumeister, A. A. The use of overcorrection procedures to eliminate the stereotyped behaviors of retarded individuals. An analysis of collateral behaviors and generalization of suppressive effects. *Behavior Modification*, 1977, *1*, 29–46.

*Rosen, A. C., & Rehm, L. Long term follow-up in two cases of transvestism treated with aversion therapy. *Journal of Behavior Therapy and Experimental Psychiatry*, 1977, *8*, 295–300.

*Rosenbaum, M. S., & Ayllon, T. The behavioral treatment of neurodermatitis through habit-reversal. *Behaviour Research and Therapy*, 1981, *19*, 313–318.

*Rosenbaum, M. S., & Ayllon, T. The habit-reversal technique in treating trichotillomania. *Behavior Therapy*, 1981, *12*, 473–481.

*Rosenbaum, M. S., & Ayllon, T. Treating bruxism with the habit-reversal technique. *Behaviour Research and Therapy*, 1981, *19*, 87–96.

Sajwaj, T., Libet, J., & Agras, S. Lemon-juice therapy: The control of life-threatening rumination in a six-month-old infant. *Journal of Applied Behavior Analysis*, 1974, *7*, 557–566.

*Schroeder, S. R., Peterson, C. R., Solomon, L. J., & Artley, J. J. EMG feedback and the contingent restraint of self-injurious behavior among the severely retarded: Two case illustrations. *Behavior Therapy*, 1977, *8*, 738–741.

*Schultz, R., Wehman, P., Renzaglia, A., & Karan, O. Efficacy of contingent social disapproval of inappropriate verbalizations of two severely retarded males. *Behavior Therapy*, 1978, *9*, 657–662.

Sears, B. R., Maccoby, E. E., & Levin, H. *Patterns of child rearing*. Evanston: Row-Peterson, 1957.

*Shapiro, E. S. Restitution and positive practice overcorrection in reducing aggressive-disruptive behavior: A long-term follow-up. *Journal of Behavior Therapy and Experimental Psychiatry*, 1979, *10*, 131–134.

*Shapiro, E. S., Barrett, R. P., & Ollendick, T. H. A comparison of physical restraint and positive practice overcorrection in treating stereotypic behavior. *Behavior Therapy*, 1980, *11*, 227–233.

*Sherry, G. S., & Levine, B. A. An examination of procedural variables in flooding therapy. *Behavior Therapy*, 1980, *11*, 148–155.

*Singh, N. N. Aversive control of breath holding. *Journal of Behavior Therapy and Experimental Psychiatry*, 1979, *10*, 147–149.

*Singh, N. N. The effects of facial screening on infant self-injury. *Journal of Behavior Therapy and Experimental Psychiatry*, 1980, *11*, 131–134.

*Singh, N. N., Winton, A. S., & Dawson, M. J. Suppression of antisocial behavior by facial screening using multiple baseline and alternating treatments designs. *Behavior Therapy*, 1982, *13*, 511–520.

Spence, J. T., & Segner, L. L. Verbal versus nonverbal reinforcement combinations in the discrimination learning of middle and lower-class children. *Child Development*, 1967, *38*, 29–38.

*Stimbert, V. E., Minor, J. W., & McCoy, J. F. Intensive feeding training with retarded children. *Behavior Modification*, 1977, *1*, 517–530.

*Teasedale, J. D., & Rezin, V. Effect of thought-stopping on thoughts, mood and corrugator EMG in depressed patients. *Behaviour Research Therapy*, 1978, *16*, 97–102.

*Thompson, T., Kodluboy, S., & Heston, L. Behavioral treatment of obesity in Prader-Willi Syndrome. *Behavior Therapy*, 1980, *11*, 588–593.

*Thorbecke, P. J., & Jackson, H. J. Reducing chronic drooling in a retarded female using a multi-treatment package. *Journal of Behavior Therapy and Experimental Psychiatry*, 1982, *13*, 89–93.

*Tryon, G. S., & Palladino, J. J. Thought stopping: A case study and observations. *Journal of Behavior Therapy and Experimental Psychiatry*, 1979, *10*, 151–154.

*Turner, S. M., Hersen, M., & Bellack, A. S. Effects of social disruption, stimulus interference, and aversive conditioning on auditory hallucinations. *Behavior Modification*, 1977, *1*, 249–258.

*Van Heuven, P. F., & Smeets, P. M. Behavioral control of chronic hiccupping associated with gastrointestinal bleeding in a retarded epileptic male. *Journal of Behavior Therapy and Experimental Psychiatry*, 1981, *12*, 341–345.

*Varni, J. W., Boyd, E. F., & Cataldo, M. F. Self-monitoring, external reinforcement, and timeout procedures in the control of high rate tic behaviors in a hyperactive child. *Journal of Behavior Therapy and Experimental Psychiatry*, 1978, *9*, 353–358.

Webster, D. R., & Azrin, N. H. Required relaxation: A method of inhibiting agitative-disruptive behavior of retardates. *Behaviour Research and Therapy*, 1973, *11*, 67–78.

*Weslowski, M. D., & Zaulocki, R. J. The differential effects of procedures to eliminate an injurious self-stimulatory behavior (digito-ocular sign) in blind retarded twins. *Behavior Therapy*, 1982, *13*, 334–345.

*Whitehead, W. E., Robinson, A., Blackwell, B., & Stutz, R. M. Flooding treatment of phobias: Does chronic diazepam increase effectiveness? *Journal of Behavior Therapy and Experimental Psychiatry*, 1978, *19*, 219–225.

*Wilson, C. C., Robertson, S. J., Herlong, L. H., & Haynes, S. N. Vicarious effects of time-out in the modification of aggression in the classroom. *Behavior Modification*, 1979, *3*, 97–111.

*Wolf, R. Systematic desensitization and negative practice to alter the after effects of a rape attempt. *Journal of Behavior Therapy and Experimental Psychiatry*, 1977, *8*, 423–425.

Wyatt v. Stickney, 325 F. Supp. 781 (M.D. Ala. 1971), 334 F. Supp. 1341 (M.D. Ala. 1971), 344 F. Supp. 373, 387 (M.D. Ala. 1972), *aff'd in part, modified in part sub nom., Wyatt v. Anderholt*, 503 F. 2d. 1305 (5th Cir. 1974).

Yalom, I. D. The theory and practice of group psychotherapy. New York: Basic Books, 1975.

Index

DATE DUE